EVERY
WEAPON
I HAD

EVERY WEAPON I HAD

A VIETNAM VET'S LONG ROAD TO THE MEDAL OF HONOR

PARIS DAVIS

WITH THEO EMERY

ST. MARTIN'S PRESS
NEW YORK

First published in the United States by St. Martin's Press, an imprint of St. Martin's Publishing Group

www.stmartins.com

Design by Meryl Sussman Levavi

The Library of Congress Cataloging-in-Publication Data is available upon request.

ISBN 978-1-250-38765-3 (hardcover)
ISBN 978-1-250-38766-0 (ebook)

Our books may be purchased in bulk for promotional, educational, or business use. Please contact your local bookseller or the Macmillan Corporate and Premium Sales Department at 1-800-221-7945, extension 5442, or by email at MacmillanSpecialMarkets@macmillan.com.

First Edition: 2025

10 9 8 7 6 5 4 3 2 1

To the gang. You know who you are.
What you did mattered. I'll never forget it.

CONTENTS

EVERY
WEAPON
I HAD

INTRODUCTION

"SOME CORNER OF A FOREIGN FIELD"

10:00 A.M.

JUNE 18, 1965

NEAR BONG SON, BINH DINH PROVINCE, VIETNAM

There was no easy way off the hill. Bullets snapped around me as I scanned the rice paddies to the north and east, watching for North Vietnamese or Viet Cong soldiers trying to circle around our flanks. The sun blazed down on bullet-riddled corpses scattered across the fields. The stench of shit and blood and smoke filled my nose. As I looked down the barrel of my rifle, my pinkie curled around the trigger because a few hours earlier, a grenade had shredded my index and middle fingers.

To my east, I saw smoke rising from the North Vietnamese rest camp we had raided at dawn, and beyond that the wide delta where the lazy waters of the Song Lai Giang River spilled into the South China Sea. The battalion we were fighting had come ashore here, part of the flow of North Vietnamese fighters into Binh Dinh Province in the northern highlands of South Vietnam. Their camp lay in ruin, a graveyard for the troops we had ambushed. But the North Vietnamese had counterattacked. We were fighting for our lives.

By the time I crouched on that hillside, U.S. advisors had already been in South Vietnam for a decade. But in mid-1965, the war was changing. The U.S. strategy of building up the army of the Republic of South Vietnam and propping up its government was failing. Fury in the U.S. over the Gulf of Tonkin Incident in August 1964, when North Vietnamese and American ships traded fire at sea, had poured gasoline on the smoldering war. President Lyndon B. Johnson, re-elected in a landslide soon after Tonkin, was frustrated over the war and impatient with his advisors who couldn't agree on how to either win the conflict or get out with honor. The loudest voices, including General William Westmoreland, the commander of U.S. forces in Vietnam, argued for more troops, more bombing, more search and destroy missions. To Westmoreland, the northern highlands where I was fighting were strategically crucial. It was here that the enemy was entering the South from the Ho Chi Minh Trail and from the sea to wage war on the tottering government and drive the Americans out. If the flow of North Vietnamese could be stopped, it had to be here.

My A-team of Green Berets, Detachment A-321, had built up a Special Forces camp not far from the village of Bong Son. For two months, we had been training a regional force of local Montagnards—the Indigenous hill people with little love for the heavy-handed South Vietnamese government—and the ethnically Chinese Nung. Our goal was to create a force able to fight the North Vietnamese and the National Liberation Front, the guerrillas in the South that President Ngo Dinh Diem derisively called Viet Cong, which meant "Vietnamese communists." The force we assembled, the 883rd Regional Forces Company, was trained and ready. When we received intelligence and aerial reconnaissance of the North Vietnamese camp to our northeast, we decided to lead the men into combat for the first time.

Eighty Montagnard and Nung soldiers in four platoons had marched with me out the gates of our Special Forces camp under cover of night, along with three other Green Berets from our detachment. We attacked at sunrise. Our dawn operation had gone exactly as planned. That is, until bugles rang out in the forest to signal a counterattack. Four hours after we launched our surprise attack, only about a dozen of those soldiers from the 883rd were alive with me on the knoll. We were pinned down, encircled by far more NVA and Cong than we had estimated. Only one other Green Beret had made it to the hill so far with me, my senior demolitions specialist, Staff Sergeant David Morgan. In our retreat, a mortar round had knocked him into a leech-infested cesspool, unconscious. I had dragged him out when he came to, his blouse soaked with shit and muck.

Another member of my detachment, Master Sergeant Billy Waugh, was pinned down in a trench in the field. A sniper had shot his foot to pieces. He screamed at me across the field to get him, calling me everything but a child of God.

My junior medic, Specialist Robert Brown, was missing. He had gotten separated in the retreat and was somewhere in the field, out of sight. I didn't know if he was alive or dead. Just before we left camp the night before, he had passed around candy cigars to celebrate the birth of his baby boy back in Ohio.

Though we were practically surrounded, we had cover. When we came under fire and retreated to the hill, we found dugouts that the NVA had abandoned when we attacked. Some of our fighters remembered their training at our camp and returned fire without hesitation. Others froze. Paralyzed with fear, they couldn't respond to the withering gunfire and the mortar blasts. I scrambled from foxhole to foxhole, quietly coaxing the men to hold their position and keep firing. I stayed in continual contact with our commos—our radio men—back at camp on a battered PRC-10 radio, relaying the NVA coordinates for air strikes.

I knew where the enemy was, and where our planes needed to lay preparations on the enemy. The NVA were dug in on high ground like ours across the rice paddies, with trees and a village for additional cover. We were running low on ammo, and I needed air support. As I surveilled the battlefield, I silently recited a line from my favorite poem, a sliver of verse from World War I that I tweaked for this war: *If I should die, think only this of me / That there's some corner of a foreign field / that is forever America.*

* * *

I had asked for this. Back at First Special Forces HQ in Okinawa, my commanding officer, Lieutenant Colonel Elmer E. Monger, had asked me to lead Detachment A-321, one of four detachments chosen to set up camps in Binh Dinh Province, where the North Vietnamese were flooding across the border and disembarking from the sea to wage guerrilla war on South Vietnam. I jumped at the chance, even after I was warned that I might have trouble. There might be soldiers on this team who would resent a Black commanding officer, Lieutenant Colonel Monger had warned me. They might be hostile. I volunteered anyway. I did it because I wanted to. I also did it because I had to. A Black soldier had to be as good as the white soldiers around him. On the battlefield, no one cared what color you were. Back home in the States, sit-ins and protests and marches over segregation and civil rights were tearing the country apart. Out here in this rice paddy, under the scorching sun of Vietnam, the only colors that mattered were the colors of your flag.

By midmorning, we had been out here for about four hours, trying to avoid being overrun. I had fought in every way possible that morning: with my rifle and my fists, with grenades and the butt of my rifle. I used every weapon I had. I wasn't sure how many Cong I had killed that morning, but I was certain there would be more.

I don't remember exactly when the voice crackled over the PRC-10 demanding an update on the battle. It came from an aircraft somewhere overhead. I didn't recognize the voice. It wasn't either of my commos back at camp, Kenny Bates or Ron Wingo. It wasn't a forward air control pilot overhead, and it wasn't my B-team commanders, Captain Claire "Tiny" Aldrich or Major Billy Cole. It wasn't anyone in Fifth Special Forces that I knew of. I didn't know who he was. But I knew *what* he was: an officer who had no business being there trying to get in on the action.

"Sir, we have two Americans who are critically wounded and the other I don't really know. I understand he might be dead," I said over the PRC-10.

"Captain, I want you go move out of the area right away," the officer said.

This had happened to me before. Colonels and even generals who craved promotions would scramble a helo when they caught wind of combat. Then they'd buzz overhead and barge into the action to try to gather extra medals and commendations. If a bullet was fired anywhere nearby, the officer was eligible for a combat infantry badge. The joke was that even if there was no incoming fire, an officer just had to say, *Did you hear that bullet?* That was good enough to qualify for a combat medal.

"Sir, I'm just not going to leave," I said. "I still have Americans out there."

Pulling out would have alerted the North Vietnamese to where all our troops were, and we would have been vulnerable. But that wasn't the most important reason for me to stay. As the commander of this operation, there was no way that I could walk away and leave injured men on the battlefield. It would have been a far more serious dereliction of duty to leave my men to die at the hands of an enemy than to cross an officer I didn't know or report to who was trying to direct a battle from the safety of the sky. There was another part of this situation specific to me.

As one of the few Black Special Forces officers anywhere in Vietnam, I found it unthinkable to walk away from soldiers of any race or color. Not to mention that as a Black man, it would be a stain that would never wash away.

The officer wasn't listening. "I'm ordering you to move out," he said again. I refused again. This time I used some choice words that I'd never used with a superior officer, or any officer for that matter. I never knew who that officer was, and I never will.

To me, I wasn't disobeying an order or defying a superior officer. I was just observing a basic principle of leadership, which was that it was both impossible for me to leave and wrong to abandon my men on the battlefield. A leader would never do that. Not only would my men never forget it, I would never forgive myself. Especially knowing that one of those men had just had a baby. If I did find Brown and get him out, at least there was a chance he might see his boy. There was zero chance of that if I didn't. When the officer gave up, I went back to what I had been doing: figuring out how to save my men.

* * *

My story has been a long time in the telling. More than a half-century has passed since that battle in Binh Dinh Province when I dragged Brown, Waugh, and another Green Beret off the battlefield to safety and killed dozens of North Vietnamese soldiers in a grueling, daylong firefight.

This is not just a story about Paris Davis. I prefer to talk about "us" more than "me." It's a story about my fellow Green Berets on and off the battlefield. These were soldiers who were with me in the quiet moments at our camp in Bong Son, who laughed as we played with our monkey, Joe, and our pet bear. These were the soldiers who fought beside me as machine-gun fire rattled around us and dirt from exploding mortars rained down on our heads. This is about soldiers like Ron Deis who flew overhead through a hail of bullets to survey the battlefield. This is about Bobby Brown, who lived long enough for his young son to walk alongside his wheelchair back home in Ohio. This is about Tiny Aldrich, who relieved me on the battlefield and stood by me when I was forced out of my command years later. This is about Billy Cole, who nominated me for the Medal of Honor for that battle. This is about David Morgan, cut down as he surveyed another battlefield three months later. This is about friends who supported me long after the war was over. This is Paris Davis talking when I say this book is about all of them.

Nor is this story only about valor and sacrifice on one battlefield. It's a chronicle of a moment in American foreign policy, a snapshot of a crucial point in the Vietnam War. As the decades slip past, this history and its meaning are vanishing. Like other conflicts that have come before this one, Vietnam is growing hazy for the generations that have come since. It's a war that escalated and spread for reasons that are hard to understand today, in a moment when communism in Southeast Asia commanded the same attention and alarm as our decades-long Cold War with the Soviet Union. This book is intended to tell the story of how my team came to be at that critical point in a critical time when Vietnam was a tinderbox, and the war was on the brink of a major escalation.

Our camp in Bong Son was considered one of the most effective anywhere in South Vietnam. It was where General Westmoreland returned again and again as he sought to build a firewall to contain the flood of North Vietnamese soldiers into the South. It was where we carried out President John F. Kennedy's strategy of using Special Forces to inoculate against communism's spread. It was where we quietly and effectively carried out operations that Congress and the American public frowned on in the open.

When I joined Special Forces, there weren't many Black Green Berets within the newly expanded Special Forces ranks. It had only been about thirteen years since President Harry S. Truman had desegregated the military. When Lieutenant Colonel Monger asked me to lead the detachment in spring 1965, the war and civil rights were fueling domestic protest back home. Eventually, the two issues became sides of the same coin as the draft sent young Black men to Vietnam in greater numbers than white ones. When a cargo plane dropped my detachment in Binh Dinh in April 1965, we arrived just weeks after the infamous march over the Edmund Pettus Bridge in Selma, Alabama, when state troopers beat marchers and unleashed dogs. The images of Bloody Sunday echoed across the globe. Opposition to both the war abroad and segregation at home became intertwined. I found myself a target of reproach as a soldier and as a Black man who volunteered to serve.

Racism didn't define my experience as a soldier, but it was always present, sure as God made little green apples. I experienced it in Airborne School and Ranger School. I saw it when a white pilot that my detachment had saved when he ditched over Binh Dinh crossed the street when he saw me coming, so he wouldn't have to introduce his girlfriend to a Black man.

Perhaps the most enduring symbol of my experience as a Black man in the U.S. military came in the fact that my nomination for the Medal of Honor was "lost" multiple times, disappearing into the Army's bureaucracy. I will likely never know exactly how that nomination was lost. My reputation in Vietnam was no secret. Charlie Black, a highly regarded war correspondent for the *Columbus Enquirer*, called me "one of the most famous Special Forces officers in Vietnam" in a 1965 article. Duty officers in Saigon tracked the events of this battle minute by minute in real time. My own commanding officer submitted my nomination not once, but twice. My advocates have told me that racism was undoubtedly behind the repeated disappearance of my nomination. While I'll never know for sure, it was probably deep-sixed in Pacific Command in Hawai'i, and never even made it to the higher-ups in the Pentagon.

Medals are so important for those of us who have served. When soldiers come home from war, it shines a light as bright as a night star on those of us who did something extraordinary. For civilians, awards and medals can seem confusing, especially when they see a uniform covered with chest candy and don't know the meaning of all those bars and pins and medals. But even when civilians don't know what each one means, they know that it shows bravery, diligence, dedication, or just patriotism. Within the military, it means more: that we have transcended duty. If there's a V for valor on a Bronze Star, that means your stuff doesn't smell. We have gone above and beyond in some way. It shows that we have worth and we did something that was extraordinary and different, that we didn't sit at a desk and work in an air-conditioned office building pushing papers and sharpening pencils. And the Medal of Honor: well, that means we've done something that no one has done before.

I finally felt the weight of the medal on my chest in March 2023. As President Joe Biden placed the award around my neck, I mouthed the words of the poem that I had recited to myself like a whispered prayer each time I went into battle: *If I should die, think only this of me.*

1

BRISTOL AVENUE

1949

CLEVELAND, OHIO

There's only one way to tell the story of my life, and it begins in my hometown of Cleveland, Ohio. Cleveland in the 1940s was a city of factories that smelted steel and iron into machine tools and sheet metal and automobiles and sewing machines and bicycles.[1] Things that lasted. Cleveland was also the city that made me. And it was the city that I had to leave as a teenager to get away from a situation that shattered my family.

When I was a kid, I had a job delivering *The Cleveland Plain Dealer* newspaper. I'd load up my wagon every morning with a stack of papers and pull the wagon from house to house. I tried to empty that wagon as quickly as I could so I could get to school.

The *Plain Dealer* was one of the most popular morning newspapers in Cleveland, and everyone read it. The job gave me some pocket money, and the paper route wasn't so bad in summer. In winter, it wasn't so good. No matter how tight I pulled my jacket shut, it felt like the wind blowing off Lake Erie was blowing right through me.

The neighborhood police took an early interest in me. As I walked along the sidewalk with my wagon, they would wave me over. They were always fishing for information. They wanted to know if I'd heard anything about a fight down the block, or who was shoplifting from the corner store.

I never had much to tell them. I'd be friendly, answering them politely with "Yes, sir" and "No, sir." They'd tell me that I was a good kid. Sometimes they'd pat my head. They'd pick up a newspaper from my stack and glance at the headlines. They'd drop a coin into my pocket.

I'd always let out a big sigh of relief after they walked away. At the bottom of the stack of papers, there was sometimes a brown envelope that I'd pick up from the one of the houses down the street. The guy who lived there ran a numbers game, a kind of illegal lottery, and he used me to courier the envelope back and forth to another house that collected the bets.

The police never did spot that envelope. Still, they were probably keeping an eye on me. They wanted to make sure I didn't get into any trouble. A few years earlier, every policeman in the city learned my family's name, along with everyone else in Cleveland.

On February 20, 1948, an above-the-fold article in the *Plain Dealer* told of a World War II vet who had shot a cop. BURGLAR KILLS HEIGHTS PATROLMAN, the banner headline screamed. That burglar was my oldest brother, Barney Davis Jr.

* * *

I was born in 1939. My family lived then on East Eighty-Fifth Street, a quiet street of two-story, clapboard homes. My parents had come to the city in the Great Migration of Black southerners who left the racism of the South for jobs in the North. My dad, Barney Sr., had grown up in Macon, Georgia. He came north with only a third-grade education. My mom, Anna, was from

Kentucky. She had more schooling, and took care of the book-keeping and the finances of the house.

Back then, Cleveland was a destination for many Black families from the South. The city's history of racial integration had been more positive than that of other cities in the North and the Midwest. A century before I was born, Cleveland was almost completely integrated for the small number of Black families who lived there.

Black tradesmen worked with white tradesmen. Restaurants welcomed Black and white patrons alike. White and Black audiences mingled at lectures and musical recitals, and even church pews were mixed on Sunday mornings. Black kids attended integrated schools. The city had been an important center of abolitionism in the lead-up to the Civil War. After the war, Ohio passed a civil rights law in 1884 forbidding discrimination in public places.

Between 1880 and 1920, the number of Black residents in Cleveland exploded from two thousand to seventy-two thousand. Segregation soon took hold in Cleveland, as it did nationally. While there was no official segregation or "whites only" signs, restaurants began to turn away Black diners. White residents policed parks in their neighborhoods and chased out Black people. The YMCA and YWCA forbade Black members. Discriminatory housing practices pushed Black residents into Cleveland's Central neighborhood. More and more jobs closed to Black workers.[2]

Still, the number of Black residents kept rising. There were 71,899 in 1930, and by 1950, when I was eleven, it had doubled to 147,847. We had hometown heroes to look up to. I went to East Technical High School, the same school where Olympic hero Jesse Owens had run track. Langston Hughes grew up in Cleveland, too.

A few years after I was born, we moved to the Kinsman neighborhood, to a house on Bristol Avenue. Kinsman was a magnet for Black families like mine. When we moved in, it was mixed. We had Polish neighbors, and there were immigrants from all over Europe and Jewish residents who had been pushed out of downtown. Railroad tracks boxed in our neighborhood. At night, we could hear the trains rumbling on their way through the city.

Kinsman was a friendly place, with lots of kids. Neighbors were special for us, because one of the things we were taught very early was that no matter what you think about the world, or the city you live in, being social is your backbone, because if you can't be social, you can't do very many things. The ladies on our street would drop by the house to borrow salt or flour from my mom. She would open her cupboard for them. When she ran short of something in the icebox, or she needed some seasonings, she'd go knock on their doors. At Christmas, we swapped holiday breads with the neighbors, and everyone decorated their houses. Our dad would crawl up on the roof to put up a cross at the peak. Our home was a big three-story house with a front porch and another in the back. When I got older, we'd sleep on the porch roof on warm nights, when cool breezes blew off the lake. The porch was also a way for my older brothers to get in and out of their bedrooms at night without my parents knowing.

Since my parents were from the South, they had a lot of babies. The house was bursting at the seams—nine of us in all, five boys and four girls. The oldest was my sister Edna. My older brother Barney Jr. came next; he was about fifteen years older than me. Then came Delores, Eleanor, Overn, and Carolyn. I arrived after them. Two younger brothers came after me, Ronald and Don, the baby of the family. Two of my uncles, P.D. and Prince, lived with us.

The 1940s wasn't an easy time for our family. We were poor, and the country was still pulling itself out of the Great Depression. The start of the war meant more hardship, more shortages.

Everyone in the family had to chip in. When my brother Barney enlisted right after his eighteenth birthday, there was one less mouth to feed, but one less set of hands to help out. With so many of us in the house, everyone had a job to do. My dad and his brothers, my uncles P.D. and Prince, constantly worked on the house, fixing what was broken and painting when it was needed. My dad divided up bedrooms so the kids would have our own rooms. P.D. and Prince helped out with the mortgage.

My dad was a foundry worker at the National Malleable & Steel Castings Co., one of the biggest employers in Cleveland. Almost all the working-age men in my family worked at the plant, and when the boys in the family got older, we worked there in the summertimes, too. I remember I had a job grinding sharp edges off the cooled castings after they came out of the molds. I figured I would work at the plant as well after I graduated from high school.

My uncles P.D. and Prince worked at National Malleable, too. Though they were brothers, they were very different men. Uncle Prince liked to drink. He would get his paycheck at the end of the week and spend it at the bar. He never backed away from a fight.

P.D. wasn't like that. Even though he had only graduated from high school, he was extremely well educated. He was unmarried, and a union man. He dressed to the nines, and he read constantly. He led our Cub Scout pack as well. He required everyone in the Cub Scout den to have a savings account, and for the first fifteen minutes of every meeting, he made us read. P.D. turned all the kids in our house into readers.

His nickname was short for Paris Darius. Like me, he was named after my grandfather. We were all named for the most famous Don Giovanni in history, Paris of Troy, whose abduction of Queen Helen launched the Trojan War. Our names came from a timeless saga of war and the siege of a faraway land.

P.D. was our family historian. He researched our genealogy and discovered that he and my dad were descendants of a mixed-race marriage. John Davis, my great-grandfather, had been a country sheriff, and he married a woman named Elizabeth Collins. Elizabeth's mother had been an enslaved servant in the Davis household, and mother and daughter were freed after the Civil War. I guess that's where my blue eyes came from.

When John Davis's father died, the couple lived on five hundred acres of his family's plantation that he inherited. The couple never went into town together. When John died, a lien on the property forced Elizabeth to sell their five hundred acres. She ended up a sharecropper on the very plantation where she and her mother had been enslaved. P.D. and my father were her grandsons.

I don't recall much about my grandfather Paris, but I do remember an expression that he often used. "The truth never moves," he would say. By that he meant that what's happened is history, and history cannot be changed, whether it was the siege of Troy a thousand years before Christ was born, or the siege of Congress on January 6, 2021. When you say something that's crystal clear, there's nothing for people to misunderstand. No matter how you color the facts, no matter how you bury information or try to twist it, the truth remains solid as a rock. That's a truth that more of us should be using now.

* * *

On Sundays after church, the family would pile into our Chevrolet and Mom and Dad would drive out to Berea, where my dad and his brother had bought a three-acre vegetable farm. As they drove, I could hear my parents speaking in low tones in the front seat about current events, whispering about news that they didn't want us kids to hear about. They didn't talk about civil rights in front of us, or what was happening in the world.

Even though we had a big family, our house was quiet, which my parents liked. My father was very reserved and didn't talk much. He was a person who paused before he acted, to make sure that things were the way they should be. He was strict, too. We went to a Methodist church on Sundays, and if we missed the services we'd go to vespers on Wednesday. My parents would tell my sisters to keep their knees together if they went out. They'd wait up on the porch to make sure that the kids got home when they said they would. Dad made sure that every one of us was at the dinner table at night. Dad would ask us questions about school and about this and that, so we really felt connected.

School, family, and church were important to my dad. He took to heart the Bible's "spare the rod, spoil the child" proverb. If one of us got into trouble, he'd tell us to go out back and get a switch. If he didn't think it was stout enough, he'd say, "No, that's not big enough, go get another." We'd get a thicker one. Sometimes he wasn't satisfied until we came back with one that seemed as big as a tree trunk, and then he'd beat the tar out of us. He scared the devil out of me.

My nickname was Chubby. I'm not sure how I got that name, but I kept it all the way through my childhood even though I outgrew my baby fat. The funny part of that was that as I got older, I was anything but chubby. Eventually I grew to be six feet tall and was very good at sports.

I was also good at fighting. I usually didn't start them. They often started because of my brother Overn. He would get into an argument, and would say, "I'm going to bring my little brother here and he's gonna kick your ass." That was me. I had more scars than I could count.

Overn was a skilled artist who could draw anything. He also had a dishonest streak. Before I had my paper route, I made some pocket change running errands for neighbors. They'd ask me to go to the store, to run an errand, this or that. I'd get a nickel or a dime.

Overn told me that if I buried my money, it would grow. So he and I dug a hole in the backyard. I put my savings in it, covered it up with dirt, and put a rock on top to mark the spot. Then I waited for my money to grow. I didn't realize that Overn had dug the money up and spent it. When my dad found out, he told Overn to go out to the backyard and cut a switch.

All of us kids played together. Since there was only about a year between each of us, every one of us had a brother or sister close to their age to play with. We didn't have a lot of money to buy fancy toys or go the movies, so we'd shoot marbles out on the street and hang around outside. We were right around the corner from Kinsman Elementary School and from the public library, where we'd go to read.

The kids tended to band together into neighborhood gangs, to keep other kids from other parts of the city off their turf. The boys in Kinsman called ourselves the Commodores. We often fought with kids who strayed from other neighborhoods. Some of the boys also shoplifted from the corner store. My friends would peg their pants and cut a hole in their pocket. They'd palm a candy bar and drop it into their pocket, where it would slide down to their socks. The storekeeper would never find it when he asked us to turn out our pockets. The Commodores were part of the reason the police were always sniffing around—there was always someone in our gang getting in hot water. But I wasn't the one who ended up in trouble in my family—not by a long shot.

* * *

My brother Barney had joined the Army in November 1941, right after he turned eighteen. He was discharged almost exactly four years later when the war was over. He returned from Europe and came back to Bristol Avenue with the rest of us.

He was even taller than me, about six foot two, and very good-looking. He spent a lot of time keeping his hair looking just right. He liked to polish his black boots. He talked about how he had been a driver in World War II hero General George Patton's famous Black armored battalion known as the Black Panthers. Barney couldn't say enough good things about Patton. If someone said Patton was a racist, Barney would fight them.

I don't know how things went wrong with Barney. I was so young. All I remember was that one day in February 1948, police came to our door. They told my parents that a patrolman had been shot to death during a home break-in in Cleveland Heights, a wealthy neighborhood on the west side of Cleveland. Barney was under arrest in the hospital with gunshot wounds. That was the day that everything went to hell in a handbasket for our family.

Eleanor had been working as a maid for a wealthy family in Cleveland Heights. The husband was a successful jeweler. For whatever reason, the family fired Eleanor and hired another maid. A week later, the family went to Atlantic City, leaving the new maid to watch the house.

The police said that Eleanor told Barney that the family would be away, drew a map of the house, and gave him a copy of the front door key. Barney went to the house with a German Luger that a friend had gotten for him from a pawnshop. Apparently when Barney arrived at the house with his accomplices in a getaway car, he tried to use the key but it didn't work. He forced his way in, carrying the Luger.

He didn't know it, but the maid and the owner's sister-in-law were staying in the house. The sister-in-law heard him and came downstairs thinking that the owner's son had come home. Instead, she met Barney on the stairs, waving his gun. He rounded up both women and locked them in a bathroom. Then he went through the house overturning furniture and throwing things to the floor, trying to find a wall safe and jewels that Eleanor had told him about. He even yelled up the stairs to the locked-up women, demanding to know where the safe was.

A neighbor heard the noise and called the police. Two patrolmen, Norman Reker and Edward Meyer, arrived in a car. The accomplices sped away. Like my brother, Reker had recently been discharged from the Army. He had only been on the force about seven months. He was at the end of his shift and was about to head home when the call came in.

The two policemen went up into the house. As they came up the stairs and turned a corner, they came face to face with Barney. Everyone opened fire. One of Barney's bullets hit Reker in the stomach. Reker kept firing as he fell to the floor. Barney collapsed with six bullets in his neck, jaw, thigh, and groin.[3] It was that night that the police arrived at our house. Over the weekend, the police arrested my sister as an accomplice.[4] For whatever reason, prosecutors decided not to bring a case against her, and she was never charged.

The day after the shooting, the news of the burglary and Reker's death splashed across every edition of every newspaper in Cleveland. I think we heard on the radio that Barney had been charged with first-degree murder, but I didn't really understand what had happened. Sometimes someone would ask me if I was related to Barney, but mostly no one talked to me about it. How was a nine-year-old kid supposed to know anything about those things?

After Barney's arrest, my mother disappeared into her bedroom for two days. I could hear her crying behind the closed door. When she finally came out of the bedroom, her eyes were rimmed with red. It affected my dad as well. He and Barney Jr.

were really close, and Dad didn't know what his son had been up to.

When his trial came up, my mom refused to let me go to court, though she went. Barney told the jury he was drunk that day and claimed he had no memory of what happened. Our mother took the stand in his defense, sobbing as she told the court about how he had been a well-behaved boy who built model airplanes, and had been eager to enlist in the Army.[5] Afterward, she rushed to his side and hugged him in front of the jury, earning angry words from the judge.

The scene she made in the courtroom didn't matter. The jury deliberated for an hour, asked for a meal of turkey sandwiches and apple pie, and returned a guilty verdict thirty minutes later.[6] Mom was there in court the day he was sentenced to death, too.

About a year later, my dad and two younger brothers went to visit Barney at the Ohio Penitentiary for the last time. It was a Thursday night in June. He talked with my dad and brothers until 3:30 P.M., ate a bacon and tomato sandwich with coffee and lemonade, and said goodbye to them. Then he walked across the prison courtyard to the death house.

When he arrived at the execution chamber, he refused to allow the prison pastor to pray for him. "I came in by myself, and I'll go out by myself," he said. Prison officials strapped him into an electric chair. The pastor read Psalm 23. Then officials flipped the switch. Barney was pronounced dead at 8:12 P.M.[7]

* * *

Barney Jr.'s death broke my parents, leaving them forever wondering whether he'd still be alive if they had done something different. The house was already quiet, and now it was silent as a tomb. Everyone spoke in hushed tones. And it wasn't just home that changed. Our neighbors treated us differently. We were no longer just the Davises. Now we were the cop-killer's family. Some neighbors were sympathetic. Others shunned us for what Barney had done: the families who lived on each side of us stopped talking to us.[8] We would hear people whispering about us as we walked by.

My parents became reclusive. My dad started working even longer hours. I think that was so that he could stay away from the house. At night, he would sleep on the sofa because my mother cried in the bed all night. He also started to drink. I knew this because when I brought the garbage out, empty bottles would clank in the trash.

My mom almost stopped going out of the house. She withdrew into herself. She no longer borrowed ingredients for meals from the neighbors, or swapped holiday breads. Sometimes she would pull me tight to her and start crying. I don't think I ever saw her with dry eyes again after Barney was gone.

I never really understood why Barney did it in the first place. He lived in a nice house with us, we always had something to eat, and he was a very good-looking guy with a paying job. I was pissed off at him even after he was gone. There's no doubt that Barney's death changed my life. Afterward, a lot of people watched out for me, looking over my shoulder to make sure I didn't take the same path. One of my teachers in particular at Kinsman Elementary School, an Italian woman named Miss Caravella, made it her mission to keep me on the straight and narrow.

Miss Caravella took a liking to me. She wanted to know why I was fighting all the time, because I seemed like such a nice kid. I told her about Overn and the fights he would get me into.

"You know, I want to meet your brother," she said. I think she wanted to straighten him out, too. I don't know if she was helping me because of Barney, but I did know she had a brother in prison. I knew that because she told me a story about how he tried to escape and couldn't figure out how to use the gearshift on the getaway car. It was a funny story, but she was dead serious about making sure that I understood that crime didn't pay.

To keep me busy, she would hire me for little jobs like cleaning her basement and she'd bring me to the museums downtown and to the library. It was because of her, and my Uncle P.D., that I grew up with a lifetime love of reading and literature. Even as an Army officer years later, I wrote down "reading" in the space for hobbies. I did pretty well in school. I was interested in everything. I read every book put under my nose because I wanted to figure out how the world turned. I did so well that I was on track to graduate from East Technical High School early.

As I got older, the neighborhood was changing around my family. After the war, wealthier and white residents of Kinsman moved out to the suburbs. A new wave of migrants arrived from the South, while redlining and downtown revitalization forced a lot of Black residents into Kinsman. The neighborhood became poorer and less mixed.[9]

I was about twelve when I started delivering the newspaper. It couldn't have been much longer after that I started my other job as a courier for the local numbers racket. They had it down to a science. Every Thursday, all the bets needed to be in for the numbers that were pulled on Saturday. I would get the envelope either directly from the man or his wife, or I would take it out of a hiding place they had in a space behind their mailbox. Then I'd go about my paper route, and drop it at the house a couple of streets away where the bets would be added up. I was perfect for it, because the people who handled the bets and the payouts were white and would stand out in Kinsman, but nobody would look twice at a little Black kid pulling a wagon loaded with newspapers.

They paid me a little bit for it, around ten or fifteen dollars a week. I gave it to my mom to pay bills and buy groceries. My mom never found out where I was getting that side money, but she had a hunch that I was up to something. "Where are you getting this extra money?" she'd demand. I told her I got tips for being so good about delivering the papers on time.

One day when I was in high school, I was out in a park near our house playing ball with some of the neighborhood kids when the police showed up with a van. They rounded us all up, put us in the back of the van, and hauled us downtown to the Cuyahoga County Juvenile Court on East Twenty-Second Street, a mile or so from our neighborhood.[10] The juvenile detention center was there in the same complex with the courthouse, filled with kids who had been caught breaking the law. I can imagine that as we drove in, young faces looked down at us through the windows wondering what we had done.

I didn't have any idea why I'd been picked up. My mind raced. Maybe they had found out about me helping the neighborhood numbers game. Maybe it was the fights I still occasionally got sucked into. Maybe it was because of our little gang, the Commodores. Or maybe it was just because they knew what had happened to my brother and wanted to keep me on the straight and narrow.

The officers led us into a room in the courthouse where lawyers talk to their clients before trial. One explained how this was going to go. "When you get into the courtroom," the officer told us, "you're going to be looking up at that judge, and you need to call him 'judge' or 'sir.' Do you understand?" he asked. We did.

As it turned out, we were getting a dose of tough love. None of us had done anything wrong, but our worried parents had given the police permission to bring us to the judge to scare the bejeezus out of us. As we were in there waiting for the judge to see us, an officer that I knew from the neighborhood wandered in and saw me.

"He's a good kid," he said, pointing to me. "He's got a paper route." I silently thanked God that my role as courier hadn't been discovered.

When we filed into the courtroom, the judge scowled at us like we were a bunch of hardened crooks or bank robbers. We hung our heads and crossed our hands nervously.

"I don't have a lot of respect for those who are in front of me that have to look up while I'm looking down," he said with a frown. He turned to me. "What school do you want to go to after you graduate from high school? You need to find a place that you can go to, where we can check on you to make sure you aren't in trouble."

In truth, I had no plans. No one in our family had ever gone to college. But shortly after the talking-to from the judge, my Uncle P.D. told me that he had a friend down in Louisiana, who worked at Southern University and A&M College, a Black school in Baton Rouge. He'd pulled some strings to get me admitted. I wasn't too excited, to be honest. None of that mattered, though, because my parents had decided: I was going to college. The judge's intervention, no matter how unfair, had both put me under the microscope and set me on a course to improve my life.

* * *

When the day arrived for me to leave for Louisiana, my mother cried all the way from our house to the Euclid Avenue bus station. Our Chevrolet was cramped. I had put on my best dress shirt and a light jacket for the trip. I had jammed everything for college into a wicker picnic basket, which was the closest thing we had to a suitcase.

"I hope this works out," Mom said to my dad through her tears. She told me that they were going straight to church to pray for a safe journey after they dropped me off.

When we arrived at the station, she fussed over me for a bit. She had packed a peanut butter and jelly sandwich with an apple for my lunch. She handed me three or four dollars for spending money, all in change. "Be very careful how you spend this money because it'll have to last you until you get down to see your uncle's friend," she said as she poured the pennies and nickels and dimes into my palm.

She had carried my bus ticket herself so that I wouldn't lose it. She handed it to the driver. "Please take care of my son," she said. "I want him somewhere safe on this bus." She had packed a second peanut butter and jelly sandwich lunch for the driver, and she handed it over to him with the ticket.

He looked surprised. "If I wasn't right here on this bus, I'd give you a hug," he told my mother.

Then my mom turned to me. "Come on over here and give me a hug and a kiss. And get on that bus and behave yourself," she said, her cheeks still wet with tears. I hugged her, then turned to my dad. He thrust out his hand to say goodbye like he might to another adult. "You're gonna be a man now. Act like it," he said. We shook hands, and I went up the stairs onto the bus.

The driver had promised my mother that he would take good care of me. He made good on that promise. He sat me down in the seat closest to the door, where he could keep an eye on me. As the bus bounced along, stopping at stations to let passengers on and off, I talked to the driver nonstop. He wanted to know what sports I played and whether I had a girl to help me take my mind off my nervousness over the long trip.

The hours passed as the bus drove south, stopping in small towns and big cities. I was so engrossed in my conversation with the driver that I barely looked at the other passengers or listened to the stops as the driver called them out. I don't know how long that trip took, but before I knew it, the driver was calling out "Baton Rouge, Louisiana." I got my wicker suitcase and stepped off that bus into a whole new life.

2

INTO THE ARMY

1956

BATON ROUGE, LOUISIANA

Dust filled my nose as I crawled across the athletic field at Southern University. The summer air was hot as a boiled cotton quilt. Wearing my rucksack, I squirmed as fast as I could on elbows and knees toward the officers in the distance, holding my rifle above the dirt in front of me.

I was coming toward the end of my sophomore year at Southern, and I was almost at the end of summer camp for the Reserve Officers' Training Corps, the U.S. Army program that pays tuition for college students as they train to become officers. Over the weekend, I'd get on a bus for Fort Hood, Texas, for six weeks of additional training under the hot Texas sun. I've always been competitive, whether it was sports, marbles games on the sidewalk, or school grades. Right now, that meant crawling as fast I could to beat the other ROTC cadets. This was no soft, turf-covered field. It was pebbly and hard, more dirt than grass. Even though I was in uniform, I could feel the sting of blood on my scraped knees and my elbows.

I didn't look behind me, but I knew that I was far ahead of the other cadets. Squinting through the sweat streaming down my face, I could see our commander, Sergeant Cook, at the finish line. He wasn't alone. More senior ROTC officers were with him. They had come to Southern to inspect our ROTC class—it was called the Jaguar Battalion—to see how we performed. Sergeant Cook wanted to make sure that they left with a good impression.

I shimmied down the field yard after yard. I shut out the throbbing pain in my arms and legs, blinking through the sting of sweat in my eyes. I focused on Sergeant Cook.

I reached the end of the course far ahead of the other cadets. Sergeant Cook held a stopwatch; he had been timing me. I jumped to my feet and stood at attention, letting my rifle fall against my shoulder in rest position. The sergeant looked pleased and a little relieved.

When the last of the cadets had crawled over the finish line, we stood at attention, exhausted and caked with dirt and sweat. Sergeant Cook reached into his pocket. He removed something that glittered. It was a gold star, an ROTC award for having completed the course. He pinned it to my uniform. The visiting officers nodded approvingly.

"Well done," Sergeant Cook said. "It's not because you're first. It's because you're setting an example for the rest of us."

* * *

I hadn't intended to join the Army when I went to college. The Korean War had reached a standstill in 1953, two years before I got into Southern. Though the draft was still in place, full-time college enrollment allowed students to defer military service. No one in my immediate family had been to college. My goal was to keep my nose clean and make sure I didn't anger the judge who had instructed me to stay in school.

Uncle P.D.'s friend who had helped get me admitted, and with whom I lived, was close enough to campus that I could walk to class. I was one of about a half dozen Southern students he put up at his house. I remember when he brought me in the front door. I was amazed at how clean and neat he kept it. Pillows in the living room matched the drapes, and the downstairs was cool and quiet. He brought me upstairs to a room in the attic, where I'd be staying. It was a nice space, though it was hot as hell when the weather warmed and the sun was high. I had to go downstairs to use the shared bathroom and shower. I paid some rent to stay there. I helped out with yard work and household chores to keep the place looking good. My Uncle P.D. would send money sometimes to help me out.

Before the semester started, I'd had to register for classes at the registrar's office. I had taken some college classes at small schools in Ohio, but it hadn't prepared me for a large institution like Southern. The bustling campus was overwhelming and more than a little intimidating. A long line to sign up for courses stretched to the registrar's window. Black students of every shade milled around me. Some were so light-skinned that they could pass for white. I couldn't help staring at the female students, the most beautiful girls I'd ever seen.

As I waited, I noticed a table off to the side. An officer in a crisp uniform there was talking with male students. He spotted me. "Would you like to join the ROTC program?" he asked. I didn't know what the hell it was. The recruiter explained what the corps was. If I successfully completed the program, I'd receive a commission as an Army officer, which would set me apart from non-commissioned officers—NCOs—the enlisted soldiers who worked their way up into the officers' ranks. In addition to the scholarship, I'd get a monthly stipend. The stipend wasn't a lot, but it was more than I had at the time. I'd also get a uniform, which meant one less set of clothes I needed to buy.

Though the Army started ROTC in 1916, our program—the

Jaguar Battalion—had only been in existence since 1948. It was almost exactly as old as President Truman's executive order integrating the U.S. military.[1] When Southern's program began, it provided officers for the Army's Transportation Corps, where many of the Army's Black soldiers ended up as drivers and mechanics. Our school's battalion reorganized in 1954 into a military science unit that commissioned officers for every part of the military.[2] That was the same year that the Army's last all-Black U.S. military unit was disbanded.[3]

I didn't learn the background of the Jaguar Battalion that day in the registrar's office. I was focused on that scholarship and how it would help me pay for college. I signed up on the spot and received my uniform. That night, I took it with me to the house to try on for size. It fit perfectly. I still remember my size—thirty-six-inch waist, thirty-inch inseam.

Sergeant Cook, my commander, was a white guy with a mustache who was about as tall as me. He was a Korean War vet who had seen combat in the war. He didn't shy away from telling us that we might find ourselves in a war one day. He talked about that all the time. If we were on the rifle range and one of the cadets wasn't paying attention, standing around with his hands in his pockets, the sergeant would kick him in the ass and yell, "What the hell are you doing? If you were in Korea right now, you'd probably be dead." More than once, he described the freezing cold in Korea, and how steam from his breath would ice up on his face and mustache. He didn't offer much information about the war beyond that. Thinking back, I suppose he wanted to avoid stories about winter battles, frostbitten fingers, and brutal hand-to-hand combat in the mountains. Little did I know that, years later, I'd be training my own men for that same kind of combat.

Being in that uniform gave me a sense of pride. The first time I polished my boots to a shine, I felt like it was something I had earned. Sergeant Cook saw that I was serious and took a liking to me. We got to know each other pretty well. We drilled outside three times a week, rain or shine.

During my first semester, I signed up for a military science class, basic math, advanced English, geography, and biology. I did well that first semester, getting all As and Bs. I took a golf class for good measure.

But some of my education took place outside the classroom. One of the first things I learned about Southern was that civil rights were woven into its history. Set up as part of post–Civil War Reconstruction, the school opened its doors in New Orleans with just twelve students. About thirty years later, it moved to Baton Rouge. It grew from one campus into five, making it the country's only historically Black university system.

The truth is that before I arrived at Southern, I didn't know much about the civil rights movement. I'd heard little about Martin Luther King Jr. and desegregation. In a few years, Southern University would explode with activity around civil rights. During the time that I was there, though, it was more a topic of quiet conversation.

I also didn't know much about what it meant to be Black in the South. Classmates from Baton Rouge and elsewhere in the South soon taught me. They knew all the unspoken rules that came from being a Black person living in a segregated society. If I was on the sidewalk and a white woman walked toward me, they told me, the safest thing to do was just get off the pavement and walk in the grass or in the street. Leave the sidewalk to the white people. Never challenge a white person no matter how wrong they are.

An incident would happen not long after I arrived in Baton Rouge that drove this home for me. I took a seat one day in the front of a city bus, not noticing when a white woman in a flower dress and a straw hat got onto the bus. All I remember is that she stood over me, looked down, and said, "Nigger, get up. I want that seat." Then she stepped back, almost bumping into the fare box next to the driver, and waited.

I remember clearly that I didn't look up at her face in that moment. I'd never had anything like that happen to me before in Cleveland. I had never been called a nigger, as far as I remember. For a long second, I stared at her feet. She wore black, lace-up shoes with low heels and worn-out, thick stockings held up with knots behind her knees. Everyone around me seemed to freeze. No one spoke. The bus was so quiet you could hear a mouse piss on cotton.

I stood and moved aside. She sat down in my seat. I walked to the back of the bus where I stood, holding onto one of the poles. Embarrassment and humiliation raced through my body. Still no one spoke. Other than the engine, the bus stayed quiet. The only sound was the rustle of newspapers as passengers flipped to a new article. Eventually, I saw the woman in the straw hat get up and exit the bus. I didn't sit down again for the rest of the trip.

The most important rule of all for Black people in the South in those days: never cross a policeman. All the power of the law lay with the police. Nothing stood in the way of a white cop taking out his baton to beat you, even if you'd done nothing. Sometimes my friends at Southern would show up to class with black eyes and bruises. No one needed to ask why, because everyone knew what could happen when we strayed off campus and into segregated Baton Rouge. On campus and among classmates, no one had to worry about that.

* * *

Partway through freshman year, Uncle P.D.'s friend got me into a new dorm on campus. My new roommate, a guy named Micheal Wayne Maxwell, was tall like me, very light-skinned, with wavy hair and a part on the side. He had a little mustache that made him look sophisticated, and he had a smile that drove the girls wild. We became fast friends. Pretty soon I had a mustache, too. I tried to mind my own business and stay out of trouble. At night, I would go right to the dorm. My uncle's friend had the dorm monitors check on me to see if I was there. He wanted to make sure that I didn't ruin my prospects or his reputation. I promised him I wouldn't.

I didn't drink. I had seen what happened when my Uncle Prince back in Cleveland would get drunk on cheap whiskey on the weekends, and I remembered the bottles in the trash at home after Barney's death. I didn't want anything to do with that. I didn't drink coffee either, and I didn't smoke. The only time I touched cigarettes was when I got a job handing out Lucky Strikes. Back then, tobacco companies handed out free cigarettes on campuses to hook students. Instead of giving them away, I'd collect the free cigarettes and then sell them on the side later for a little cash.

Mike joined ROTC, too, and wanted to be a helicopter pilot. When rush began, the two of us started looking at the fraternities on campus. My Uncle P.D.'s friend had been a member of Alpha Phi Alpha. He suggested that I join, too. Mike went in a different direction and pledged Kappa Alpha Psi.

Both fraternities were well respected and members of what were called the "divine nine": the nine original Black fraternities and sororities. A lot of prestige came from being members. APA had a pedigree and a long history of civil rights activism with famous members. One of them was Martin Luther King Jr. Another was Thurgood Marshall. W. E. B. DuBois was an honorary member, and so was the singer Paul Robeson. As part of my pledge initiation, I had to learn all the history of the Alphas and write papers about prominent members. That's how I learned about MLK, Marshall, and the other famous Alphas.

While I educated myself about civil rights, I didn't get involved.

My uncle had pulled strings to get me in there, and the last thing I wanted to do was to get in trouble with the law or get arrested, which would probably have gotten me expelled.

Instead, I focused on campus life, and especially on my academics. I spent a lot of time in the library reading just like I had learned to do in Cleveland. I was never lonely in the library because there were always books to keep me company. And it wasn't just the stories on the pages; I also became friendly with the librarian, who I'd visit with and spend hours talking to.

I didn't take summers off during college. I just kept taking classes all through the academic year. First semester of each year, which spanned winter and spring, bled into the summer session. Then I'd start second semester classes starting in September. I'd work right through the holiday, and start again in the new year. Even though I had a heavy course load each semester, I kept up my grades, mostly As and Bs, with a sprinkling of Cs, and one D in French.

I recall that I only went home once the entire time that I was at college, for Christmas of my sophomore year. I missed my family, but I had so little money that there was no way to travel home. Collect calls were expensive, so I rarely even heard my parents' voices. When I did talk to my mom, she would cry every time. Her heart was still broken.

I soon became well known on campus. In my junior year, I was elected parliamentarian of the Alphas, and president the following year. I also worked for the school newspaper, *The Digest*, as a columnist and editor. I also got involved with student government.

ROTC was the thread that ran through it all. The basic ROTC training lasted from January 1956 through June 1957. Advanced ROTC went from September 1957 until graduation.

In summer 1958, at the end of the school year and right after our crawl across the football practice field, I got on the bus to Fort Hood for ROTC camp after my junior year ended. There were students from other schools as well, like Louisiana State University. That bus ride was as close to hell as I could have imagined. When a sergeant at Southern called my name, I climbed on and took the seat the officer pointed me to. The bus had no air conditioning, and every seat was filled with a sweaty young man headed into the unknown. Our nervous stink was so overpowering that a rat looking for crumbs would have fled holding its nose.

It took about half a day for the bus to cross Louisiana and head west to Fort Hood. When we arrived, we climbed down as NCOs yelled names off their lists. I was assigned to a barracks, and less than three hours later, we stood in formation outside the building while a sergeant went down the line of recruits barking out our assignments.

When the sergeant reached me, he got up close to me and asked, "Do you know anything about shit?"

I wasn't sure exactly how to respond. "Are you talking about when you defecate, sir?" I asked.

"It comes out of your ass," he yelled at me. "If you have any problems with that, let me know. Because you shouldn't be here if you don't know what it is." My job was scrubbing toilets. I got to work.

Every day at Fort Hood, I ran from sunrise to sundown. I trotted to the mess hall. I jogged to morning exercises. I ran double-time between classes. Everywhere I went, sergeants yelled at us to go faster. *Go over here, go over there.* There wasn't a moment that went by when we weren't being told what to do. We felt like idiots, but we did what we were told.

We didn't know our asses from our elbows. Some of the men in my company would shoulder their rifles on the left shoulder instead of the right, or would get their feet all tangled during cadence. Our annoyed sergeant would stop us to correct our behavior. "That is so fucked up," he would yell. Then, he'd make us do it all over again.

He drilled respect for rank into us, telling us we had to salute anytime we saw a star—meaning a general. We were so terrified of him that some of us saluted staff sergeants who ran the mess hall because they had a star under their chevrons.

All of us cadets got to know one another pretty well. I met ROTC recruits from all the other schools in the area, like Louisiana State University. The LSU students looked like America—Asian-American soldiers came from there, alongside white and Black soldiers.

Race didn't come up. Or I should say, almost never came up. One time a white soldier complained about how he wasn't ready for an upcoming test. Maybe he'd been out drinking or dancing—I don't know. All I know is that I told him that I'd be happy to help him with the exam, if it was an open-book test.

"Really?" he asked, looking stunned. He was genuinely shocked that a Black soldier would offer to help him.

"I'm happy to help," I told him. After the exam, he and a couple of his buddies asked if I wanted to join them for a hamburger at one of the off-fort diners.

"Isn't that going to be a problem?" I asked. He realized that no restaurant in Killeen, Texas, would ever serve a hamburger to a mixed-race group of soldiers, even if all of us were wearing the same uniform.

"Well, maybe we could do something else, some other time," he said. I never did get that hamburger.

* * *

One day during my senior year, I was taking a walk off campus and saw a girl washing her family's car in the driveway of their big brick house. She was a beauty with a wide smile and eyes shaped like almonds. I caught her attention because I was so light-skinned that she thought I was a white man walking through her neighborhood. We didn't talk; I just gave her a little wave and kept walking.

A few months later, I saw her a second time. I was having lunch with a group of friends when the girl came up again to talk to an Alpha Kappa Alpha sister at the table. She recognized me from our encounter on the street. We smiled at each other again, and again didn't say anything to each other.

When the campus Greek Week rolled around, I stood with my Alpha brothers watching the new pledges marching around campus singing their fraternity and sorority songs. As I watched the Alpha Kappa Alphas go by, I saw that same girl in their ranks. I stared at her as she went. On the last night of pledge week, the Alphas traditionally built a bonfire for the AKAs and Alphas to celebrate their new members together. I spotted the girl for the fourth time. It was raining a little. She was holding an umbrella. Finally, I walked up to her and introduced myself.

She told me her name was Delores, and her friends called her "Dee." She was a junior. A year younger than me, she had grown up right next to Southern, where her mom worked, and her father had built the house where I had seen her washing the car. She lived at home. Even though I would soon graduate, we began to date and started going steady.

Her dad was the minister of not one, but two Baptist churches. He was very strict. He made it perfectly clear to me that because of his standing in the community, he had high expectations for me. I couldn't do anything that would reflect badly on her or on him.

I don't think he liked me at first, but I won him over. When I'd visit her at home, I'd bring a bouquet of flowers for Dee's mother. We'd sit in the living room and sip Cokes. When we went out together, her dad would drop her off and pick her up. I got to know her family well, and I think it was her father who gave me a new nickname, "the Buz," probably because of my buzz cut. I never really talked about my family. It would be years before Delores met anyone in my family.

With graduation on the horizon in 1959, Sergeant Cook asked me if I had a job lined up. I told him I didn't. "If you're in ROTC, you have a job," he told me. On Valentine's Day, I applied for an appointment as a reserve commissioned officer, listing my schooling, my scholarship, and my major. It also included my race—"negroid."

When I went to New Orleans for a physical, an Army doctor noted scars on my right forearm and left wrist, but otherwise found me in top physical shape. "Physically qualified for appointment," the office of the surgeon stamped on the report.

On June 1, 1959, I received a letter through Southern ROTC that I had received my commission in the U.S. Army. "The secretary of the Army has directed that you be informed that by the direction of the President, you are appointed a Reserved commissioned officer of the Army," the letter read. The letter came with an oath of office. After I signed it, I would be a second lieutenant infantry officer.

"I will support and defend the constitution of the United States against all enemies, foreign and domestic, that I will bear true faith and allegiance to the same," the oath read. I signed it that same day.

* * *

On July 10, the Army sent me my first active-duty assignment. In November, I would report to Fort Benning, Georgia, for the infantry officer training course. Several of my Southern classmates received the same assignment. I would report first to Fort Dix in New Jersey, and then on to Georgia from there.

As spring turned to summer of 1959, I had six months before I had to report for duty. I graduated on June 1 with a bachelor's degree in liberal arts and social sciences. I had just turned twenty. I decided I'd have an adventure before my two years in the Army began. I had only traveled in Louisiana, Texas, and Ohio. All across America, the pulse of the country was speeding up. New York City felt like the beating heart of it all. I wanted to see for myself. I bought a bus ticket for New York City to find summer work and see what the city was like.

Young people like me streamed into the city in the summer of 1959. Members of storefront churches met the buses as they pulled into the Port Authority Bus Terminal to help people like me find work and housing. I got a delivery job in the Garment District, carrying fabric and clothes between the city's bustling factories, which still made most of the clothes worn in the country. My lodging was a room in a cold-water walkup in Midtown, near where I worked. I've never hated anything like getting under that freezing water that sprayed out of the rattling pipes over my head.

During those five months or so in New York, I saw America as I'd never imagined her. The city was electric with energy. Beat writers like Jack Kerouac and Allen Ginsberg had taken up residence in Greenwich Village. I could hear poetry on the street corners and arguments over philosophy in the parks. James Baldwin lived there, too, bringing Harlem's energy into the Village. In the daytime, soapbox radicals on the sidewalks railed about how something was rotten in America. At night, jazz spilled out of bars. Censorship was withering away. What was once considered shocking and dirty was out in the open.

The old politics of the country were changing too. Before I arrived, Fidel Castro had come to New York on a victory tour of the Cuban Revolution, which had ended on New Year's Day. Thronged with fans, he lunched on Wall Street, visited the Bronx Zoo, and spoke to thirty thousand spectators in Central Park.[4] In July, Mike Wallace's documentary *The Hate That Hate Produced* introduced the Nation of Islam and Black power to the country.

On July 8, something happened thousands of miles away that barely made any headlines in the United States. In a tiny country in Asia that I probably couldn't have found on a map, communist guerrillas attacked an American base for military advisors. The raid in Bien Hoa, Vietnam, killed two U.S. officers. They were the first American deaths in Vietnam since 1945. *Time* magazine published a short article about the deaths, but otherwise it received little coverage.

I didn't know anything about this as I packed up my bags in New York City and headed to Fort Benning. It had been in heavy use in World War II, home to Patton's Second Armored Division and the Infantry Officer Candidate School. The fort shrank with the war demobilization, but the Korean War had pumped new life back into it.[5] Enormous three-story barracks housed thousands of soldiers. The Army built a 250-foot parachute tower based on an amusement park ride and erected it in the center of the installation as a jump tower for paratrooper trainees.[6] Then they built three more.

The Infantry Officer Basic Course lasted about three months through the end of 1959 into early February of 1960.[7] Flush with my first real salary, I bought a big Buick with an eight-cylinder engine that guzzled gas like a race car. On long weekends, I'd drive from Georgia to Baton Rouge to spend time with Delores and her family. We hadn't yet talked about marriage, but we wanted to spend as much time together as possible.

While I was still at Fort Benning, something happened that pushed students into the center of the civil rights movement and sparked a generation of protest. A group of students at North Carolina Agricultural and Technical State University in Greensboro went into a Woolworth's and bought a few things, and then approached the store's whites-only lunch counter, sat down on the stools and refused to get up.[8]

The sit-in inspired students nationwide. One of them was Delores. The next month, she marched with her friends from the Southern campus to the S. H. Kress & Co. five-and-dime store, where they sat down at the lunch counter just like the students in Greensboro. They were refused service, and eventually returned to campus.

That student movement was a world away from me. Protest was the antithesis of my new, regimented Army life. After I finished the Infantry Officer Basic Course, no one seemed to know what to do with me. To this day, I'm not sure what happened—maybe my paperwork got misplaced or lost in transit. I reported to this office and that office, trying to figure out where I was supposed to go. My name didn't appear on any of the rosters with an assignment. All around me, soldiers were training, running in formation, improving their marksmanship. I felt lost, like a book on a shelf that no one wanted to read.

As I tried to figure out where to go next, a sergeant major who had his eye on me told me he had an open slot in Airborne School he needed to fill. A candidate had dropped out. He asked me if I wanted the spot. I told him I was still waiting for an assignment. I hadn't realized yet that Airborne School was a prestigious honor and one of the first steps toward becoming a Green Beret. He looked disgusted at my hesitation.

"Dumbass," he said, as if it was the most obvious thing in the world that I would want to jump out of planes. "What's your name?"

"Second Lieutenant Paris Davis," I said.

"Paris?" He looked at me like I was crazy. "Are you sure your name is Paris? That kind of sounds like a girl's name."

In my short time at Fort Benning, I had seen those jump towers rising over the installation and learned something about Airborne School's training for paratroopers, the soldiers who parachute into hostile territory from airplanes. I had watched Airborne students climb the towers, parachute to the ground, and gather and fold their chutes after they landed. I might even have wondered about jumping off those towers myself. Jumping out of planes hadn't exactly been on my hit list, but now it was about to be.

3

SPECIAL FORCES

FEBRUARY 1960

FORT BENNING, GEORGIA

I couldn't hear myself think over the roar of the plane. Thousands of feet over Georgia, I was strapped in a seat against the fuselage, divvied up with the other jump school candidates into two groups called "sticks" facing each other. I was in the first stick, maybe the fourth or fifth in line.

We had practiced the routine over and over on the ground: stand up, hook up. Check your line, inspect your equipment. Walk to the hatch when your number is called. Watch for the light to change from red to green.

Some men held crosses and prayed. Then it was my turn. The jumpmaster called my number. "Stand in the door," he yelled. I said a little prayer to myself: *Lord, just let me make it out of this aircraft and let me not be hurt.* I wasn't sure if He was listening or not.

The wind screamed in my ears as I reached the open doorway of the plane. I adjusted my feet into the stance I had learned in training. Looking down, I could see the red clay farmland far below. The light turned green above me. I threw myself out the door. My suit snapped in the whipping wind. I was in free fall for less than a second before the static line yanked out the chute.

I was alone, 12,500 feet in the air. It was strangely peaceful two miles above the earth. I tugged on the toggles to steer the chute. Shapes slowly emerged from the indistinct landscape below—roads, buildings, and trees, growing larger by the second. The landing zone below me got closer. I flared the chute. The balls of my feet hit the ground, I rolled as I had been trained, and I was standing on that red clay again. I had landed safely, without a scratch.

"How'd you like that night jump?" the jumpmaster asked us afterward. He was poking fun at us because so many of the men had shut their eyes in terror. I was just glad I hadn't peed myself. Some of the other men who weren't so lucky held their bundled-up chutes in front of themselves.

* * *

I had ended up in jump school almost by accident, leapfrogging past soldiers begging to be admitted to paratrooper training. When I took that spot offered by the sergeant major in Fort Benning, I didn't realize that I would be taking one of my first steps toward becoming a Green Beret.

In that winter of 1960, I also didn't know that huge changes were coming to the military and Special Forces. U.S. Special Forces had existed since World War II to train strike forces to conduct stealth attacks on the Nazis behind enemy lines. The First Special Service Force, as it was called, was known as the Devil's Brigade. It was reactivated in 1952 as the Tenth Special Forces Group, based at Fort Bragg.[1] In 1957, President Dwight Eisenhower's administration activated the First Special Forces Group on Okinawa and trained fifty-nine Vietnamese commandos—the first group of Vietnamese trainees. Most

Americans had never heard of Special Forces, and even though I was in the Army, I hadn't either.

Despite their superior training, Special Forces were almost an afterthought to the military, looked down upon as cocky and undisciplined. But Special Forces would soon have an outsized role in U.S. military policy, and especially in Vietnam. While I was in jump school, guerrilla fighters aligned with communist North Vietnam began stepping up attacks on South Vietnamese Army troops. By May, another thirty Special Forces instructors would depart Fort Bragg to set up training for the South Vietnamese Army.[2]

My focus at that time was on trying not to fail out of airborne training. I was the only Black paratrooper candidate in my class, and the students weren't there to make friends. The sergeants did everything they could to get under our skin, to find our weak spots and root out the candidates who shouldn't be there.

That included making sly references to my race. *Have you ever been in a line with a white person?* they'd scream at me, trying to provoke me. *Have you ever seen a white person?* I stayed quiet and took it all in, always keeping my eyes focused forward. I'd learned to never let myself get angry or get discouraged. There were plenty of other eager soldiers waiting for my spot if I dropped out.

The first part of the course was on-the-ground training, learning the five points of contact on a landing—balls of the feet, calves, thighs, butt, and shoulders. I learned how to retrieve equipment, what I should do if I landed in a tree. I drilled in a training plane and learned the instructions I'd get from the jumpmaster. Next, I went up those towers and came down with ropes, rappelling with big jumps into space as our NCOs yelled instructions, and eventually parachuted from the top. In the last part, I jumped from airplanes.

I was done with airborne school on March 3. After I got my

wings, the same sergeant who'd offered me the spot in airborne training told me he had a place for me in Ranger School. This time, I wasn't dumb enough to ask what that meant.

Ranger School was the kind of training people think of when they imagine Special Forces: close-quarters combat, martial arts, orienteering. We became experts in Morse code. We learned how to improvise radio equipment. We learned to survive in the bush and forage for food.

This training had three parts over eight weeks. The first segment was at Fort Benning, for conditioning and endurance. We ran everywhere double-time, went out for evening training runs before dinner, and stood shoulder to shoulder as we tossed telephone poles back and forth.

For the second part of the training, we boarded trucks and went to Florida for water and jungle training, where we waded through swamps and waterways with our weapons in the air, stormed beaches at night, and learned how to survive in the jungle by cooking snakes and turtles.

For the third part, we got in trucks again and travelled to the Blue Ridge Mountains of northern Georgia for mountain training. We rappelled down cliffs, slept in treetops, crossed rivers on swaying ropes, and crossed a timber bridge high over a river while grenades detonated around us.

One exercise had us ride a rope zip line over a river, and then drop into the water. It was known as the "death drop." When one trainer demonstrated the exercise for us, he fixated on the tree at the far end of the zip line course and forgot to let go. He slammed into the tree at about fifty miles an hour and fell to the ground. I never found out if he lived or died.

One time, we had an exercise where we had to infiltrate a built-up area in the dark. We found out quickly that the instructors had set up all kinds of obstacles for us—trip wires a few inches above the ground, barbed wire, booby traps. When we were done, I was covered in scrapes and my knees had been bloodied. But you couldn't say anything about it. If you complained in a debriefing, they'd mark it down and hold it against you. They didn't give a damn.

If I thought the sergeants in jump school were hard-asses, the instructors in Ranger School were even worse. They did everything they could to break us down, goad us into a mistake and force us to leave. *What the fuck are you looking at me for?*, they'd yell. *If you keep this up, I'm going to call your mama.*

I made it through, bloody knees and all. After I got my Ranger tab—the patch sewn on the shoulder of my uniform proving that I had graduated—I was sent up to Fort Dix in New Jersey, assigned to Company A of the Fourth Training Regiment. Fort Dix was the largest of seven Army training centers, home to the Ninth Infantry Division, the Sixty-Ninth Infantry Division, and the United States Army Infantry Training Center.[3]

After almost three months of elite training, I was now working with confused draftees. As one of the COs, I had to be out of bed around 3:30 A.M. to shower and dress, so that I could meet the soldiers at 5:30 A.M. Every day, we tried to prepare these kids, get their shoes tied and their gig lines straight, assign them to platoons and squads, get them to the rifle range or their classroom, and somehow turn them into soldiers. I had volunteered for the Army, but these boys had reported for duty after their numbers had come up in the draft. They were disoriented and frightened, unsure of why they were even in the Army or what they were doing. By the time I arrived, almost forty-seven thousand trainees had passed through the course.[4]

The training at Fort Dix was a return to a more conventional military career path, and not one that excited me. It felt like a demotion, because I had had a taste of what it meant to be a different kind of soldier. I think that experience showed in my performance. In those few months, I began to gain the attention of my superior officers. In my September evaluation, which the Army calls an Officer Efficiency Reporting, my rating officer wrote that I possessed "an unusually fine code of ethics and sense of military discipline and justice."

"A well-coordinated, mature and quiet officer of good military bearing and appearance who accepts responsibility unhesitatingly and has demonstrated unusual self-reliance, determination, common sense and drive in his diligent and untiring application to produce highly effective results," the captain wrote. "Morals above reproach."[5]

Though I received high marks for my performance with the Fourth Training Company, I knew that I didn't want to be stuck forever filing the rough edges off green recruits. The way out of that was to seek a new assignment. That opportunity arrived in the fall, when I received a new posting that would send me almost seven thousand miles away, to a tiny, poor country in Asia that had split in half in a brutal war over communism: South Korea.

* * *

I arrived in Korea in September 1960. It had been seven years since the armistice had stopped the fighting in the Korean War. But the war had never really ended. A tense stalemate existed between North and South Korea, with the U.S. defending the South and China backing the North. The two sides, armed to the teeth, bristled at each other across the demilitarized zone not far from the camp where I was stationed. Each side studied the other through telescopes day and night, watching for hostile moves or signs of aggression.

I was assigned a platoon in Company C, Second Brigade, Fourth Cavalry. The camp quarters were Quonset huts, which looked like steel soup cans cut in half with the round side up, perched in rows on a hillside overlooking a barren parade ground. My hut held four bedrooms for about eight officers total, and a shared living room. Our division's executive officer, Major Clarence Cummings Jr., was Black like me. It was the first time I had had a commanding officer who wasn't white. He would check in with me every so often to ask how everything was going. "Come see me if you ever have problems," he said. I was grateful for the offer.

The company was based near a tiny town called Munsan-Ri in a hilly region about thirty miles northwest of Seoul. Our camp lay in a thumb of land—a salient—tucked into an oxbow of the Imjin River. It was a desolate, deforested area, with barely any vegetation other than grass. South Korea was incredibly poor, and locals had hacked down most of the trees for timber or firewood. There were clear lines of sight between each of the three company camps, which were only a few hundred yards apart, with overhead power lines strung between them. A huge water tower loomed over our camp. On a nearby hillside, two enormous Buddhist statues poked up above the hilltop, gazing out of the landscape, and craggy mountains peaks rose in the far distance. The Freedom Bridge, the span built between North and South Korea for prisoner exchanges, lay about three miles to our west. The demilitarized zone between North and South lay a few miles to the west of the bridge, with the North Korean army on the other side itching to finish the war that had ended in stalemate in 1953.

I wrote to Delores as often as I could. In May 1962, she sent me a photo of herself in a light-colored blouse and pleated skirt, her hair short and a radiant smile on her face. "To Paris with all my love," she wrote on the back in pen.

I think that shy smile of hers helped keep me warm, because the South Korean winter was cold as a witch's tit. We bulked up with layers of clothing under our jackets, and wore heavy black leather gloves to prevent frostbite. Some of us wore fur hats with ear flaps and goggles to keep the wind and dust out of our eyes. It was so frigid that sentries on camp guard duty had to rotate every half an hour so they didn't freeze to death. But it wasn't an option to stay inside. We needed to maintain constant visibility in our area, because the North Koreans were always watching. In camp, my rifle platoon drilled on the frozen parade ground, and we practiced firing mortars. We kept a constant presence in the countryside too, roving on daily patrols with our South Korean counterparts, splashing through the muddy, rutted dirt roads, and across the Imjin River. We even drove up to the demilitarized zone, where a massive stone slab marked the Thirty-Eighth Parallel beside a low stone wall with rice paddies stretching far into the north. We trained out in the countryside with every kind of weapon, heaving rocket launchers and machine guns up the hillsides and draping ammo belts around our necks. Every so often the men would light a bonfire on the roadside to keep us from freezing between maneuvers.

We made sure that our presence was visible in the sky, as well. During the change of command when one battalion rotated out and a new one arrived, we would put on a show of force for the North Koreans, turning out in formation as fighter jets streaked over the South's airspace. But there were strict rules about what we could and couldn't do. A wrong move could be misconstrued as an act of aggression and trigger an unexpected response. Sometimes we'd consult with the North Koreans guarding the border about our maneuvers, to make sure there were no misunderstandings. We wanted to keep them guessing, but at the same time, no one wanted to accidentally spark a new war.

* * *

In February 1961, I met one of the new arrivals, a second lieutenant named Ambrose Brennan. He had grown up in the Bronx, the son of a U.S. government inspector, and had graduated from

West Point the year before. Like me, he had earned his Airborne wings and graduated from Ranger School. He was straight as a glass of water, short and fit with flaming red hair.

Ambrose headed an infantry platoon in Company B. Even though we weren't in the same company, we got to know each other. We bonded for a reason that had nothing to do with the military: we were the only two officers in the camp who didn't drink. When we gathered at the officers' club, we ordered cherry cola, while other officers downed beer or liquor at the bar with pictures of pinup girls in bathing suits stuck on the wall behind.

When I transferred to Company B in April 1961, Ambrose and I became roommates. Because we rarely left the base for R and R and didn't drink, we spent a lot of time in our barracks. There wasn't much to do at night except drink cherry soda, stay alert for a North Korean attack, and keep our eyes peeled for the thieves that everyone called "slicky boys."

They were boys and young men from the nearby village who would slip into unlocked windows and rob us blind. They snatched anything that they could get their hands on—booze, cameras, boots, whatever might fetch a buck on the black market—and tossed them out the windows to buddies waiting outside. One night I chased one all over camp in my shorts and slippers, but he got away. When we did catch them, there wasn't much we could do other than let them go.

Their ingenuity was incredible. One night in the middle of winter, they broke into the officers' club, which was on a bluff overlooking the river, and stole a grand piano. They somehow managed to carry it down an icy cliff in the snow, wheel it across the frozen river, and load it onto a waiting vehicle.

The slicky boys weren't the only sign of the area's extreme poverty. Late one night, we heard a commotion outside the razor-wire-topped fence at the back of the compound. When Ambrose and I went out to investigate, we found a group of five or six prostitutes in the darkness trying to get the attention of the soldiers. Since they were outside the compound, we called the police in the nearby town. An officer arrived and started beating the women mercilessly with a heavy flashlight. The worst part was that they weren't looking for money. They were offering up their bodies in exchange for food.

Amid this misery, we still managed to have fun. To help with morale, I took over the battle group sports program and organized football and basketball games between platoons. Sometimes we got entertainment from outside the camp. The USO brought shows to the camp, and we'd have a performance with music and dancing. We had to be careful not to have too much fun. Most of the women at those events were white.

Our executive officer, Major Cummings, warned the Black soldiers like me not to mess around with white girls. "I don't want there to be any fighting or anything," he said.

Ambrose and I got to be good friends. Aside from not having a taste for alcohol, we had a lot in common. He did everything by the book, and to prove it, he always had Army field manuals on hand that he flipped open at a moment's notice. He sure as shit didn't care if I was Black.

My superiors noticed that while I got along well with the other officers, I didn't generally socialize much with them. Many of them were commissioned officers and West Pointers. I didn't belong to that group. I didn't want to be in a place where I felt as though I was out of my depth. It didn't affect my duties, though, and Ambrose and I had our own entertainment because Ambrose brought a record player, an amplifier, and a tape recorder with him to Korea. The slicky boys relieved him of the turntable and the amp, so we guarded the radio in the hooch with our lives.

Ambrose was a huge John F. Kennedy supporter. Not long after I arrived in South Korea, John F. Kennedy had defeated

Richard Nixon in the presidential election, a victory that illustrated that the country was hungry for a new kind of leader. We never talked about politics in the Army, but we were sure as hell expected to vote. Like my friend, I, too, had voted for Kennedy in November 1960.

Kennedy was young, telegenic, and liberal in some ways. But his margin of victory had been thin over Nixon, who had accused him of being soft on communism.[6] Before leaving office, Kennedy's predecessor, President Dwight Eisenhower, had warned Kennedy about Soviet influence in Laos. But Kennedy saw the situation differently: he viewed Vietnam as Southeast Asia's bulwark against communism.[7] He came into office a dedicated Cold Warrior, readying the nation to contain communism and insurgencies around the globe.

Kennedy saw the need for deterrence everywhere—in our submarines, in our nuclear arsenal, in our Air Force and our Navy. He saw something else: the need for unconventional forces to quietly train homegrown, anti-insurgent forces among Indigenous populations. With communism spreading across the globe, it was more effective and less expensive to train, equip, and advise local populations than to deploy U.S. troops to every hot spot on the planet.

While we were in Korea, we got a taste of the instability that Kennedy warned against. In May, a coup toppled the South Korean government.[8] For a day or so, we were on high alert. We broke out all our live ammunition, preparing for an attack. We nervously cleaned our weapons over and over. We didn't know if an attack would come from the North or the South. It was a tense time, everyone worried that the stalemate on the border was about to break into open warfare. But after a day or so, the crisis ended, and we went back to our normal routine.

One night in spring 1961, we gathered to listen to Kennedy speak to Congress. A few weeks earlier, he had told Congress in another speech that he intended to make changes in national security and defense spending.[9]

Now he was discussing details of those changes. As we listened in our hooch, he laid out plans for a huge expansion of paramilitary operations around the globe.

"I am directing the Secretary of Defense to expand rapidly and substantially, in cooperation with our Allies, the orientation of existing forces for the conduct of non-nuclear war, paramilitary operations and sub-limited or unconventional wars," he said.

"In addition, our special forces and unconventional warfare units will be increased and reoriented. Throughout the services new emphasis must be placed on the special skills and languages which are required to work with local populations."[10]

Ambrose and I sat up and took notice. Members of U.S. Army Special Forces were a different breed from conventional soldiers. Every member of Special Forces graduated from Airborne School and Ranger School—as I had—but the final and most important step was to successfully complete the Special Forces Qualification Course, or the "Q Course" for short, at Fort Bragg. Only the best soldiers graduated. Born in World War II, Special Forces were specially trained to survive behind enemy lines, train guerrilla soldiers, and wage unconventional warfare. They learned how to survive in the wilderness. How to suture their own wounds. How to withstand torture. How to use any weapon imaginable.

But what really grabbed me about Special Forces was that they really weren't fighters—first and foremost they were teachers. Their goal was to work with local populations and show them how to repel invaders and fight on their own behalf. To defend themselves. To stand on their own two feet. Their motto was *De Oppresso Liber*—Latin for "To free the oppressed."

Kennedy gave Special Forces a name. Before his speech, it

wasn't something that everyone knew about. Because of him, that changed. Later in 1961, Kennedy would make a trip to Fort Bragg. When he arrived, Brigadier General William P. Yarborough wore a beret that he had long sought as a symbol of the Special Forces but that the Defense Department had not approved as official uniform. Kennedy liked the look, and noted the general's personal touch when he wrote to thank Yarborough. "I am sure that the green beret will be a mark of distinction in the trying times ahead," Kennedy wrote.[11]

Yarborough took that as official approval and ordered thousands of the berets from Canada. Kennedy tipped his hat to the beret again in April 1962, calling it "a symbol of excellence, a badge of courage, a mark of distinction in the fight for freedom."[12] The green beret became a universal symbol of U.S. Army Special Forces.

Right after Kennedy's speech, I wrote to Cummings to volunteer. I wanted to be in that elite force. Soon I'd be wearing a beret myself.

* * *

Not long after, I was promoted to first lieutenant. I was busy in the camp, planning the relocation and renovation of classrooms, installing a diesel fuel tank, and completing the renovation of ammunition bunkers. A few times, I even stepped in as company commander when Cummings was away.

The commanders in the Fourth Cavalry began taking notice of my performance. I was given an executive officer position with my company in addition to training my rifle platoon. We had a live fire exercise in which my platoon outperformed all the others, and periodic inspections showed that our group was one of the best organized and trained in the company.[13] One of my raters called me versatile and energetic, and inspections of my work yielded excellent ratings.

In January of 1962, I got on a plane in Seoul and returned to the U.S. for the Q Course at Fort Bragg. Two years earlier, when that sergeant major asked me if I wanted his open slot in jump school, I didn't even know what Special Forces was. Now I knew. They had a lot of smart people who wanted to do good things for the Army. They were people who thought very highly of America and wanted to do what they could for their country.

When I got to Fort Bragg, I had a pretty good idea when I got to the course that there weren't going to be a lot of Black guys like me, and I was right. I was one of only three Black guys in my class. Pretty soon I was the only one. Not long after the start, the other two tried to sneak out of a formation without being noticed. They got caught. Within a few minutes, they had packed their bags, loaded them onto a jeep, and left. Now I was the only Black student in the course.

My assigned partner for the course was a huge white guy, big as a fullback, with blond hair. We did everything together: physical training, jumps, close combat exercises, martial arts. I don't think it was an accident that he was assigned to me; I think the instructors paired the only Black guy with the biggest, strongest white guy for a reason: to try to force me out of the course. He was strong as hell, and he worked me over. He tossed me all around the judo mat when we were practicing hand-to-hand combat. Split my lip in two places so badly that I couldn't talk. But I kept going. I think he saw that I wasn't going to buckle, and I think he felt sorry for the hell he was dishing out. "Forget about what I'm doing," he told me. "Keep going."

That's what I did. I pushed through all the exhaustion and doubt and pain until I had completed the course. I didn't mind working my butt off to get there, because it wasn't handed to me. I had to work hard with everyone else. My reward was a Special Forces long tab to sew on my left sleeve. It also gave me the right to wear the beret. *De Oppresso Liber.*

Ambrose had left Korea a few months after me, and arrived at Fort Bragg as I was finishing up the course. During the time that we overlapped, we would sometimes go into town together. We tried to go to a movie one time. As I remember it, when Ambrose went to the booth to buy tickets, the person at the counter said that we couldn't sit together because the theater was segregated. We sat together anyway.

Being stateside meant that I could see Delores again. As often as I could, I would drive my Buick the nine hundred miles from North Carolina to Baton Rouge. She had been hard at work while I was gone, building her own career separate from mine. After Southern, she'd received a master's degree in speech pathology at Northern Illinois University. On one of my visits, I went to see her when she was back home preparing to start a job at Southern University's New Orleans campus. I brought her to a car dealership and made a down payment on a fire-engine-red MGB convertible.

We talked about getting married on my visit. There was no drama, no getting down on one knee. We just decided that we wanted to spend our lives together, and I asked her to marry me. She wanted her engagement ring to also be her wedding ring, and described exactly what she wanted: a gold band with embedded diamonds spelling out her initials. That was the ring that I got her.

We didn't get married right away, though. A few days after Christmas of 1962, I stepped off a plane in Vietnam for what would be my first tour. I was assigned to Vietnam as our involvement in the country was deepening. Before 1960, almost no one in America even knew where Vietnam was. They probably couldn't find it on a map if they tried, because world atlases still labelled it French Indochina.

Though it wasn't widely known, U.S. involvement in Vietnam had begun not long after the 1954 agreement that ended fighting between the French Expeditionary Corps and Ho Chi Minh's communist Viet Minh. The two sides withdrew into a stalemate on each side of the Seventeenth Parallel, much like in Korea, but with active and fierce guerrilla activity in South Vietnam. The first U.S. military advisors who had gone to South Vietnam in 1957 discovered that the Army of the Republic of Vietnam—the ARVN—was completely unprepared for insurgencies and guerrilla warfare.

The South Vietnamese government and army were corrupt and brutal, and out of touch with the realities in the countryside where insurgent sympathy easily took root. There were also deep-seated religious differences that worsened that divide. Most rural dwellers and farmers were Buddhist. City dwellers and government elites were largely from the Catholic minority. Eventually, government crackdowns on Buddhists would lead to protest and destabilization, disorder that the North Vietnamese and the Viet Cong—guerrilla fighters in the South aligned with the North—would exploit. The government was in a constant state of turmoil, and the instability would cause the government to collapse more than once in the years to come.

Secretary of Defense Robert McNamara had made his first trip to the country in May 1962.[14] Robert Kennedy visited too, telling the press "we are going to win."[15] American helicopters and weapons began flowing into the country that fall, giving President Diem a false sense of security. The weakness of the government forces became obvious when a contingent of Viet Cong destroyed a better-armed and supposedly better-trained South Vietnamese division south of Saigon.[16]

Diem was deeply unpopular, especially after brutal crackdowns on Buddhist monks. The public saw his regime as weak and corrupt, but he didn't care, believing that the U.S. would keep him and his government safe. When Kennedy sent an advisor to the country right before I arrived, the advisor returned stateside with a bleak assessment that after the U.S. had spent $2 billion in seven years, the situation in Vietnam was getting worse.

I was assigned to a detachment at a Fifth Special Forces camp called Bu Gia Mop. My commanding officer was a former officer in the British SAS, the English version of special forces. He drank constantly. Every time I went to Saigon, he would order me to bring back Scotch whiskey for him. He spent all his time in his hooch. I was handed a full complement of duties the moment I arrived, handling camp construction, organization funds, supply, and weapons control. A month in, we started a campaign to convince Vietnamese in the area to abandon guerilla warfare, and it worked—many Viet Cong defected to our side.[17] I had to work closely with South Vietnamese officers, and I discovered that I had a knack for getting along with them.

I was good at small unit combat operations as well, though we never saw any combat. Kennedy had said in early 1962 that the U.S. wasn't fighting in Vietnam, and that was true for me a year later. The Viet Cong just weren't the threat they would be a few years later in 1965. I remember one patrol, when we captured four or five Viet Cong. We took their ancient weapons, kicked them in the ass, and told them not to come back before we let them go.

The time that I was in the country saw the start of the strategic hamlet program, a harsh South Vietnamese program that forcibly relocated rural farmers and peasants into stockaded villages intended to cut off guerrilla access to the local population. This was predictably unpopular and created more anger toward the government and greater support for the Viet Cong—the exact opposite effect of its goal. But we had a job to do, and we did it. We cleared fields and felled trees. We built new bamboo hooches surrounded by stockade fences with sharpened stakes facing outward to keep out intruders.

Our role was to support the government's anti-insurgency

efforts with tangible help in the countryside. The idea was to stave off the lure of communism with benefits that helped people's lives, such as medical facilities, education, and social services.[18] We also trained Indigenous tribesmen, the Montagnards, to fight the Viet Cong. We set up a training course that mimicked Special Forces training, with sharpened bamboo stakes and tunnels for the trainees to crawl through, and barbed wire fences for them to shimmy under. As part of my duties, I helped start a civic action program near the camp, building schools, medical clinics, and bridges. On my officer evaluation for that period, the rater who reviewed my performance wrote that I did it so efficiently that I ended up saving the U.S. government money.[19]

All the while, I stayed in touch with Dee. I collected snapshots of our camp, and every so often I'd send one home to her. I sent her one snapshot of me sitting shirtless on my cot, which was in open air outside a hooch surrounded by piled sandbags. "How about that suntan, Freeman—I look sort of sexy huh? I love you much—The Buz," I scrawled on the back.

In another, I crouched in uniform beside a Montagnard villager in a loincloth sitting with his back to the camera, his long hair pulled up and held in place with a stick. "The man with his back to you is a Montagnard. Very little is known about their race except that they come from Cambodia," I wrote. "P.S. Everything is made out of bamboo."

I made such progress that my commanding officer was eager to claim responsibility. When I went out on patrol, he would bring me in afterward, and debrief me to find out everything I had done that day. Then when he met with his higher-ups, he would report everything I had done as though he had been there. They got the impression he was doing all this hard work himself, and I was just a lieutenant assisting him. It bothered me that he claimed credit for my work, but I didn't piss and moan about it. Plus, the officers who actually mattered knew exactly how hard I was working, and they weren't going to forget it.

* * *

After six months in Vietnam, I returned to the States in June of 1963. When I got back to Baton Rouge, Delores and I decided to finally become husband and wife. We didn't have much time because I only had a few days of leave, and so we had a hurried ceremony right there in her house. Her father married us in the living room. She wore a wedding gown with a veil and I wore my dress blues. It was just a small wedding with her family and a few friends. We were in such a rush that I decided to go ahead without inviting anyone from my family. One of Delores's co-workers was her maid of honor, and Delores's brother stepped in as my best man.

We packed the MGB and drove to visit Delores's sister in Detroit, and then headed west. I was supposed to report to the Defense Language Institute in Monterrey, California, to study Burmese, as Burma was also an insurgent hot spot in Southeast Asia. The MGB took us as far as Ely, Nevada, where it broke down. We left the car there and continued by bus to California.

We got an apartment in a house in Pacific Grove just north of the Defense Language Institute. We settled into a life as new-lyweds, getting to know each other in a way that we hadn't been able to while we were separated by thousands of miles. The apartment was walking distance to the beach. Sometimes we could see whales sounding in the surf.

The institute was on a long finger of land extending almost into the middle of Old Monterrey, with the easternmost side facing over the bay. It hosted an intensive language program set up after World War II, when the attack on Pearl Harbor put us at war with an adversary who spoke a language that few non-Japanese

Americans spoke. We would soon have a similar problem with Vietnamese. Even though the institute began teaching Southeast Asian languages in 1955, the institute only taught fifty-two Vietnamese speakers in 1955 and 1956. By 1964, there were still only about two hundred Vietnamese speakers throughout the armed services.[20]

Just as in my French-language studies during college, I turned out to be a very bad Burmese student. Even though I spent six hours a day in classes and studied for three hours more, I got a blunt letter from the commandant's office reporting that I was making unsatisfactory progress. My academic work "indicates severe deficiencies in all areas."[21]

Things were heating up in Vietnam, meaning that my Burmese language abilities began to feel less and less likely to be needed. In November 1963, our government backed a coup that toppled President Diem's government in South Vietnam. Diem took refuge in a Catholic church and was shot dead when he tried to surrender. Three weeks later, President Kennedy went to Dallas with his wife. Lee Harvey Oswald fired two bullets that took his life, and Lyndon Johnson became president.

I was still at language school on August 2, 1964, when North Vietnamese torpedo boats fired on the USS *Maddox* in the international waters of the Gulf of Tonkin. The *Maddox* had been offshore monitoring a covert U.S–South Vietnamese operation to launch Special Forces attacks on North Vietnamese coastal defenses. At 11 A.M., three North Vietnamese patrol boats raced to intercept the *Maddox*. When the *Maddox* started firing, the patrol boats launched torpedoes and fired machine guns. Jets launched from a nearby carrier sank one of the NVA boats and damaged the other two, which returned to shore. The entire episode lasted about twenty minutes.

A cat-and-mouse game began between the U.S. vessels and the North Vietnamese, with the *Maddox* and another ship provoking the North Vietnamese in a kind of naval game of chicken. On the stormy night of August 3, the captain of the *Maddox* reported intercepting radio traffic about a new assault. Amid thunderstorms and choppy seas, the *Maddox* and the other ship began picking up blips on their sonar. Believing they were under attack, both ships began firing at what they thought were enemy targets. A pilot overhead saw no boats, no torpedo wakes, no gunfire. There had been no attack. The whole confrontation had been imagined, a result of malfunctioning equipment and jangled nerves.[22]

But in the press, the phantom attack was real, an international incident. Major news outlets described a white-knuckled battle, the air filled with automatic weapons fire and torpedoes shooting through the waves.[23] President Johnson, in a tough election campaign with Republican Barry Goldwater, opted to take a hardline position and demonstrate American resolve. He addressed the nation on live television.

"As President and Commander in Chief, it is my duty to the American people to report that renewed hostile actions against United States ships on the high seas in the Gulf of Tonkin have today required me to order the military forces of the United States to take action in reply," he said.[24] The next morning's *New York Times* reported on the president's speech under the headline, U.S. PLANES ATTACK NORTH VIETNAM BASES; PRESIDENT ORDERS LIMITED RETALIATION.[25]

Even though details of what happened in the Gulf of Tonkin were still sketchy, he sent the Gulf of Tonkin Resolution to Congress the next day. The resolution essentially gave Johnson carte blanche against North Vietnamese aggression with no approval or oversight from Congress. Johnson was now free to escalate U.S. involvement with no checks or balances.

"Resolved by the Senate and House of Representatives of the United States of America in Congress assembled, That the

Congress approves and supports the determination of the President, as Commander in Chief, to take all necessary measures to repel any armed attack against the forces of the United States and to prevent further aggression." Two days later, the House of Representatives approved the resolution unanimously, while the Senate passed it with only two dissenting votes.[26]

The war wasn't the only big news. On the day after the president's speech to the nation, *The New York Times* ran another banner headline: F.B.I. FINDS 3 BODIES BELIEVED TO BE RIGHTS WORKERS. In the summer of 1964, students from around the country travelled to Mississippi to register Black voters. The bodies were three student civil rights workers who had been abducted and murdered by members of the Ku Klux Klan and buried in a dam.[27]

The Gulf of Tonkin Incident, not the murders in Mississippi, was the talk of the school. All of the students speculated that full-scale war in Vietnam was imminent. I never did get to use my Burmese. In October, I got back on a plane, this time for Okinawa.

4

THE ROCK

The sun warmed my face and the smell of the sea filled my lungs as I stepped through the doorway of my plane into the humid air of Okinawa. I started down the steps to the tarmac at Kadena Air Force Base, the main airfield serving Okinawa. A sergeant in civilian clothes waited for me at the bottom. "Are you Captain Paris Davis?" he asked.

"Yes, I am," I said.

"Why don't you follow me?" he said. "We'll pick up your duffel bag and we'll take you over to your quarters." Carrying the small bag I had brought on the plane, I walked with my escort to the rear of the aircraft, where the crew had unloaded my duffel with the rest of the cargo. I picked it up and followed the sergeant to a waiting jeep.

Everyone in the military called Okinawa "the Rock," but it was a rock in paradise. Outside Kadena, the road wound through grassy hills and gullies covered with low pines.[1] The airfield wasn't far from the First Special Forces Group compound, where

I had been assigned. The sergeant drove to a neat residential area where three low, flat-roofed buildings—one for each company—were nestled into the neighborhood. The compound lay about one hundred yards from the shore, across a wide, grassy playing field. There were no gates, no barbed wire fences. I could see Navy destroyers anchored offshore in the deep water. Tiny figures of sailors sunned on the decks.

The sergeant parked and brought me inside the Company C headquarters. On my way in, I walked past a glass case on one wall displaying neat rows of memorial plaques. Each wooden plaque bore the image of a Green Beret, along with the name of a First SFG soldier.[2] They had all been killed in Vietnam. Two weeks after I arrived, there would be another name for the wall, Private First Class William Toth.[3]

Inside HQ, the staff processed my housing papers and asked me to check everything over to make sure there were no errors. Everything was in order. They handed me a key, and the sergeant brought me to the barracks. My tiny apartment had a small sitting area with a desk and a separate bedroom, as well as a kitchen and bath. It was spartan and clean. It had everything I needed.

After I changed and freshened up, I went back to the headquarters to call on my commanding officer, Lieutenant Colonel Elmer E. Monger. I waited outside his office until I heard his voice on the intercom saying he was ready for me. An aide brought me in, and I stood at attention when I reached his desk.

Monger had a whitewall buzz cut, and his narrow eyes burned intensely. His desk was perfectly clean and orderly, the top polished to a gleam. We chatted for a while, and he asked me if I needed anything. I told him no, I just wanted to get started, see the training areas and meet my staff.

"We'll take care of all that," he told me. For now, I should kick back, get a hamburger, and enjoy the ocean views. I probably should have taken him up on that. It would be the last time for a while that I would have that kind of time on my hands.

* * *

When I arrived in Okinawa in the fall of 1964, the crisis over the Gulf of Tonkin had subsided to a smolder. President Johnson didn't want to plunge into full-scale war and limited the response to one day of air strikes. But diplomatic efforts aimed at negotiations with North Vietnam collapsed. South Vietnam was a tinderbox. The government there was in constant turmoil. In the aftermath of Tonkin, the prime minister declared a national emergency and throttled dissent. Catholics and Buddhists were up in arms against one another. Protests and riots rocked Saigon.

With Election Day approaching, Johnson chose not to make any risky moves that would inflame his critics, especially on the right. His calculus seemed to add up. On November 3, he beat Barry Goldwater in a landslide. The lopsided victory handed him a mandate to carry out his Great Society program. But he also had to deal with what he called "the damn little pissant country" of Vietnam.[4]

One of his top State Department advisors warned that the South Vietnamese government could collapse, and proposed a gradual escalation of pressure on North Vietnam: ARVN commando raids, resumption of patrols in the Gulf, air strikes against overland Communist routes into Vietnam. But others in Johnson's administration feared that ramping up the U.S. commitment would end with U.S. soldiers deployed in a ground war. Johnson brought advisors together to thrash out a path forward. In September, the Joint Chiefs of Staff conducted a war game to gauge the outcome of an air offensive. The grim conclusion was that American pressure would not deter North Vietnam. The North Vietnamese were too determined, and the air attacks only strengthened their resolve.[5]

On the Rock, the debate in Washington was a world away. My

life was taken up with the routine of Army life. Each morning I'd get up early, put on shorts and sneakers, and go for a run before breakfast. I kept my apartment as spartan as the day I arrived, so that if I had to leave in a hurry, there was nothing valuable to leave behind. Officers like me had our own apartments, but the enlisted men lived in barracks, group quarters with footlockers at the end of their beds. In a letter I sent to Dee in November, I enclosed a snapshot of myself grinning in front of a Quonset hut. I stood next to a massive sergeant major who towered over me. "I'm not short, it's just that the sgt/major is 6′6″," I wrote on the back. I pointed out the bulletin board in the photo that advertised an upcoming talent show sponsored by *Playboy.* "Jazzy, huh!"

I was assigned to be an intelligence officer called an S2. My job was to help with preparations for a joint exercise between U.S. and Korean Special Forces. It was the largest unconventional warfare exercise anywhere in Asia, covering thirty-eight thousand square kilometers of South Korean land ripe for counterinsurgency. Even though I had no experience with that kind of work, I was tasked with providing intelligence to the exercise commander. I cheerfully worked long hours.[6]

In December 1964, I got a new assignment, this one as a liaison officer between the Army and the Air Force's Eighteenth Tactical Fighter Wing at Kadena Air Force Base. This was a new area for me, helping coordinate airstrikes with direction from reconnaissance aircraft. It was a product of Lockheed's famous, top-secret Skunk Works, a high-altitude intelligence-gathering plane called the A-12 Oxcart. Its other nickname was the "Habu," named after a vicious venomous snake on Okinawa. I was learning on the fly, and it paid off once again. My higher-ups noticed how I was able to quickly learn new skills and use them effectively.

"In possession of these qualities he presents a complete

military man capable of meeting the challenges of his time," one of my evaluators wrote, adding that I became "one of our ablest team members."

In the background, the war continued to raise alarms in Washington. On Christmas Eve of 1964, the Viet Cong had a series of major military wins, occupying a village, destroying two companies of South Vietnamese rangers. But the one that most alarmed Washington was a bomb set in a Saigon hotel that housed U.S. officers, killing two Americans and wounding fifty-eight others.

"We are on a losing track," Ambassador Maxwell Taylor wrote in January. "To take no positive action now is to accept defeat in the fairly near future."[7] Johnson's National Security Advisor McGeorge Bundy felt the same. After conferring with Secretary of Defense Robert McNamara, he sent a memo to Johnson that read "both of us are now pretty well convinced that our present policy can lead only to disastrous defeat."[8]

As I worked and studied, I would sometimes feel someone watching me. When I turned to look, Monger would be observing silently with those piercing eyes. We didn't talk often—he was in charge of the whole company, after all—but he watched me like an owl, taking in whatever I was doing. I wasn't the only one. Monger watched all the men closely, constantly judging our training and preparedness. He could laugh at a joke, but he didn't suffer fools. I didn't know it yet, but he was silently weeding out candidates for a mission that Westmoreland would deem critical to the war, as a bulwark against the advances of the North Vietnamese. For that, he would need the very best.[9]

* * *

Monger would be far more than just my commanding officer. A seasoned soldier from Pipestone County, Minnesota, he had registered for Army service on August 1, 1945, his eighteenth birthday. Five days later, the U.S. dropped a nuclear bomb on Hiroshima, and then Nagasaki three days later. World War II was over. Five months later, he enlisted anyway.

Like me, he had already had a tour in Vietnam under his belt. His assignments as a Special Forces officer would stitch his career to the growing U.S. commitment in Vietnam. On his way up, Monger had held about every position imaginable, from food service supply to munitions officer to mess officer. Eventually, he ended up at Fort Campbell with airborne divisions, and then Fort Bragg with the Seventy-Seventh Special Forces Group.

When the first U.S. military advisors had gone to South Vietnam in 1957, they discovered that the Army of the Republic of Vietnam—the ARVN—was completely unprepared for insurgencies and guerrilla warfare. The South Vietnamese forces, centrally controlled out of Saigon, trained for a conventional invasion across the Seventeenth Parallel. Most ARVN troops were poorly trained and often used old and defective French equipment. Grenades didn't explode, mortars were rusty and corroded, and ammunition dated back to the French colonial era. In 1959, the North Vietnamese–sponsored Viet Cong stepped up guerrilla attacks. In 1960, the number of clashes between the ARVN and the Viet Cong tripled.[10] Assassinations skyrocketed, from 1,200 in 1959 to 4,000 in 1960.[11]

It was clear to American leadership that this poorly trained fighting force, with its outdated equipment and weapons, was ill-prepared for unconventional war. The Army's Military Assistance Advisory Group, based out of Okinawa, coordinated what they called Mobile Training Teams to instruct South Vietnamese rangers in counterinsurgency warfare. Monger's unit at Fort Bragg, the Seventy-Seventh Special Forces Group under Lieutenant Colonel William Ewald, was selected to train the South Vietnamese. Thirty Special Forces instructors in all were sent to three training stations, in Da Nang, Song Mao, and Nha Trang. Monger, then a captain, was Ewald's deputy in Nha Trang. The training was even more challenging than expected. The Americans found that ARVN training had done little to help the South Vietnamese prepare for guerrilla warfare. The ARVN ranger candidates disliked operations that had required any discomfort, such as night, jungle, or swamp maneuvers. Many lacked fundamental skills. They didn't know how to read a map, navigate overland, or patrol. Faulty and failing equipment compounded the problem. At one camp, not a single French compass still worked.[12]

But as the training began, the Americans saw steady improvements. New American equipment eventually replaced the faulty ARVN supplies, and the Vietnamese trainees saw the gusto of their instructors and began to emulate them. Soon the trainees were taking command of the program, leading the instruction and filling out new Special Forces teams.

When the Seventy-Seventh returned to Fort Bragg in late 1960, its mission complete, Lieutenant Colonel Ewald became an evangelist for using Special Forces in the way that the just-completed mission demonstrated.[13] The mission became a template for the deployment of Green Berets to South Vietnam, and when Monger arrived in Okinawa just before I did in 1964, he was ready to put it into action.[14]

* * *

For Green Berets in Okinawa, life wasn't bad. There was underwater demolitions training or paratrooper training with high-altitude, low-opening jump instruction. Some of the most junior men pulled KP duty or assisted with the training. Everywhere we went on the island, our green berets brought attention. Regular army soldiers looked at us with awe. Marines sometimes tried to pick fights if our men ended up in the wrong bar on the weekend.

The U.S. had held Okinawa since defeating the Japanese in World War II, and most of the U.S. Forces elsewhere in Japan transferred there in the 1950s. By the 1960s, the island offered anything that American soldiers, their officers, and their families needed. There were churches and schools, restaurants and bars, theaters and ballparks. During downtime on the weekends, some men in the company would pull on wetsuits, grab snorkels and spearguns, and swim offshore to fish. The water was shallow for about a mile. Then the coral would suddenly drop away into deeper water. The men would spend half a day bobbing in the water before hauling lobsters and fish back to shore.

They brought their catch to the huge VFW hall a few miles down the road—it was rumored to be the biggest VFW in the world. For fifty cents, the chefs there would cook up the seafood, add a side of potatoes or vegetables, and the men would have a meal with rum and Cokes that cost a quarter. Other nights, the men would hire a taxi to take them to nearby towns, where Okinawan girls flocked to the bars looking for dates. For the price of a beer or two, the soldiers could go home with one.

That wasn't for me. I still didn't drink, I mostly kept to myself, and I didn't socialize much. My preferred activity was to go to the library on base and read. When I felt lost or lonely, I could always find a friend on the shelf to keep me company. That's how it had been for me since I was a kid in Cleveland. I've always believed that when you're reading, you're having a conversation.

I was browsing the shelves one day and I found a poetry anthology. I'm fond of World War I history and poetry about the war. This was both. I flipped the pages until I stopped at a poem called "The Soldier," from an English writer named Rupert Brooke. He had served briefly in the Royal Navy Volunteer

Reserve and wrote his most famous patriotic poems while he was serving.

> If I should die, think only this of me:
>   That there's some corner of a foreign field
> That is for ever England. There shall be
>   In that rich earth a richer dust concealed;
> A dust whom England bore, shaped, made aware,
>   Gave, once, her flowers to love, her ways to roam;
> A body of England's, breathing English air,
>   Washed by the rivers, blest by suns of home.
>
> And think, this heart, all evil shed away,
>   A pulse in the eternal mind, no less
>   Gives somewhere back the thoughts by England given;
> Her sights and sounds; dreams happy as her day;
>   And laughter, learnt of friends; and gentleness,
>   In hearts at peace, under an English heaven.[15]

I'm not sure that I made it past the first two lines. I read it over and over. Something unexpected boiled up inside me. I'm not sure exactly what reservoir of emotion it tapped, but that poem brought tears to my eyes. While it's about England, it perfectly captured how I felt as an American and a soldier. I might fall in some foreign field one day. If I did, it would be because I loved my country.

I checked that book out and brought it back to the barracks so I could memorize the poem. Eventually, I returned the book to the library—with overdue fees, because an operation made me return it late—but those words have stayed with me ever since. I would recite it quietly like a prayer, but with a tiny change: "a foreign field/That is forever America."

* * *

In early 1965, the tempo of Army life on the island quickened as the U.S. involvement in Vietnam deepened. A surprise VC attack on Special Forces troops in Pleiku in early February killed eight Americans and wounded more than a hundred others. The attackers also destroyed ten U.S. aircraft. The raid triggered new waves of bombing of North Vietnamese targets. It began as a retaliatory operation called Flaming Dart. Days later, Flaming Dart was renamed Rolling Thunder, an ongoing bombing program that would last for three years.[16]

These events led to the war's first commitment of combat troops. On February 22, Westmoreland requested two Marine battalions to protect the American airfield at Da Nang, where many of the bombing flights originated. On March 8, 3,500 Marines waded ashore at Da Nang. It was a strange scene. The Marines waded ashore like U.S. troops in Normandy, and were greeted by girls with flower garlands and welcome posters. Westmoreland, who wanted the Marine presence to remain discreet, was not happy. [17]

Johnson granted another of Westmoreland's demands. Rather than continuing to restrict U.S. combat troops to defensive roles, as his other advisors urged, Johnson quietly approved a change of strategy. Westmoreland wanted U.S. soldiers on patrol, out in the countryside. This, he believed, would allow them to flush out the Viet Cong and the North Vietnamese, rather than sitting passively in their bases and compounds waiting for attack. Johnson didn't talk about this publicly, didn't address the nation about this escalation. On paper, the U.S. was still in Vietnam in strictly an advisory and defensive role, only attacking when fired upon. He ordered his aides to avoid publicizing it.[18] But in reality, the mission had changed.

Okinawa was crucial to the new U.S. push. Over the course of the year, tens of thousands of troops poured into the island. B-52s and Caribous lumbered in and out of Kadena all day, and jeeps and military trucks clogged the roads. On the weekends, the bars filled up and grew raucous with fights. Some of the men quietly complained that the influx of new soldiers had caused the price of a date to triple.

The Rock was also the secret heart of the Special Forces engagement in Vietnam. In January 1964, the Military Assistance Command, Vietnam—which had absorbed the decade-old Military Assistance Advisory Group—added a new branch with a deliberately inconspicuous "Studies and Observations Group." MACV-SOG, as it was known, was more than it appeared. It was the nerve center for clandestine Special Forces operations in Vietnam to counter the gathering force of South Vietnam's guerrilla insurgency. SOG was mostly Army Green Berets, but it also included other branches of Special Forces like Navy SEALs, Marine Recons, and Air Force Special Operations pilots.

Unlike regular Army platoons, Special Forces were organized into small twelve-man detachments. Originally, they all started with "F"—FA, FB, and FC teams. In 1961, the Army dropped the F, turning the detachments into A-teams, B-teams, and C-teams.[19] A-teams are the fighting units, the operational detachments which go in the field on combat missions. Specialists made up each team, two of each type with extensive training in specific fields. Two intel officers, two radio experts who we called "commos," two light weapons experts, two heavy weapons experts, two medics, two explosives guys. Twelve in all. B-teams staff the command headquarters for the missions. The C-teams are the commanders who have oversight over both the A- and B-teams.

In Vietnam, Special Forces focused on building counterinsurgency capacity among what the Army called Civilian Irregular Defense Groups, or CIDGs. These were local paramilitaries, including South Vietnamese villagers and Indigenous populations like the Montagnard hill people and the ethnically Chinese Nung people. Rather than breeding more resentment toward the government, which was more of an occupying force in the countryside because of the ARVN's heavy-handed security and corruption, we wanted to train these groups to fight the Viet Cong.

Each U.S. detachment operated independently. No one talked about their missions. Orders came in and a detachment would slip out of Okinawa without so much as a goodbye. Beds in the barracks would suddenly empty, and officers' quarters went vacant. The twelve members of the detachment vanished like ghosts in the nighttime. Six months later, they'd be back, and no one would have any idea where they had gone, and no one would ask. Because the missions were all classified, no one ever knew how many people were on base at one time, and how many had been sent on any given mission. Even though half the company might be gone, the kitchens were still stocked with food for a full company. We had so much grub that we could eat steak for breakfast, lunch, and dinner if we chose.

* * *

In early April 1965, a flight from Thailand landed at Kadena. An exhausted officer stepped out of the plane. Major Billy Cole, the son of a Baptist minister and a farm girl from the Ozarks, had started his military career in the Arkansas National Guard before clawing his way up the ranks of the Army through sheer grit and determination. Assigned to First Special Forces Group, he had first arrived in Okinawa in January 1965, and immediately went to Thailand for a counterinsurgency mission.

He had been stationed in Korat, in the northeastern part of the country. His job had been to conduct a threat assessment of communist infiltration in the region, visiting rural towns to speak with village chiefs. At the end of the demanding mission, he concluded that the area was ripe for a Chinese-sponsored insurgency. The temporary duty concluded with a parachuting competition and a celebratory banquet.

When he returned to Okinawa in that first week of April, he was drained and looking forward to a visit to one of the island's steam baths. Instead, the deputy commander of First Special Forces Group was there to meet him at the airfield. The deputy ordered him to report to First Special Forces headquarters in the morning to see Colonel Francis J. Kelly, commander of the group. *And don't mention it to anyone*, the deputy added.

When Cole arrived at 7 A.M. the next day, Kelly showed him a map of Vietnam with the coastal province of Binh Dinh highlighted. Binh Dinh had become one of the most volatile regions in the country. It was a major North Vietnamese infiltration point from the Ho Chi Minh Trail through Laos, and MACV estimated that two thousand or more Viet Cong were in the province. Other than north–south Highway 1, most of the province was under Viet Cong control. In early February, the Viet Cong had blown up a hotel in Quy Nhon that MACV was using as a barracks. The blast killed twenty-three Americans—the largest body count of Americans in a single incident to date. Binh Dinh would be the focus of a new, high-priority mission.

The mission would involve dropping four A-teams of Green Berets into Binh Dinh Province to build new Special Forces camps to train the Indigenous residents—what the Army called CIDGs—and extend the U.S. military presence into areas thick with Cong and North Vietnamese. The B-team would be based in Quy Nhon to the south. "The mission is Top Secret and all activities involved with it will be treated as Top Secret," the deputy commander told Cole.

The operations officer of the B-team—the rear detachment that ran operations for the A-team in the field—was Captain Claire Aldrich. His nickname was "Tiny," and he was anything but. As tall as John Wayne, he was a physical powerhouse who had lied about his age to enlist in the Korean War when he was fifteen. Tiny was a ferocious fighter. Off the battlefield, he was an extrovert, a loud man who loved pranks and practical jokes. Whenever Cole was about to leave on a dangerous mission, Tiny would say, "Hey sir, if you get zapped, can I have your watch?"[20]

Six other officers made up the top personnel of the B-team: a logistics officer, a physician, a psyops officer, an operations sergeant, an intelligence officer, and a commo sergeant. Kelly summoned all of them to a conference for lunch and told them to put together four A-teams to carry out the mission in Binh Dinh Province. A first lieutenant and three captains had been selected to head the four teams. I was one of them.

Monger called the three others into his office first to tell them their assignment. He then called me in separately. I remember waiting outside until his voice came over the intercom to send me in. I stood ramrod straight in front of him.

He told me he was assembling four Special Forces teams to establish training camps near the North Vietnam border. The A-teams would train up regional forces to fight the Viet Cong and the North Vietnamese troops that were flooding south across the Seventeenth Parallel. He had already selected three of the teams. He asked me to head the fourth detachment, A-321.

Before I could answer, though, he needed something from me. "Paris, you're going to have an all-white team," he said. "Can you handle it?"

"If I can't, I'll learn how before you find out that I couldn't," I said. He laughed.

A couple of things to understand here. I believe that I was the only Black Special Forces officer on Okinawa at the time. I didn't talk to anyone about race. I didn't have anyone to talk to. And so for Monger to say what he did meant that he understood—or at least acknowledged—that I could face racism as a Black commanding officer. We were reading from the same sheet of music. There was something else more profound to understand: I had to say yes. I wasn't blind to what was happening with civil rights back in the States. I had heard on the radio and read headlines about Alabama State Police viciously attacking Black civil rights marchers in Selma, Alabama, on March 7 as they tried to cross the Edmund Pettus Bridge outside the city.

Police used clubs, whips, and tear gas against marchers who looked like me and only wanted to vote. Fifty-seven people were injured, including women beaten to the ground. Afterward, the march became known as Bloody Sunday. John Lewis, the head of the Student Non-Violent Coordinating Committee and the future congressman, was cracked on the skull. Before he went to the hospital, he made a speech aimed right at Johnson.

"I don't see how President Johnson can send troops to Vietnam—I don't see how he can send troops to the Congo—I don't see how he can send troops to Africa and can't send troops to Selma, Alabama," he said.[21] Two days later, Dr. Martin Luther King Jr. joined the protest. An agreement between the city and the protestors allowed the march to proceed about a mile before it was blocked again. This time, the marchers turned around and there was no violence.[22]

Though I didn't talk about it, I closely followed what happened with Bloody Sunday, along with everything that happened with civil rights in the U.S. I was no protester, but everything I read in the news bothered me. It did something else: it made me even more determined to be the best soldier I could be. I wanted to show that as a Black man, I was as capable or better than any other soldier. I didn't know what was in store for me, but I knew that I had to say yes to Monger.

After he and I spoke, I was summoned into a conference room to talk with Cole and Aldrich. They gave me the rundown and approved me as the A-321 leader. At the end, Cole ordered a major and an intelligence officer to provide a briefing on the mission in Binh Dinh and the strategic importance of the province. He brought in maps and charts. Colonel Kelly, the First Special Forces commander, joined us.

The room went silent as the sergeant major told the group that there were probably more than two thousand Viet Cong fighters in Binh Dinh. A still larger group of almost six thousand was believed to be hiding in the northwestern corner of the province.

The sergeant put up another map. This one showed two thick red arrows into the province, the transit routes of the North Vietnamese from the Ho Chi Minh Trail. The North Vietnamese Army was pouring troops into the area, the major said, tapping the map with his pointer. Intelligence reports suggested that an entire regiment of North Vietnamese troops had infiltrated the neighboring Kontum Province. General Westmoreland believed that Ho Chi Minh intended to launch an offensive there that would cut South Vietnam in two, absorbing the northernmost provinces and leaving a rump nation of southern provinces. Our mission included a total of ninety-five men in all.

At the end, Colonel Kelly stunned everyone in the room again with the timeline: the detachments would leave on April 10. In four days.[23]

Soon after Lieutenant Colonel Monger called me in to his office, I summoned the members of our Detachment A-321 for the first time. Even though all of the men were in Company C, I had never met them, and most had never met one another. The detachment's other commanding officer was First Lieutenant Walter Pierson. I didn't think much of him. He asked too many questions and thought he knew more than he did. I was against him being there. We didn't want anyone around who didn't know what the hell they were doing.

Master Sergeant Billy Waugh, another member of the team,

was already a Special Forces veteran by that time. During World War II, he had run away from home at age fifteen to try to join the Marines. When he was finally old enough to enlist, he went to Korea, where he got a taste for combat. He earned his beret in 1954, and went to Laos in 1961, running clandestine operations in the very earliest years of the war.

When the Army put together the Studies and Observations Group (SOG), he was tightly wired into the CIA, going back and forth between Okinawa and Vietnam on mysterious missions. He was loud, boisterous, and funny. He didn't just love combat; he loved to kill Viet Cong. In 1965, he was already a legend throughout Special Forces for his ferocity in battle. He was also famously brash and difficult. No one could tell Billy Waugh what to do, and he had the support of the CIA and the top brass of Special Forces. It wouldn't be long before I would soon find out that he was the detachment member that Monger was indirectly warning me about.

The youngest member of the detachment was our junior demolitions specialist, a kid from Dayton, Ohio, named Ron Deis. Deis was smart as a whip. He always had lots of opinions that he never hesitated to offer, but unlike Pierson his opinions usually had merit. He had been going through advanced infantry training at Fort Polk in Louisiana when he was ordered to report to a classroom. The Green Beret sergeant there told him about the specialized training for Special Forces, and about the conflict in a country called Vietnam. Then the sergeant showed him a picture of a Green Beret eating a snake in the jungle. Deis signed up on the spot. After Monger asked him if he wanted to be a member of A-321, Deis told Monger he would give his left nut to be on the team.

Deis was close with another member of the team, Specialist Robert Dennis Brown, our junior medic. Shy and very bright, the Troy, Ohio, native was about four years younger than me.

He was lean and wiry, with a big grin. He and Deis had grown up only a few miles apart in Ohio, and met in Washington, DC, where they had been sent to study French at the Berlitz School of Language. They rode the bus together from the Navy Yard to downtown, where the school was located a few blocks from the White House. Brown's family called him Denny, but we called him Bobby. His wife back in Ohio was pregnant and due in June.

My senior demolitions expert was an outgoing Oregonian, a staff sergeant named David Morgan. He was three years older than me, with a lot of combat experience. Small, probably not more than 140 pounds, Morgan was fearless in a firefight. Except for Billy Waugh, he had seen more combat than anyone else on the team. I would come to rely on him. Sergeant Hugh Hubbard was the senior medic.

Our light weapons specialist was Sergeant First Class Burrell Wilson, nicknamed "Rat" because he had once fallen asleep in the jungle and woken up to a rat chewing on his ear. His heavy weapons counterpart was Staff Sergeant Brooke Bell. He didn't last long with the detachment. Our two commo guys were Staff Sergeant Kenny Bates and Sergeant Ron Wingo. We had a twelfth member of the team, but just before we were to embark to Vietnam, I decided he wasn't ready for the mission and I ordered him to stay behind. Eleven men would go to Bong Son.

Our first meet and greet was a hike. It wasn't a long hike, maybe an hour or two around the base, but it gave us a chance to learn one another's names. Everything else would have to wait.

5

BONG SON

APRIL 27, 1965
BONG SON, BINH DINH PROVINCE, VIETNAM

Shortly after that hike, we left for Vietnam. As our CV-2 Caribou thundered toward Bong Son, the pilot turned in his seat and held up five fingers. Deafened by the roar of the engine, I sent the message down the row of my men in the belly of the cargo plane bracing themselves for a rough landing in Binh Dinh Province, just south of the Seventeenth Parallel. *Five minutes.* Webbing strapped me to the fuselage, along with the rest of Detachment A-321. If we had been able to look out the windows, we wouldn't have seen much below. *Two minutes.*

I'd had just days to prepare for the mission since Lieutenant Colonel Monger had put me in charge: studying maps, making equipment lists, meeting my men. Billy Waugh had flitted back and forth between Okinawa and Vietnam with Air Force intelligence fed from the CIA about the landing site, the terrain, the regional forces we would be recruiting, the proximity of North Vietnamese troops, Viet Cong activity in the area. Parachuting into Binh Dinh at night risked separation and injuries in the hostile territory in the dark. The best way to infiltrate was to fly in just before nightfall.

Air Force bombers had pinpointed a landing spot in Bong Son, a treeless field long enough for the lumbering plane to land, turn, take off on the rudimentary runway that would be waiting for us. We flew first to Quy Nhon, where we spent time training and preparing before boarding up for the trip to Bong Son.

As the pilot counted down, we checked our weapons, making sure they were loaded and ready. When the cargo door opened, we didn't know what we'd find—an ambush, Viet Cong waiting for us, God only knew. All we knew was that we had no time to spare once the plane was on the ground. *One minute.*

"You're going to have fifteen minutes to get your shit out of here," the loadmaster warned us. "And if you don't have all your shit unloaded, whatever's still on the plane is going back with us."

We held our weapons at the ready as the plane bumped onto the runway and came to a stop. The pilot cut the engine. The ramp at the back went down, the loadmaster cracked his whip, and we got to work. We removed towers of rolled concertina wire, enough ammunition to restock a depot, M-60 machine guns, mortars, bags of cement, and everything else we needed to build a training camp in hostile territory.

We moved as quickly as we could. The sun was going down as we helped turn the plane on the bumpy, rutted runway. When the Caribou was reoriented, the pilot restarted the engine and the plane lumbered to life, gained speed, and lifted off the ground. The sound of the engine receded into the distance. It was just us now, dropped into a hotbed of Viet Cong and North Vietnamese activity.

As darkness fell, we huddled together, curling up on the ground next to the landing field in our fatigues with our weapons close. Everyone on the team was collected and calm, even our youngest member, Deis. All we knew was that when dawn broke, we would start building the camp that we would call home for the next six months.

Work began at first light. We found ourselves in the middle of wide-open highland dotted with trees. The rainy season was months away, so the fields were parched and dusty in every direction. In the distance, hazy hills rose up to meet mountains. To the northeast lay Bong Son village and the Song Lai Giang River, which emptied into the South China Sea.

David Morgan and I walked the perimeter of what would be our camp. Our first task was to set up a fence line. While some camps were geometrically shaped in a star pattern, ours had more of the shape of a kidney bean. We began cutting trees and digging post holes to string up the towers of barbed wires piled on the outskirts of the camp. The area was forested when we arrived; soon we had cut down nearly every tree.

As word of our arrival spread, curious Montagnards arrived to watch. I talked with the regional chief of the area villages about hiring local workers to assist us with the camp. Soon we had a small army of Montagnard laborers helping us pound fence posts, dig artillery pits, and excavate the footprint of what would be our underground tactical operations center—the TOC—that we'd enter through tunnels. Tunnels also connected machine gun and mortar positions. We put up a mess hall, built a radio hut, and rigged up a shower out of a fifty-five-gallon drum. After the buildings had all been erected, Billy Waugh crawled up on one of them and painted "Fuck Communism" on the tin roof.

When I had built the camp in Bu Gia Mop in 1962, we constructed almost everything from bamboo—fences, buildings, towers. This time we were building something much more permanent, and much more solid. The camp was a feat of engineering. The buildings were concrete with roofs made of galvanized tin instead of leaves. We used steel rail ties to reinforce the roofs of the underground bunkers, and we piled layers of sandbags on them to withstand mortar fire. While the other camp had sharpened bamboo stakes as defenses, Deis and Morgan, our demolitions specialists, strung up ingenious defenses in Bong Son, stringing trip-wire flares and setting booby traps. Among these traps were napalm cannons, fifty-five-gallon drums partly buried in the ground at an angle and facing outward from the camp, the fuse wires running back to a board in the tactical operations center. When the circuit was tripped, the cannon blasted a fan of flame that went about a hundred feet in the air. They also set up Claymore mines, facing outward, that spewed a deadly spray of ball bearings.

Deis became our unofficial photographer. He wore a camera around his neck just about everywhere he went, snapping pictures of every waking moment for the detachment, and some when we weren't awake. He documented visits from Westmoreland, briefings with the Montagnard soldiers, and the ongoing construction of the camp. He got us in the mess hall, playing cards. Since he was sometimes a spotter on operations, he took photos of the camp from the air.

After we had been in Bong Son more than a month, one member of the detachment, Brooke Bell, abruptly returned to Okinawa. Sergeant First Class John E. Reinburg III—a huge guy—returned to take his place as my heavy weapons specialist.

We had tried to slip into Bong Son unnoticed, but it was impossible to keep our presence a secret for long. Soon after we arrived, one of our commos—I think it was Ron Wingo—called me over to our radio.

"Listen," he said to me. It was tuned to Radio Hanoi, the propaganda transmission of the North Vietnamese. Hanoi Hannah, the station's host who heckled and taunted U.S. troops with her anti-American broadcasts in English, was welcoming us to the war. She called out Billy Cole and Tiny Aldrich by name, and welcomed our four A-teams to "liberated territory."

My high school yearbook photo.
Davis Family

A photo of me from my senior yearbook at Southern University,
from a section about campus leaders. I was president of our
campus chapter of Alpha Phi Alpha, one of the "divine nine" Black
fraternities that included Martin Luther King Jr. and Thurgood
Marshall in its membership. *Archives, Manuscripts and Rare Books
Department, John B. Cade Library, Southern University and A&M
College*

My official Army portrait. *Davis Family*

One of the ways we passed the time in
Vietnam was by playing with a series
of camp "mascots." Here I am with a
tamed monkey during my first six-month
deployment in late 1963, at a Fifth Special
Forces camp called Bu Gia Mop. Much
like in my later tour of Vietnam in 1965,
we were training villagers to fight back
against the Viet Cong, although at the
time the threat wasn't as dire as it would
become in a few years. *Davis Family*

That runway in front of our camp is 1500 ft. long.

We built all this in 3½ months. Some of the buildings you can't see, there under ground, also we have a tunnel system. & it already has the reputation of being one F of the best camps in Viet-Nam. When we arrived the whole area was covered with trees, I've still got a few to cut down.

An aerial view of the Detachment A-321 camp at Bong Son. Our location in Binh Dinh province was one of four chosen for Special Forces camps to bolster the U.S. presence in the northern highlands of South Vietnam, where North Vietnamese troops were infiltrating the south from the Ho Chi Minh Trail and the South China Sea. *Ronald Deis*

A test detonation of napalm defenses at the Bong Son camp. Specialist Ronald Deis created these napalm booby traps out of 55-gallon drums buried in the ground at 45-degree angles. If the camp were attacked and in danger of being overrun, fuses in the tactical operations center would ignite the napalm, blasting a plume of fire about 100 feet in the air. By one historian's estimate, the U.S. dropped about 388,000 tons of napalm in the war, and its use resulted in the iconic 1972 Associated Press image of a crying, burned, naked girl running down a road. The UN restricted its use in civilian areas in 1980. *Ronald Deis*

This is a drum of napalm I set off on our perimeter one night to see its effectiveness. It sure makes the VC think twice about coming in this camp

View of Binh Dinh province near the Special Forces camp in Bong Son. Deis snapped this photo while standing at the end of our camp's airstrip, most likely facing southward. Ordnance dropped on a target from an A-10 Thunderbolt "Warthog" can be seen in the distance. *Ronald Deis*

Sergeant Ronald Wingo and I taking a break in a partially completed machine-gun nest in the camp. Wingo was one of two radio specialists, or "commos," in the detachment. *Ronald Deis*

Detachment members resting on "moving day," when construction was mostly finished and equipment, supplies, and weapons were being moved into the completed structures in the camp. I'm to the left, in a T-shirt. First Lieutenant Walter Pierson, the detachment's second in command, is behind the jeep. Staff Sergeant Kenny Bates is in the foreground. Sergeant Hugh Hubbard, senior medic, is in the back seat. Specialist Robert Dennis "Bobby" Brown, junior medic, is in the driver's seat. Sergeant Ron Wingo is in the passenger seat, face concealed. *Ronald Deis*

Master Sergeant Billy Waugh, in the driver's seat, trying to free a stuck jeep on "moving day." Staff Sergeant David Morgan is at the rear of the jeep. I would later pull Waugh off the battlefield in the June 18, 1965, firefight. Morgan was killed in the September 1965 ambush that left me badly injured. *Ronald Deis*

One of the three mascots we had in our camp, a pet sun bear. The bear usually stayed in a cage, but sometimes we'd let him out to roam around. *Ronald Deis*

Specialist Fourth Class James Branecki with another camp mascot, Joe the monkey. Branecki replaced medic Bobby Brown, who I dragged off the battlefield during the June 18, 1965, battle for which I was nominated for the Medal of Honor. *Ronald Deis*

Staff Sergeant Kenny Bates seated at the radio in the "commo hut" at the camp at Bong Son. *Ronald Deis*

Specialist Ronald Deis posing with a rifle in the camp at Bong Son. Deis, the junior demolition expert in the detachment, was the spotter for the forward air controller on the day of the June 18, 1965, battle. The youngest member of the detachment, he was also our unofficial camp photographer. *Ronald Deis*

Specialist Robert Dennis "Bobby" Brown, our junior medic, relaxing. Just before the operation in which he was critically wounded, Bobby got word that his wife back home in Ohio had given birth to a baby boy. We shared candy cigars the night before the raid, and my commanding officer still had his cigar in pocket the next day when Bobby was injured. *Ronald Deis*

Members of Detachment A-321 after the June 18, 1965, battle. Back row, left to right: Master Sergeant Danny West, Billy Waugh's replacement; Sergeant Hugh Hubbard, senior medic; myself; Specialist Ronald Deis, junior demolition expert; Specialist Fourth Class James Branecki, junior medic. Front row, left to right: Staff Sergeant Kenny Bates, Sergeant Ronald Wingo, Sergeant Charles Matulevich, Sergeant First Class Burrell "Rat" Wilson. The sign above reads, in its entirety: "Det A-321 has 120 years in the U.S. Army, 60 years in Special Forces, 17 years in Viet-Nam. We hope you are here to agree with us." *Ronald Deis*

General William Westmoreland visited the Bong Son camp on numerous occasions in the spring of 1965, as he saw the surrounding rural Vietnamese highlands as a strategically crucial area for cutting off the flow of North Vietnamese soldiers into South Vietnam. On this trip, Sergeant Hugh Hubbard acted as his bodyguard. I got to know the general well during my Vietnam years, and I was saddened when he was relieved of duty after the 1968 Tet Offensive. *Ronald Deis*

A photo of me handing a certificate or graduation diploma to a Vietnamese trainee. The camp trained the 883rd Regional Regiment, made up of rural highland residents known as Montagnards and ethnically Chinese Nung villagers. Waugh, Morgan, Brown, and I accompanied the 883rd Regional Forces Company on the pre-dawn raid on June 18, 1965. *Ronald Deis*

The injury to the man on the stretcher I'm holding most likely occurred during a patrol of the countryside outside of our camp, when we often came under fire. Accidents and injuries of all kinds were frequent. Once, a regional recruit tried to use a live 55-caliber round as a tent stake, and was badly injured after it exploded while he was pounding it into the ground. *Ronald Deis*

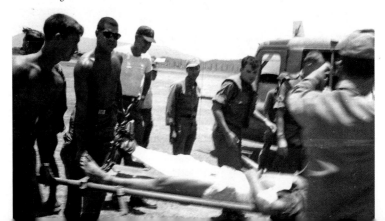

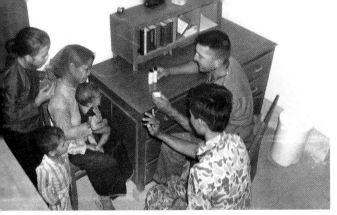

Medic Hugh Hubbard attending to a family of Vietnamese villagers. His services in the camp clinic were in high demand in the area among Montagnard and Nung villagers, who had little access to medical care. *Ronald Deis*

A photo of me receiving the Silver Star in December 1965 for my actions in Bong Son the previous June. This would stand as my highest decoration for the events of that day for more than fifty years. *U.S. Army*

A family photo with, clockwise, my wife Delores, daughter Stephanie, son Paris Junior, and daughter Regan. We later adopted a second son, Chris, who passed away in 2005. *Davis Family*

A photo of me with Senator Ted Kennedy (D-Massachusetts) at Fort Devens, Massachusetts. I served at Fort Devens twice, first as a battalion commander in the Tenth Special Forces Group from 1975 to 1977, then as group commander in 1980. The latter command was short-lived; mounting friction between my group and the commander of the fort led to my relief in the fall of 1981, a move that my fellow officers and the men I commanded protested fiercely, to no avail. *Davis Family*

I met Secretary of Defense Lloyd Austin in March 2023. After a decade of renewed efforts to revive my nomination for the Medal of Honor, Austin approved the medal upgrade and sent my packet to the White House for President Biden's approval. *U.S. Department of Defense*

President Joe Biden shaking my hand after hanging the Medal of Honor around my neck on March 3, 2023, almost fifty-eight years after the battle in Bong Son. *White House*

Then she called me out by name, along with the other three detachment commanders, and promised that "in a short time," the North Vietnamese would welcome us.[1] We had a good laugh about that.

Two nights later, we got that welcome. After nightfall, the Viet Cong began launching 60mm mortars at us from a hidden position some distance away in the darkness. Another detachment, at Binh Khe, was also taking fire at the same time; unlike us, they faced a genuine assault that required nighttime air support. I radioed Major Cole to let him know and sat tight, because there was no indication that an assault was imminent. The Cong were only testing us. I ordered my men not to return fire, because it would expose our weapons positions and increase our vulnerability. The expressions on their faces showed that they weren't convinced this was a wise tactic, but they followed my orders.

* * *

Our primary goal in securing the province was to train the local Indigenous population in how to fight, and we now got started on that process. The Viet Cong and NVA owned the countryside in Binh Dinh. Because of the dysfunction in the South Vietnamese Army and the tension between the Army and the rural population, we believed that the only way to beat the Viet Cong was to have competent local fighters. We worked with the regional chief to find men who wanted to resist the North Vietnamese and the Viet Cong. The Army called these Indigenous fighters Regional Forces and Popular Forces, or "Ruff Puffs," though we never called them that.

Our job wasn't going to be easy. The villagers in Binh Dinh were no friends of South Vietnam's heavy-handed, corrupt government, but they weren't necessarily sympathetic to the Communists, either. The problem was that they didn't have an alternative to Diem's government, and we wanted to provide one. We recruited through leaflet drops around the province, and by signing up up-rooted Montagnard men who streamed into refugee camps near Quy Nhon. We had to be careful that we didn't enlist Viet Cong infiltrators. The recruiters figured out crafty ways to identify po-tential spies. For example, they deliberately disabled automatic weapons so that they didn't fire. If a recruit knew how to fix it without instructions, odds were good they were an infiltrator ex-perienced with weapons.[2]

The mission of our detachment was much more than just standing up local militias and defending against the North Viet-namese; we were there to create alliances with the local popu-lation by providing services and assistance as an alternative to Ho Chi Minh's vision for the country's future. General West-moreland, the commander of U.S. forces in Vietnam, made his first visit to the camp not long after we began. He was tall and lean, with bushy black eyebrows and a jaw as square as a brick. He flew in by helicopter to congratulate us about starting the encampment, and we gave him a tour. Though he was an im-posing presence, he was genuinely concerned for the welfare of his troops. Major Cole often flew with the general on reconnais-sance flights, and the general always had a bag of sandwiches and chips that he shared.

I got to know Westmoreland well on his return trips. Every-where he went, he gathered information about the officers he met—their names, whether they were married, and the names of their children. Soon after, the officers' wives would write to say that they had received a kind letter from Westmoreland. The next time Westmoreland saw those NCOs, he always remem-bered their names and would ask about their families.[3]

On one of his visits, our chief medic, Hugh Hubbard, served as the general's bodyguard, following him around the camp with a rifle and keeping guard outside the mess hall as we briefed the general. It was a little funny to see Hubbard guarding the general, because Hubbard would become one of the most important humanitarian links to the local population around the camp. He quickly became the physician for every Montagnard, Nung, and Vietnamese farmer in the whole province. He easily saw one hundred patients in a day. Mothers brought their sick small children. Pregnant women came for prenatal checkups. Others had their injuries bandaged and diseases treated. Some days I'd stick my head into the clinic and find entire, multigenerational families crowded around Hubbard.

Among the local villagers, Hubbard was probably one of the most popular detachment members, and it wasn't just because of his medical skills. He had a tiny monkey named Joe who wasn't much bigger than a coconut. He had lured Joe into camp and trapped him, then domesticated him with a diet of fruit. Hubbard turned Joe into an assistant, training him to fetch medical supplies. He color-coded items in the clinic, and would tell Joe to go fetch bandages that had, say, a red label, or gauze that had a green label.

We joked that Joe was smarter than all of us. We taught him how to use a knife and fork to eat. We even gave him honorary jump wings. Someone had the smart idea of putting poor Joe in a harness hooked to a flare parachute. They took him up over the camp in a plane and tossed him out the door. He screamed all the way down, but landed safely with his parachute and didn't seem to hold a grudge against us.

Joe had other skills. When we had visitors to the camp, smokers usually carried their cigarette packs in their breast pocket. Joe would jump onto their shoulder, which they liked at first. They were less happy when he reached down, dipped a paw into their pocket for their Lucky Strikes, then scampered up a tree where he would sit and eat all the cigarettes.

And then there was our Malaysian sun bear, which never got a name. Sun bears are small creatures, the adults the same size as black bear cubs in the United States. I'm not sure how it ended up in the camp in the first place, but sun bears had been the mascot of another Special Forces detachment, A-312, which had included Ron Wingo, one of our commos. The year before, Wingo's detachment had kept their bears in Okinawa, where they were illegal, and Wingo eventually smuggled them onto a plane to Vietnam.[4] Our bear may have been one from this group. The third member of our little zoo was a pet civet, a kind of cat that looks a little like a raccoon.

The three animals provided constant relief from the tension of our everyday routines. My favorite act involved the civet trying to get into the mess hall by bounding up the screen door with its claws, pushing the door open at the top, and then descending the inside screen. The problem with that was that its tail would sometimes get caught in the closing door, so the cat would hang on the screen with its tail outside. Joe would then jump up and hang off the cat's tail, and both animals would be shrieking and squealing at each other.

One day an American jet shot over us on a low strafing run. As we watched, a long tongue of flame thirty or forty feet long shot out of the engine. Clearly the plane was in trouble. The pilot pulled up on the stick and rocketed up almost vertically, then ejected. His chute came out immediately, and he began to drift down. Unable to steer, he drifted away from the camp. The plane began to tumble toward earth, spiraling away from our camp and then back toward it. For a moment, we were certain that the plane and its 250-pound bombs were going to land right on top of the camp. Luckily, it landed a few hundred yards away. The impact followed by the detonation of the bombs shook the ground like an earthquake.

We sent a team out to get the pilot. It was risky, because he could easily have been snatched up by the Viet Cong. But we reached him first and brought him back to camp dazed but safe.

After we got him out of there, our resupply plane arrived for the next few Sundays with a case of beer and newspapers courtesy of the grateful pilot. The crash also gave us some other unexpected dividends. The pilot's ejected seat proved to be considerably more comfortable than any other chair in the camp. We dragged it over to our bonfire site and argued over who would get to sit in it beside the fire. We also found the cockpit canopy and hauled it back to camp, turned it upside down, and used it as a bathtub. The bear in particular liked to splash around in it.

* * *

The weeks passed, and we grew closer as we got to know one another. When you're in a situation like ours, in constant danger, you've got to bond quickly. You don't have a lot of time—we were constantly in harm's way. We went out on patrols every night, and every night we came under fire. We were shelled almost every day with mortars. Fortunately, this incoming fire almost always missed, to the point where we didn't pay it much attention. Everyone slept separately in the camp, so that if there was a successful nighttime attack, we couldn't all be killed at once. I slept underground, in the tactical operations center. Hubbard slept in the infirmary. Deis slept in a mortar pit that filled up like a bathtub when it rained. We were aware that any one of us could be killed or injured at any moment.

Even though we faced constant danger, we had our fun as well and managed to make the best of the situation. We had feasts with our South Vietnamese counterparts, and one time we roasted a whole pig on a spit. One of the Vietnamese soldiers had a guitar, and we'd sing country songs and laugh together as we sat around the mess hall. Every so often, we'd have poker games, using the big round quinine pills we took for malaria as chips. For a time, we had an incredible chef we recruited from Bong Son. "Cookie" would bring back canned peaches and apples from Quy Nhon, and he'd bake us delicious pies in a charcoal oven we'd built. He wanted to be a soldier and begged us to go out on patrol. When we finally let him, he was shot and killed. That was the end of the pies.

I became very friendly with the regional chief, who worked with us closely. I called him chief, and he called me *đại úy*, which is Vietnamese for "captain." He would join us on patrols, and his wife would always wait for him to return at the gate, holding a little jar of dark liquid that was probably liquor to celebrate his safe return. The team got friendly with the Montagnard soldiers as well. Ron Deis in particular was friendly with the 'Yards, as we sometimes called them. One night they invited him into a hooch for a party game. About a dozen men were there with a platter with a lid. They spun the covered platter until it stopped. They lifted the lid, and under it was a chicken head. Whichever soldier the decapitated head faced had to drink from a rum bottle. Since all of us had lost about twenty pounds from the stomach problems that came from being in a foreign country, it didn't take Deis long to get drunk as a skunk. That was the first and last time he had a drink in Vietnam.

For the most part, members of the unit got along, and operated with mutual respect. But there were exceptions. Walter Pierson, the other detachment commander, didn't have much of a presence in the camp, and stayed in the background. When he did venture anything in the way of leadership, his input was usually dismissed. The men soon viewed Pierson with the quiet contempt reserved for leaders without experience or the respect that came with it. As for their other commander—me—I had the sense that the men weren't quite sure what to make of me. I didn't smoke, I didn't drink alcohol or coffee, and I didn't talk much about my family or life back home. I didn't tell them I was married. Though I had been in Vietnam and Korea, I didn't have combat experience like Billy Waugh and David Morgan. But my instincts were always sound, my common sense was solid, and my attention to detail and planning led them to trust me.

And I did do my best to make sure they were prepared. I told all the men to have two rucksacks at the ready: one for day-to-day use, and one that was always packed with essentials in case we were overrun and had to make a lightning-fast escape. I made sure that everyone was cross trained in all the skills of every other member of the detachment, so my commo men could suture a wound and my demolitions guys could handle artillery. This would prove essential soon enough.

The biggest challenge to my leadership, the source of Monger's warning, came from Billy Waugh. I had deep respect for this soldier who had gone to Korea at the age of fifteen more than a decade earlier, who had fought in so many battles and had such self-confidence. He knew what he was doing. I was glad to have someone on my team with his skills and expertise, and having him in the camp meant that we had the confidence and support of MACV behind us.

But there was a downside. He knew he had earned his stature in Special Forces, and he was cocky as hell. He had no hesitation about challenging my leadership. This is a tough thing for a leader, obviously, particularly when the person in question has the battle experience to back it up. Waugh would sometimes tell members of the detachment to do things contrary to what I had ordered, rather than approaching me with a suggestion. Given my race and the fact that we were all still getting to know each other, I often had to walk a fine line of respecting his experience while maintaining discipline in the camp.

One time Waugh demanded to know why I had put one of my soldiers up for an award after a firefight, saying that the soldier didn't deserve it.

"How the fuck would you know? You weren't there," I told him.

He looked at me like he wanted to strangle me on the spot. "Do you know who the fuck you're talking to?" he said. But he hadn't been there—he was gone on one of his mysterious missions—and he had to back down. From my perspective, our relationship never fully recovered from that, though Waugh's experience was important to the group. He was hard on members of the team, too. One time, he chewed out our junior medic Bobby Brown after a tough firefight, because he didn't think Brown had showed enough spine. I didn't like that, because it wasn't right to talk that way to a teammate.

It was obvious to me that the friction with Waugh wasn't simply over which of us had more experience. I didn't have a single doubt in my mind that he was prejudiced and resented having a Black commanding officer. One time when we were in Quy Nhon I went to find him in a pool hall. When I arrived, he was facing off with four or five Black soldiers. He had smashed a whiskey bottle on the side of a pool table and was holding the bottle by the neck, waving the jagged edges to hold the other men at bay. When he saw me, he snarled, "Which side are you on? Theirs or mine?" It ended when MPs arrived to break up the fight, and I was able to drag him away to bring him back to camp. Sometimes we'd have fistfights to settle our disputes. Sometimes the only way to end the fight was to let him land a roundhouse on my jaw. Then he could say he had won.

Waugh's efforts to undermine me didn't affect my relationships with the rest of the detachment. They saw that I did exactly the same jobs that they did. I took the garbage out, I washed dishes. During the camp construction, I stripped off my shirt and helped dig foundations. I slept out at the gate of the camp in my boots when other members of the detachment were out on patrol, so that I could meet them when they came back. Some officers might have stayed safe in camp, but I went out on patrols with them. When I did, I often walked in front, the first to engage when we ran into the enemy. If everyone's doing the same thing, nobody can piss and moan about it. The only thing I didn't do was prepare food, because I was a terrible cook. For that, they were grateful.

It was also obvious that I would put my life on the line for them. On May 15, an aviation fuel truck jackknifed near the camp as it went around a curve. It tipped over onto its side, pinning the driver behind the steering wheel. The truck began to burn. I ordered the men with me to stand back, threw off my gear, and ran to the truck.

The driver's side door was jammed shut, so I ran to the other side and climbed inside. The driver was pinned between the steering wheel and the door. As the flames licked higher, I kicked out the jammed driver's door. Then I told him to exhale deeply. When he did, I yanked him as hard as I could and pulled him from behind the wheel. I half-carried, half-dragged him away from the crash. Seconds later, the truck exploded in a fireball.[5] I might have died that day. But if I hadn't done what I did, the driver would definitely have died. No one in camp forgot that.

Still, I needed to remind them every so often that our lives hung by a thread. One day we were bringing equipment east across the river. We had found a shallow area where we could ford the river, and brought across a rope to use as a zip line to send over equipment that couldn't get wet, like our radio. I was on one side of the river and the three other members of the patrol were on the opposite bank. It was Morgan and one other Green Beret—I think Wingo—and a Nung trainee. I waited with the equipment while the men on the other bank fucked around, trying to figure out how to secure the line to bring the equipment across. They were taking so long that I finally waded across the river, furious, and dressed them down.

"What the fuck are you doing over here?" I yelled at them.

"We're trying to tie the right knot to get the rope secure," one of them said.

"Stop fucking around," I ordered them, and did it myself. We weren't in a Boy Scout camp; we were in enemy territory. The wrong knot, a wrong turn, a missed signal, could mean the end of all of us.

Hugh Hubbard and David Morgan came to see me in my hooch that night. Hubbard told me that he had something important to talk to me about. The senior medic was a warm, sunny person with a big smile, but he had a serious expression on his face that evening. The men respected me and my leadership so much, he told me, that they wanted to do everything they could to make sure that I didn't leave. So here was what he was going to do: if I got injured, he would treat me right here at the camp without reporting my injuries to higher-ups in the chain of command. The reason was that if he reported that I was injured, he said, I would probably be transferred out and another officer installed as head of the detachment. None of the men wanted that.

Surprised, I thanked Hubbard and Morgan, sent them on their way, and went to sleep. But I was flattered. I had no idea then, though, what their confidence would come to mean.

* * *

As fighting increased in the province, our camp gained a reputation for our effectiveness. Our part of the province had one of the best kill ratios anywhere in Vietnam. We heard that the Viet Cong circulated "Wanted" posters for Waugh and put a price on his head because he was such a feared fighter. After a while, we heard that there were posters with my face on them, too.

Visitors to the camp were often taken aback by the dangers we faced. One day, a C-123 taxied on our airstrip right into a helicopter that was idling with its rotors going. The rotors were the same height as the wing on the C-123, and they slashed right through the plane's wing, shattering the rotor and flinging pieces of shrapnel in every direction. Ron Deis was in the camp when one of the rotor shards whipped past him. It would have cut him in half if it had hit him. The Air Force sent in a team to repair the C-123. They were with us for about four or five days, putting a new wing on the plane. They were scared shitless the whole time, worried that they would be caught and killed in an attack. By now battle-hardened and used to the daily attacks, we found their fretting a little amusing. "Welcome to our world," Ron Deis put it.

As we gained recognition, reporters from stateside swarmed Binh Dinh, looking for stories, and we had to be careful about what we said around them. Photographers constantly photographed the Montagnard women, who went shirtless. I convinced Westmoreland to bring in shirts for the women to cover them up for the photographers. We also had celebrities drop in as well. Raymond Burr, the dashing TV actor who played Perry Mason, came through the camp on a tour of Vietnam, and posed in a jeep with Bobby Brown.

I'd like to think that one of the reasons our team was effective was because of a democratic spirit I encouraged among the men. After we planned a mission, I would invite them to provide their opinions and suggestions. Some had more experience than I had, and this collaborative approach to leadership improved our performance and created more cohesion. One of the rules of my briefings was that everyone got heard, no matter what. The men knew I was listening to them and wanted their opinions. You could say anything so long as it was constructive.

That didn't mean that my approach always went smoothly. One time, I held a briefing for my men that happened to be on a day when Secretary of Defense Robert McNamara was in Binh Dinh. He had come to the camp with Major Cole to learn more about the situation in the province. McNamara was standing in the back of the room as I briefed the men.

Standing in front of a chalkboard, I described the mission and what we were going to do. I don't recall the specifics of the mission, other than the fact that it was planned for difficult, hilly terrain. After I gave my presentation, Brown raised his hand. I pointed at him. "Sir, this is all fucked up," he said. The steep hillsides and rugged topography would make the plan unworkable, he said. I heard McNamara break out laughing. I told Brown to get his ass up. As he came up, I gave him a hard look and tossed him the chalk. "When he leaves, I'm going to kick your ass," I told him.

The dialogue I encouraged about what worked made us more effective in combat, too. During an ambush we conducted, a group of Viet Cong soldiers chased our patrol as we retreated in the direction of camp. For hours, we stayed ahead of them. After a long time, we paused to catch our breath. As we stood under the trees, our chests heaving, one of my guys approached. I'm not sure which one; maybe it was Morgan. He had been listening for our pursuers, and he had heard nothing.

"I think they're resting," he told me. Another soldier might have suggested trying to use the lull to get as far ahead of them as possible, but he had other ideas. "I've been talking to a couple other guys—here's what I'd like to do. I'd like to turn around and ambush 'em right now."

It wasn't exactly a by-the-books strategy. The Viet Cong were looking for us, armed to the teeth and angry. But I trusted Morgan's experience and instincts, and if he was right, we could catch them off guard.

We began retracing our steps, slightly offset from the path we had taken earlier. We walked slowly, guns up, step after careful step, trying to be completely silent. After a few minutes, we came across the VC, sprawled out on the ground sleeping where they had dropped in exhaustion. We stepped out from the trees and quickly padded among the sleeping soldiers, gingerly picking up their weapons. Someone in our patrol then fired a pistol to wake them. They bolted upright, startled into wakefulness. We trained our guns on them, bound them up, and started our march once again—slower this time. When we got back, the district chief was amazed. "I have never heard of anyone doing that in my life," he said.

I also learned a lesson that would later earn me even greater respect from my team: the higher-ups weren't always right. I couldn't always obey their orders in good conscience. Sometimes it was silly stuff, like the rule that when we were in camp, we were supposed to wear shirts at all times. That was a stupid rule, because it was hot as hell and we were working all day long in the sun if we weren't sleeping or on patrol. Early on, a colonel made a surprise detour to the camp along with my boss, Major Billy Cole, when I was working shirtless alongside the team.

"Captain Davis, were you told about my policy regarding wearing the fatigue shirt?" the colonel snapped at me after he walked to me from his chopper.

"Yes, sir," I said.

Major Cole broke in to explain that my team didn't have enough funds to pay workers to build some of the structures, which were urgently needed. Because there was no money for laborers, my A-team and I had to do it ourselves in the blazing heat. The colonel seemed chagrined. He said to me before walking back to his chopper, "Carry on and do not mention my visit to anyone." Within a couple of days, we had a few hundred thousand piastres—the South Vietnamese currency—to pay for more laborers.[6]

Sometimes the stakes were higher. Once, we were passing through a village when we spotted a wounded American soldier lying motionless on the ground. From a distance, we couldn't tell the severity of his injuries or whether he was conscious. Overhead, helicopters carried generals who had come up from Saigon to observe our activities. Westmoreland was on one of the choppers.

One of our men got on our radio, a PRC-10, with one of the helicopters to report that they had found an American casualty.

"We'll come back and get him," one of the generals on the helicopter said.

I took the radio. "I'm not going to do that, sir," I responded.

The general didn't like that. "You're disobeying a direct order," the general said, anger in his voice.

"Well, then I'm disobeying an order," I said.

That really ticked him off. "You know what? I have never, ever liked Special Forces," he yelled into the radio. "I hate these fucking Special Forces guys. You all think you're so fucking tough. What I really would like to do is get out of this helicopter and come out there and kick your ass."

"Well, you know something sir? There's a lot of room down here," I said. Over the radio, I could hear the other generals in the helicopter chuckling in the background. We stayed with the soldier until a medevac came for him. I never was disciplined. Later I found out that General Westmoreland was listening in on the exchange.

Westmoreland came to Binh Dinh frequently, and I came to know him well during his trips to our camp. He came in for a graduation ceremony we held for the regional forces, and looked on as I passed out certificates to the Montagnard men we had trained. We'd pop open an awful-tasting Vietnamese soda that was the temperature of warm tea, and he'd confide in me his frustrations with the conventional troops he commandeered. They just didn't seem to understand what was needed to win the war, he complained.

On one of Westmoreland's trips to the province, I drove him by jeep to the district headquarters. He told me that he had heard I had a good rapport with the locals, and he wanted to see for himself. When we arrived at the village, children and adults ran out to greet us and began to clap. Westmoreland was amazed.

"Captain Davis, you are a real rarity. I have seen displays of admiration by villagers before, but nothing quite like this. What's your secret? How do you do it?" he asked.

I chuckled. "Oh sir, they have just never seen a blue-eyed Negro before." On their flight back to Quy Nhon, Westmoreland told Cole that I was one of the most outstanding officers he'd seen in his entire career.

* * *

As enemy activity picked up in the province, Westmoreland and the MACV leadership began to send conventional troops into the area through Quy Nhon. A helicopter battalion set up at the airport, and the Seventh Marine Battalion made camp nearby. Field depots popped up all around the airport to supply the new American troops streaming into the countryside.

At first, there was little response to this increased American presence from the North Vietnamese and the Viet Cong. But one day on patrol, we detected a huge enemy movement toward our northwest, and close to one of the other camps. I alerted Major Billy Cole, and he and Tiny Aldrich went up in a spotter plane to track them. Cole and Aldrich quickly came under fire, and they called in air support. Waves of A-1E Skyraiders followed by F-100s dropped cluster bombs and then sheets of napalm. The attackers slowed and then scattered.[7]

Over May and June, North Vietnamese and Viet Cong activity grew even more consistent. The VC launched attacks across South Vietnam on May 11 and briefly seized a provincial capital, Songbe, only about fifty miles from Saigon. Not long after, the Viet Cong wiped out two South Vietnamese battalions and attacked a U.S. Special Forces camp, fighting their way all the way into the compound.[8] In one attack, a Viet Cong force ambushed a much smaller Vietnamese ranger battalion with a single American advisor. The advisor called in a B-52 air strike, which annihilated the Viet Cong regiment. Helicopters evacuated the rangers and their American advisor, a young captain named Norman Schwarzkopf. He would one day lead American troops in the first Gulf War.

Around that time, the South Vietnamese government collapsed again. Catholic militants in the army forced the resignation of Premier Phan Huy Quat and another top official, Chief of State Phan Khac Suu, on June 12.[9] To General Westmoreland, the political instability and military losses meant only one thing: the U.S. needed to commit even more combat troops if it intended to win the war. [10] He estimated that it would require 180,000 men on the ground. That was just to stop the bloodletting. Another 100,000 U.S. soldiers, and maybe more, would be needed in 1966 and in the years after.[11]

Westmoreland visited Binh Dinh Province more frequently, sometimes as often as three times a week. He was convinced that Binh Dinh Province and Vietnam's Central Highlands were the key to preventing a Communist victory. The North Vietnamese were moving battalions, regiments, and entire divisions into the region in an effort to defeat government troops. Guerrilla attacks were also increasing as the Viet Cong tried to destabilize the countryside and destroy outposts of the Diem government.[12] We needed to be a bulwark against the tide.

Then in mid-June, we received intelligence that squared exactly with the general's fears. Aerial surveillance had spotted a North Vietnamese camp to our northeast, near a village close to the South China Sea. NVA troops had recently come in by sea. We decided to mount a stealth attack on the camp, intending to rout the North Vietnamese there.

On June 17, we prepared for the raid on the camp. We held a briefing on the operation—where the camp was, who was doing what. Four of us would lead platoons from the 883rd Regional Forces Company—one Green Beret for each of the four platoons of Montagnard soldiers. I would be one of them. Billy Waugh, Bobby Brown, and David Morgan would be the other three. We had trained the troops well, but they had never seen combat. This would be their first test. If the mission went well, we would cut through the camp and kill as many NVA as we could before they knew what happened.

The rest of the detachment would remain at camp, except for Ron Deis. I told him that he would be our spotter in the operation. Spotters have a crucial role in any operation. They fly overhead with a pilot called the forward air controller, or FAC, to view the action from above and help coordinate reinforcements or air support. Deis would be able to see what was happening as the operation unfolded, and the FAC would have radio contact with me on the ground, with our commos at Bong Son, and with the Air Force, if we needed to call in bombers.

As we were getting ready to go, an accident in the camp made for a foreboding start to the mission. A Vietnamese sergeant was cleaning his rifle that evening when the loaded weapon discharged and the bullet went through his head. Bobby Brown attended to him all night, and even managed to restart his heart when he went into cardiac arrest. It wasn't a great start to the night; Deis chewed out the South Vietnamese soldiers about the importance of unloading a gun before cleaning it.

As he ministered to the soldier, Brown was as cheerful and steady as always. He had just gotten word that his wife back in Ohio had just given birth to a baby boy. He passed around a box of candy cigars to us. Most of us ate them on the spot. Cole put his in his pocket for later. Brown was so proud. The new papa couldn't wait to get home to see his baby boy.

6

BUGLES

The night of the raid, stars spilled across the clear night sky above us. We walked out of the camp gates around 10 P.M., marching in silence through the brush and grass, two by two. Night sounds swirled in our ears: croaking geckos, cackling birds, whirring cicadas. The air was almost ninety degrees and thick with humidity.[1] Sweat soaked our uniforms.

We planned for a straightforward search-and-destroy mission. We would walk to the camp not far from where the Song Lai Giang River emptied into the South China Sea. With the rising sun behind us, we would attack the camp at dawn, kill as many Cong and NVA as we could, raze the camp and seize as many of their weapons as possible. We expected stiff resistance, but with stealth and surprise on our side, we were confident that it would be successful.

We walked northeast, cutting across the wide-open grassland encircling the camp. I was point man, first in the line of march, the tip of the spear. Behind us were a group of roughly eighty Montagnard and Nung soldiers from the 883rd Regional Forces Company. The regional force commander walked at my side, with one platoon of Montagnard soldiers close behind. Others walked silently to my right and left flanks, watching for ambushes or lookouts. One of them carried the PRC-10 radio that was our link to the camp and the air support we might need.

Waugh walked behind me, a regional soldier with an AK-47 beside him, to make sure that we had enough firepower in case we ran into trouble. The rest of his platoon followed. Brown led another platoon of regional forces. David Morgan covered my six o'clock, heading the fourth one in the rear.

I carried my M-16 rifle and ammo and grenades. I had tucked my bayonet blade in my boot and had my M1911A1 pistol on my hip. I had my map and compass. Before we left, I had slipped some beef jerky in my pocket as a snack. As always, I didn't carry anything personal that I might lose in a battle.

As we walked through the brush, I silently recited my version of the Rupert Brooke poem I had memorized in Okinawa: *If I should die, think only this of me / That there's some corner of a foreign field / That is forever America.*

After less than a kilometer, we entered the woods. Walking through the brush, we connected with a trail roughly parallel to the Song Lai Giang River, heading northeast toward the coordinates of the North Vietnamese rest camp. We walked beside the path to avoid mines or booby traps. After about fifteen minutes, the company paused for an equipment and ammunition check. Using flashlights masked with dark cloth, we peered at our compasses to make sure that we were oriented in the right direction. Then we continued, creeping through the foliage along the western bank of the river. I had forbidden smoking, which would have betrayed our location. We communicated with hand signals passed silently from the front of the line to the back.

Closer to the river, dense undergrowth slowed our march. We drew closer together to keep visual contact. In the moonlight, every shadow seemed to be a person waiting to ambush us. Every tree limb was a phantom arm holding a weapon. Animals called out in the dark, and every rustle and bird call overhead halted us in our tracks. Every so often, I heard a quiet slap in the darkness, the sound of someone in our company swatting at insects.

After about two kilometers, we reached Highway 1, the long north–south road that ran up the coast to Hue. The highway was dirt then, and it was open and wide and dangerous. We paused to look in both directions. It was quiet. We found a spot where trees came right up to the shoulder. I crossed first, and my men slipped like ghosts across the road in small groups. The undergrowth on the far side swallowed us up.

We continued in the direction of the village of Bong Son. The area was thickly settled, with bungalows along the roads and lining the rice fields. We stayed in the deep brush along the river, avoiding buildings. Though the village was still and silent, we could sometimes see candlelight in the darkness. Villagers didn't stray out of their homes after dark. There was no electricity to guide their way, and it was dangerous, with Viet Cong everywhere. We stayed vigilant for spies, fearful that dogs might alert others to our presence. We didn't hear a single bark as we moved past the village.[2]

Every step required precision. Mines or traps could be anywhere underfoot. The Viet Cong owned Binh Dinh Province. I paused at every snap or rustle in the undergrowth. I ignored the invisible insects swarming us in the darkness and kept on.

Eventually, the river curved east before dipping south. Our column followed the same route as the river, hugging the banks as we crept through the undergrowth. We waded across a tributary before we reached a bend in the river around midnight.

Then, I heard a sound in the bushes off to one side. I raised my arm to stop the march. The silent signal passed down the column. Everyone froze, listening.

In the quiet, I heard the unmistakable sound of snoring just off the trail. Holding my pistol, I slipped off the path. In the gloom, I found a sleeping sentry leaning against a tree, a Chinese-style rifle propped next to him. He was sleeping so soundly that I could have punched him in the nose and he wouldn't have woken up.

I slid up next to him and grabbed him in a chokehold. He didn't have a moment to cry out before his eyes opened. With my hands still on his throat, I took the barrel of my pistol and put it in his mouth. He didn't make a sound. I could see the terror in his eyes.

I slowly slid the pistol out of his mouth, then reached up with my left hand and pinched his lips tightly closed, as if to say, *Don't make a fucking sound.* He cast around and put his hand on a bag of food beside him. A district intelligence officer came up, snatched the bag away, and handcuffed him.

The man was not a Viet Cong soldier in ragged gear and outfitted with used equipment; he was a North Vietnamese regular. Billy Waugh had been in Vietnam for twenty-seven months already, and this was the first NVA soldier he had encountered.[3] The regional commander quietly interrogated the soldier. He said he had been posted as a lookout. There were many North Vietnamese soldiers in the area, he said. The commander sent him to the rear. He would accompany us as a prisoner.

We continued up the trail, one cautious step after another. We were heading northeast again, peeling away from the river into open fields and rice paddies. There were fewer dwellings here, but we were more exposed. We walked slowly, creeping forward a short distance before I would halt the column with a hand gesture to listen, motionless. After another two hours, we had covered only another kilometer or so. A grove of trees lay ahead of us, with a cluster of huts around a road following the river to our east. We entered the trees. I heard another noise in the brush. I stopped the column with a hand signal again and crept off the trail in the direction of the sound.

A few yards off the path, two North Vietnamese sentries slept soundly on their watch. One had an automatic weapon beside him. The other had a medical kit and a sidearm. "Look at what this son of a bitch has on him," Waugh whispered to Morgan. Unlike the Viet Cong, these soldiers had top quality gear. The medical kit looked like first aid equipment that Brown or Hubbard would have carried. His gear, his boots, his helmet—all new.[4] We disarmed them and prepared to send them to the back. As with the other prisoner, the regional commander interrogated them.

He whispered to me the intelligence he'd learned from the sleeping sentries. There were hundreds of North Vietnamese soldiers in the rest camp, not the dozens we expected. A full battalion's worth of soldiers had infiltrated Binh Dinh from the South China Sea. They were well trained and heavily armed with both small arms and machine guns, and were resting before travelling farther south. The information changed nothing. The scope of the operation had grown, but our mission was the same.

We kept going. Now we were headed due north, past more villages. The river curved toward the east, and we followed a tributary that ran along the base of heavily forested hills. We were near the coast now, where the river delta spilled into the South China Sea. After about two more kilometers, we encountered evidence that the camp was close. Sometimes we'd hear voices in the darkness, conversations in Vietnamese about military movements and preparations. We moved even more slowly, stepping like cats through the brush and stopping even more often to listen.

We arrived at the camp's perimeter just before dawn. We approached from the east. When the sun came up, it would be at our backs and in the eyes of the enemy. In the dim predawn light, I could see about thirty low huts with grass roofs, some arranged in an orderly grid, others halfway built and scattered in random spots, as if slapped up in a hurry. We could see candles flickering. Some had stone fireplaces outside. Smoke rose from the fireplaces, a sign that breakfast was underway. Clothing hung on lines to dry. To my surprise, I could see women's and children's clothes alongside black uniforms. A sign that the NVA rest camp was alongside a village filled with families.

There was no gate, just a makeshift fence. I slipped in through a gap. On the other side, I spotted a North Vietnamese soldier turned away from me. He had probably just awakened, because he was relieving himself against the fence, his legs spread wide. I crept up behind him, wrapped one arm around his throat in a chokehold, and put a gun to his head. He let go of his joint and raised his hands. His black pants slipped down to his knees. When I turned him around, I stepped on his toes, and he squealed in pain. When I looked down, I saw that he was only wearing one rubber sandal; the foot I had stepped on was bare. Like the others, the regional commander interrogated him quietly.

He told us that a command unit was asleep in a nearby hut, in charge of an entire infantry battalion that had come in by ship from the South China Sea and disembarked on the shore to our east. There were dozens of NVA soldiers in each hut in the camp, preparing to move south to bring the war to the Americans. We handcuffed him and moved him to the back of the column with the other prisoners.

Sunrise was about forty-five minutes away. I passed word down the column that combat was imminent.[5] I didn't need to look at them to know that adrenaline was lighting up every man in the company, their hearts pounding in their chests. With Billy Waugh close behind me, I slipped inside one of the nearest hooches. On a wide sleeping mat near the wall, shapes moved rhythmically under the covers, heads facing the wall. I crept inside, trying to move around the bed undetected in the gloom. A table beside the bed held opened cans of beer, suggesting that it was the hooch of an officer, maybe even a general.

One of the shapes suddenly sat up. It was a naked woman, and she had spotted me while in the middle of having sex with the man in the bed. She didn't scream or cower—quick as a soldier, her hand darted down next to the bed and produced a pistol. Without a pause, she aimed and fired at me in the half-darkness.

She missed. In that moment, I could see the strap of a rifle or a semi-automatic leaning against the bed. I didn't need to worry about her reaching for the rifle because Billy Waugh fired past me, shooting the woman several times. Then the man stood, naked, and reached for the weapon. I killed him.

With the gunshots, our advantage of stealth and surprise evaporated. The silence exploded into chaos and gunfire. As we ran from the officer's hooch, we could see North Vietnamese soldiers racing through the camp, jumping into defensive bunkers with their guns. Bullets began to snap through the air around me. I heard machine-gun fire.

Much of my platoon, experiencing hostile fire for the first time, immediately lost their battle discipline and scattered. My heart sank as they ran; I yelled at them to come back, but they either couldn't hear me or pretended that they couldn't. Maybe they were spooked, panicked at the shooting. Maybe they got confused and forgot our contingency plans for regrouping. It didn't matter why they ran; I had to get them back. One of those men had our PRC-10 radio. Without the radio, no one would know where we were and there would be no way to call up air support. I couldn't see them anywhere because the scattered buildings and the undergrowth obstructed my vision.[6]

A small number of soldiers had stayed with me, and we started fighting our way through the camp, the rising sun behind us now

doing its job blinding the enemy. My other three platoons—
which were still intact—fanned out according to my plan. We
couldn't see each other, but we all knew what to do. Billy Waugh
went ahead of me to the north, Dave Morgan stayed behind to
the south, and Brown was off to my side. In front of me, a group
of North Vietnamese soldiers who had been eating breakfast
outside a hut jumped to their feet. I opened fire with my M-16,
killing five of them. Gunfire poured out of the closest house, and
grenades detonated around us. I ran to a window, pulled a pin on
one of my grenades, and tossed it inside. The explosion blasted
smoke out the window. I ran through the door.

Inside, injured soldiers screamed and coughed in the
smoke-filled hooch. Shapes darted and bobbed in the haze. I
sprayed the men with my M-16. When the bullets ran out, I
used the rifle butt as a club, smashing the soldiers one by one
as I came to them. A bullet grazed my right forearm—my first
combat wound.

Adrenaline raced through my body. I felt as though I was su-
perhuman, that nothing could touch or harm me. Grenades continued to explode, and mortars streaked toward us from hidden
enemy positions while gunfire from AK-47s zipped from hidden
bunkers and sniper's nests. With a few of the regional soldiers
still by my side, I went from hut to hut, tossing grenades through
doorways and windows. There were dozens of NVA soldiers in
some of the huts, and their screams soon filled the air.

The other platoons did the same. Waugh, Morgan, and Brown
led their men between the hooches, first tossing in grenades
then leveling their M-16s through the doorways and spraying
the interiors. Empty magazines littered the ground as they re-
loaded. Later, Billy Waugh would recount that he was surprised
by how well the NVA soldiers were equipped, their huts packed
with modern gear and weapons. *I don't like the look of this*, he
thought.[7]

As we pressed westward through the camp, flames billowed from the huts. From out of the smoke and noise, four more North Vietnamese soldiers charged at me. I used my rifle butt and my fists to fight back. I killed all of them. As I dashed between buildings, I surprised more panicked North Vietnamese, who still had no idea of the relatively paltry force they faced. I used my rifle, my fists, my rifle butt. I killed everything that came at me.

Waugh and Morgan had run into the trees toward more of the huts, tossing grenades inside and strafing the interiors. They managed to surprise still more of the North Vietnamese as they rushed to mobilize. They also heard a new sound: the thunder of boots on the forest floor as hundreds, maybe thousands, of soldiers rushed into attack formation. [8] Morgan and Waugh quickly ran low on grenades and ammo, and withdrew toward our rally point.

We reached the far side of the encampment. The machine-gun fire had quieted, and mortars had stopped falling. A lull fell over the camp. The battle was over. We had cleared the camp and routed the entire battalion. In the hour since fighting broke out, I had killed eighteen or nineteen North Vietnamese soldiers and captured weapons positions. The NVA had left behind thousands of rounds of ammunition and four or five machine-gun emplacements. Any moment, we expected to hear the drone of our spotter plane carrying Ron Deis up from Bong Son to survey our work.

Giddy with excitement, Waugh, Brown, Morgan, and I began to laugh and joke, as our adrenaline dissolved into relief. I felt like King Shit, mastermind of the successful operation. The regional troops began collecting the weapons that the North Vietnamese had dropped or abandoned: Russian-made RPDs; AK-47s and ammo; and radios.[9] I started back to find my men who had run, and the radio that had gone with them. It was time to withdraw to safety.

Then the horns sounded.

We stopped in our tracks. The bugle notes rolled out from some invisible point in the forest to the north, across the wide rice paddies to the west of the camp. The rally point we had chosen was on the opposite side of the fields, on a hill overlooking the burning camp. We didn't realize it, but the huts we had struck had only been a small part of the camp. Many more buildings stretched into the forest. The huge force that we had learned about from the sentry weren't all dead, and they hadn't vanished. *Shit*, I thought. They were regrouping.

7

THE KNOLL

6:50 A.M., JUNE 18, 1965
BINH DINH PROVINCE, VIETNAM

Back at camp, our junior demolitions specialist Ron Deis awoke before dawn. He had gone to bed long before we left camp with the expectation that he would have a bird's eye view of a seamless operation in the morning. He hadn't expected anything unusual with the mission. The 883rd was going into combat for the first time, but the mission included me and A-321's two most experienced men—Waugh and Morgan—taking on what we thought was a relatively small force, so Deis assumed that everyone would be home safe soon.

In his hooch at the bottom of a mortar pit, Deis jumped out of bed, yawned, and stretched before putting on his glasses, boots, and uniform. He walked to the mess hall for some grub. Deis had been assigned to be on the small spotter plane with the forward air controller, or FAC, an Air Force captain named Howard Bronson III. Deis knew him well. Bronson was well-liked at the camp, and often stayed over, sometimes sleeping in one of the outbuildings across the landing strip. The plan was to leave for the NVA camp at sunup.

After eating, Deis gathered his M-16, grenades, and ammunition and walked out to the airfield to meet Bronson. Even though it was barely dawn, the weather station in Quy Nhon already notched ninety-seven degrees. Deis, his rifle in tow, got into the backseat of the Bird Dog, a single-engine plane often used for spotting. He sat down on his flak jacket and put on his headset. Bronson started the engine. Moments later, the Bird Dog was airborne.

As the plane rose to cruising altitude, the camp fell from Deis's sight and Binh Dinh's highlands stretched to the north. Bronson flew over Bong Son with the river to the right, as forest gave way to rice paddies and turned back into forest. With the plane's cruising speed of about 105 mph,[1] it took Bronson less than five minutes to fly to the camp coordinates.

The FAC was a crucial part of ground operations, coordinating movements on the ground with air support. The planes carried multiple radios: an FM radio to talk to troops on the ground, a UHF radio to communicate directly with fighter jets and bombers, and a VHF radio to make requests and get approvals from the Air Force. Deis's headset allowed him to talk to Bronson and no one else.[2]

Even before the plane reached the coordinates, Deis could tell that something had gone wrong. Looking down out of the plane's right side, he could see plumes of smoke billowing from the burning huts, and huge numbers of North Vietnamese soldiers below. While the plane was too high to make out specific people on the battlefield below, he could see that the company was pinned down and in trouble.

Bronson talked to one of the commos back at camp—most likely Kenny Bates—while describing for me what he could see from above. *Smoke! We need smoke*, Bates yelled to the pilot, who conveyed the instructions to Deis.

As the plane circled over the camp, Bronson told Deis to get ready to drop a smoke grenade. He pulled the pin on one and held it out the window of the Bird Dog. When Bronson gave the sign, Deis dropped it, watching as it tumbled to the ground. Then it seemed to disappear. For a moment, Deis wondered if he had thrown a dud. Then he saw it—red smoke billowing out of the windows and doors of one of the huts. The grenade had gone right through the hut's thatched roof.

As the Bird Dog circled, Deis spotted something that we couldn't see on the ground that made his blood freeze. To the north of the rice paddies, a long, well-constructed trench stretched from east to west. In the trench, two to three hundred North Vietnamese soldiers crouched shoulder-to-shoulder holding AK-47s. The soldiers were so close that Deis could see their faces. He could also see their weapons, which were trained on the exposed Americans and the soldiers from the 883rd.

Over the radio, Deis asked Bronson to bring him closer. The plane buzzed lower. As the Bird Dog dropped toward the ground, Deis pulled up his M-16, poked the muzzle out the right-side window, and began spraying the surprised North Vietnamese soldiers below with bullets.

The soldiers' heads whipped upward. They saw the plane for the first time and turned their AK-47s skyward, firing at the Bird Dog. As the bullets pocked the fuselage, Deis thanked God that he had remembered to sit on his flak jacket. Within seconds, Bronson told Deis over the radio that they were losing oil pressure; one of the bullets had pierced the oil pan. They needed to return to the camp at Bong Son before they crashed. The plane veered south and out of sight.

* * *

Just minutes earlier, I faced the result of all of those bugles sounding. Within moments, North Vietnamese soldiers began charging toward us, dozens of them. Automatic weapons fire rattled, and bullets snapped all around us. Artillery exploded, small mortars that the Vietnamese fired from a distance. The withering gunfire scattered what remained of our company. The three platoons still in the camp were spread too far apart to coordinate movements and reassemble in an orderly way at our rallying point. The pre-raid calm was gone. We had plunged into a deadly fun house of billowing smoke, tracers and mortars showering us from above, and automatic weapons fire everywhere.

We knew for certain that the intelligence reports we had received had woefully underestimated the number of North Vietnamese in the area. Even the information from the soldiers we captured didn't fully capture the scope of the camp, which was mostly hidden under the forest canopy.

The members of my Montagnard platoon who had fled toward the shore and away from the fighting had taken the radio with them. Without it, I couldn't call in backup. As the three other platoons fought back under withering fire, I ran to search for the rest of my men. Several minutes after they had turned tail, I finally found them off to the east on a path that led toward the river and the shore. A South Vietnamese officer with them had failed to keep them from running, but had managed to keep them together in a cohesive unit, even if they weren't on the battlefield. The men looked exhausted and terrified. Even though I was furious, I didn't let my anger and frustration show. I just let them rest for a moment, and pulled the officer to one side.

"What the fuck happened?" I asked him, trying to stay calm.

He hung his head and kept his eyes on the ground, rather than meet my gaze. "They started running," he told me, as if that explained everything.

"Why the fuck didn't you stop them?" I asked quietly.

"They started running," he said again.

I wasn't going to get a better explanation. To this day, I'm not sure why those men ran. All I knew was that I needed to get them back to the battlefield. Our retreat route was through the firefight raging in the distance, and the only way these men would get home alive that day was to go back to where they had just run from.

I let them take another sip of water and rest for a few more moments before I got them back onto their feet and into formation. I told them that we were going to move quickly back in a westerly direction toward the fighting, and we'd pick up the pace as we went along. As I reached the camp again, a soldier from the 883rd ran toward me. The rest of the company was pinned down and under attack, he yelled.

The sound of explosions, machine guns, and screaming filled my ears, so I couldn't hear the engine of a two-man prop plane overhead. I probably couldn't have seen it through the smoke if I had. But somewhere above us, Specialist Ron Deis was looking down out the window at us.

After he tossed the smoke grenade, I saw the red plumes billowing from the hut but didn't realize that the spotter plane had taken fire. We had our hands full on the ground. Two North Vietnamese soldiers charged at me, and one threw a grenade. I got a shot off at the one who threw it and he fell, then he got up with a knife. I shot him again. And then the grenade went off.

After it detonated, I looked at my hand. The blast had blown off the top of my middle finger on my right hand and ripped open the tip of my index finger—my trigger finger. I saw the tip of my middle finger on the ground. I picked it up and put it in my pocket. I tasted blood in my mouth; I eventually realized that the explosion had knocked a tooth down my throat. I shat that tooth out later.

Blood was everywhere—mine, my attackers', and God knows who else's. Blood mixed with the sweat that soaked my uniform, and now we were caked in dirt and mud. The loss of my trigger finger was a problem; I needed to be able to fire a weapon, and I wasn't proficient with my left hand. I tried to wipe the blood from my hands, and curled my injured fingers so I could use my pinkie to pull my trigger.

A kind of calm came over me. Something happens when you get wounded on the battlefield. There's no way to explain it. If your body is still working, you find that you can keep going in a way that you couldn't off the battlefield. Even as the blood pours from your wounds, and you find pieces of yourself no longer there. You keep going.

The only way for me and my platoon to reach the high ground to our west, the rally point, was to cross the rice paddy in front of me. Because of the trench to our north and the NVA machine gun and mortar placements, trying to make that run would be like trying to cut across a firing range. It would likely be suicide. But it was the only way.

With about a dozen members of my platoon, I set out across the field. I crouched low, my M-16 muzzle facing north and my back to the south as I scuttled toward the hill. In a few months, that paddy would have been flooded with water. Now it was mostly dry and grassy, only muddy at worst. Not far from me—I wasn't sure where—Billy Waugh, David Morgan, and Bobby Brown were also trying to sprint across the shooting range. Waugh was focused completely on reaching the hill. Bodies were everywhere, mostly our regional recruits who had left themselves exposed. The stench was awful, a combination of the shit that the Vietnamese used as fertilizer and the acrid bite of explosives in the air.

I reached the hill at about 7:45 A.M., about two hours after our attack had begun. The knoll was shaped like a camel's back, with a hump in front about thirty meters high, a dip, and another rise that continued to a ridgeline stretching to our west. The hill was partially forested, with stands of trees giving us some cover, and shrubbery and grass between. As we reached the hill, we discovered dozens of foxholes dug into the hillside, including a trench at the base of the hill. When we sprang our surprise attack, the North Vietnamese had abandoned them, believing a much larger force was attacking. Now, the North Vietnamese held similar high ground to our north and east, across the wide rice paddies.

We made for the foxholes. I was the only American among the fifteen or so regional fighters who made it to the hill. I organized what was left of my men into defensive positions in the earthen dugouts, going up and down the line shouting at the remnants of the company to keep firing. Some did, keeping their heads down as they held their guns over their heads and fired blindly. Others were paralyzed with fear.

From our elevated vantage point, I could look out over the entire terrain of the camp and see our position for the first time. I finally got eyes on Waugh. He was in the middle of the rice field about two hundred yards away, lying in a muddy ditch. He had been running across the rice field when a round from a Russian-made RPD machine gun hit him in his right knee, knocking him to the ground. He had managed to crawl forward behind a low levee that bisected the field. After a few meters, he rolled into a shallow trough in the field, an indent on the ground called a buffalo rub, where oxen would roll in the dirt. It wasn't deep enough to provide cover for his whole body; one leg was sticking out and visible to snipers. Later, he claimed that he was sharing that rub with an ornery buffalo who wasn't happy with having a roommate. I never saw a buffalo. Maybe he was hallucinating.[3]

I kept scanning the field. I still wasn't sure where Morgan was. A few moments after I reached the hill, I was relieved to finally locate him. I heard him yelling for help south of where Waugh was trapped. It turned out he had been knocked unconscious on his way across the rice field. Now Morgan was trapped, too, but in a very different situation.

He had fallen into a cesspool of human shit so deep that he was afraid he might drown. I'm not completely sure how he got in there—he either fell in when he was knocked unconscious, or crawled into it after he regained consciousness, thinking it was safe. However he got in, he couldn't claw his way out because it was so deep and slippery. As for Brown, I didn't have any idea where he was. He could have been anywhere—behind an embankment or a tree, down a foxhole, dead behind a hooch.

The PRC-10 that came back with the platoon had been shot to hell, but it still worked. I got on the radio and told Kenny Bates back at Bong Son that we were running low on ammunition and needed to be resupplied. We also needed air support from above and artillery from our two 155mm howitzers in the camp. I could barely hear Bates over the din of artillery and automatic gunfire. As I yelled at him, I watched for attackers, trying to keep my men in fighting position.

For a time, there was nothing I could do but try to keep our position from being overrun. The dozen or so members of my platoon were all that remained with me of the eighty soldiers of the 883rd that we had left camp with. I made sure the men were stationed at strategic distances to defend our flanks and every approach to the hill. Though they were well-trained, their inexperience under fire was obvious. The only way to keep our position from being overrun was to dash back and forth from one pocket to another telling them what to do and how to do it.

If they couldn't do it, then I had to do it myself. When I heard fire coming on our right flank, I ran toward the shooting and discovered five North Vietnamese soldiers climbing over our trench. I opened fire with my M-16 and killed all five.

I heard shots fired on our left flank, on the far side of the hill.

I ran toward the sound of gunfire and saw about a half-dozen stealthy attackers moving toward our position. I grabbed a grenade from my belt, pulled the pin, and threw it. The grenade killed four of them. Two kept coming, but my M-16 had jammed. I drew my pistol and shot one of them. When the other got close, I used the butt of my M-16 to beat him to death.[4]

I'm not sure when it dawned on me that we were surrounded on that knoll. It wasn't just a matter of avoiding the incoming gunfire from the dugouts and the artillery fire to the north. We were an island under siege, and we needed to defend the entire hilltop from all directions. The North Vietnamese were as likely to try to sneak up behind us from the west and from the south as they were to attack us directly from the north. I have an expression for situations like this: a goat fuck.

* * *

Down in Saigon, the duty officer at the MACV command center was having a busy morning. Every few minutes, he took down incident reports from around Vietnam, recording the details in the log book. At 10 A.M., he recorded that a razorback reconnaissance flight investigating mortar fire in Cu Chi found nothing. Soon after, he took a report of a B-team destroying a cache of rice believed destined for the Viet Cong. At 10:21 A.M., a report came in of another mortar attack in Cu Chi.

Then, he made a brief entry at 10:25 A.M. A Special Forces captain had radioed in with fuzzy details of something going on in Binh Dinh Province. One U.S. soldier wounded in action. One victim killed. "No other info available now," the duty officer wrote. He moved on to the next report.

8

"I REFUSE TO GO"

The thump of rotors midmorning meant that help had arrived. A "slick"—a stripped-down Huey chopper with no armaments other than door guns—came up over the hill behind us to the south. The chopper from the 117th Assault Helicopter Company had been on its way to Bong Son on a "hash and trash" run—a general support mission to return some Green Berets to the camp and bring in mail. The moment the Huey landed at the camp, the pilot and crew were redirected to bring ammo to us and bring out our wounded. The pilot got a short briefing in our tactical operations center while the helicopter refueled. Four boxes of ammo went onto the slick, and the pilot took off to the north.[1]

I spoke to the pilot on the radio as he followed the river. I gave him the coordinates and advised him to approach us from our six o'clock; otherwise they'd run straight into North Vietnamese fire. The crew could hear the urgency in my voice, and the sound of rounds detonating and gunfire over it. They knew we were in trouble.

They didn't realize until the slick had nearly reached me how much trouble we were in. The pilot approached the hill from the rear, just as I suggested. I didn't even have time to get to the helicopter. The moment the skids kissed the ground, gunfire began to spray the Huey. The pilot on the left side took most of the fire, because of the angle of the chopper. The crew chief took the worst of it. A bullet ricocheted through the cockpit and hit him in the arm. It hit a vein or an artery, and blood sprayed everywhere inside the helicopter. Whipped by the rotor wash, blood splattered the instrument panel, the pilot, the interior roof.

Another bullet that went through the instrument panel nicked Chief Warrant Officer Bob Baden. A third bullet that shattered the chin bubble went through the heel of the pilot, who started screaming that he'd been shot. Baden grabbed the controls of the helicopter and lifted off, turning down the backside of the hill. He yelled at the gunner to toss the ammunition out of the helicopter. The gunner flung the ammo boxes out of the helicopter as it gained altitude and flew back to Bong Son, carrying the bleeding crew chief.

I'm not sure how many of those boxes made it out of the helicopters, but the ones that did were like gifts from heaven. We needed every bullet.

* * *

With my remaining men organized on the hill, I used the PRC-10 to radio our location to Kenny Bates, who had guided the slick with the ammo resupply to our position. I stayed calm and focused as I gave the coordinates of the Cong to Bates to target with artillery. Across the rice paddy, the North Vietnamese had an elevated position like ours. It was advantageous high ground, but it was also an easy target. Even as bullets snapped around me, I knew the men at camp were jamming 155mm shells into the breech of our howitzer and training it on the enemy locations I was feeding them. The metal would be scorching hot in the sun, and the men would be handling the shells as quickly as they could. Then they would turn away as the gun thumped the shells toward the enemy positions eight kilometers to the north.

The shells travel faster than the speed of sound. That means there isn't much time between hearing the whistle of incoming artillery and the detonation of the shells. Hearing a whistle meant that a shell was passing over my head. If I didn't hear the shell, it was landing on me. I heard the whistle. I ducked low and pressed my face against the dirt, as if I was trying to bury my head in the soil. A deafening blast. A shock wave. A tremor in my bones. I raised my head.

About thirty yards from me, the shell from the howitzer catapulted a fountain of earth and foliage high into the air. For a moment, a quiet fell over the battlefield as the fighting paused, as if both sides were holding their breath. Then the sound resumed. The screaming of injured men. The rattle of machine-gun fire.

The racket of the artillery was a welcome addition to the ear-splitting chaos. We had been fighting since before 6 A.M., and I wondered how much longer we could last without air or ground support. The midmorning sun spilled over a battlefield littered with bodies from our regiment. While we were holding our own, we had no idea how many North Vietnamese were still hidden in the forest readying for an attack. The rising heat baked the battlefield. The stench was overpowering. With every blast and concussion, flies rose in clouds. Vultures wheeled high overhead.

Out in the rice paddy, Waugh remained in the buffalo rub. He hadn't exhausted all his ammo, and he was firing at the North Vietnamese, giving us cover on the knoll.

Most of his body was in the ditch, but his leg was still exposed. The NVA gunners went for that leg. A tracer round went through the bottom of his jungle boot. The bullet bored up through his foot and shredded his toes, punching out through his ankle. As he described it later, he had never felt such pain. His foot and ankle were a bloody tangle of blood and sinew, the bone shattered and jutting through his skin. Shrapnel filled his knee, and leeches were soon feasting on his leg. *Damn, my military career is over. I'll never see combat again*, he thought.[2]

As he lay bleeding, I could hear him as he cursed God. Bullets kicked up dirt around him as he screamed, "Goddammit, God, don't you know what the fuck is going on down here? They're shooting me. Where the fuck are you? Whose side are you on?" He was talking like God was right there beside him in the rice paddy, hanging on his every word.

He wasn't only cursing God; he was screaming at me, too, calling me everything but a child of God. I swear that boy from Texas was calling me the N-word as he lay there in the dirt, screaming for rescue. "What the fuck are you doing?" he yelled at me. He was trying to point to a sniper in a tree. "Why the fuck haven't you killed him?" he shouted.

I tried to turn to look, but I couldn't see where he was talking about. There was incoming fire from every direction. The artillery blasts were coming more frequently now, sometimes in quick succession. It was impossible for me to pick out where the gunfire might have been coming from. "I don't know where the fuck he is," I shouted back.

"Well, Goddammit, you know, it's about time you tried growing up and being a Special Forces soldier," he shouted back.

Waugh got the sniper before I did. As he lay in the field bleeding, he managed to get the sniper in his sights. Waugh steadied himself and got a shot off that knocked the shooter from his perch. The wounded sniper slipped down from his position. Waugh got his barrel up and took another shot. The legs stopped dancing.

Waugh and I yelled back and forth as the minutes ticked by, trying to communicate over the noise of the battlefield. I decided I could make the attempt if I had a shield of suppressing fire; artillery and air support were one of the few ways I had to interrupt the blizzard of lead and mortars that the Vietnamese were raining down on us.

In a lull, I crawled on my knees down the hill. At the bottom, the field was a stinking soup of mud and shit. I slithered through the filth until I reached Waugh's ditch. Dead members of our regional forces company lay around him. I told him I was trying to assess the situation so that I could get him the hell out of there. He saw that he was entangled in some vines. I tried to pull him free.

Waugh was still spitting mad, angry as hell that he was still out there in the open. All the bad blood between us, the hostility and friction over who should be in charge, came pouring like blood from a ripped-open wound. Waugh considered himself my superior, and now his life was in my hands. I imagined that must have pissed him off, maybe even more than his injury. "If you're not out here to help me, what the fuck are you out here for?" he spat at me. I wanted to yell back, *Saving your stupid ass*, but I didn't say anything. "It's about time you did something with that brain of yours," he went on.

The incoming automatic weapons fire was too heavy to attempt to rescue him. I told him that I needed more covering fire and air support if I was going to attempt to rescue him, and said I'd be back. I left him where he was and pressed into the rice field, crawling back toward the hill. Partway back, I took a round in the arm. I ignored the pain and kept going, willing myself up the hill and into the dugouts.

Back on the hill, I kept ordering up more artillery and air support, and told Bong Son that we were running low on ammunition. We would need more ammo soon, and heavy weapons. Back at the camp, we had a 105mm recoilless rifle, a massive weapon that's more like a cannon than a gun, which would have given us a tactical edge. We'd also need a dustoff—a medevac helo—to bring out our wounded when I could finally get them.

Morgan had come to. From out in the paddy, he yelled to me that he was taking fire, too. I had more luck finding that gunman, who was concealed in an underground sniper's nest. I located the camouflaged sniper hole he was pointing to and crawled over. When the sniper lifted the sod covering, I shot him. Then I slipped in a grenade, dropped the top, and put my head down as the ground shuddered under my body from the underground blast. The blast killed two more Cong who were also in the nest.[3]

I heard a new sound: the roar of engines overhead. My requests for air support had been relayed to the Air Force. OV-1 Mohawks streaked over the battlefield. As I watched, the Mohawks rained ordnance down on the trench lines on the other side of the open field. The roar of the planes deafened me as they shot past, followed by bone-rattling concussions and a mushroom of flame that turned to a plume of smoke. Now at last the planes had delivered the preparations that I needed to crawl out onto the battlefield to try to bring my men back alive.

The ordnance lighting up the North Vietnamese positions gave me an opening to drag Morgan to safety. He was still trapped in the shit pond to my east. It wasn't far from the earthworks at the base of the hill, but I was exposed to the gunfire to our north. I found a piece of rope and told the regional forces with me to give me covering fire. I began to crawl toward the pit.

When I reached Morgan, he was still confused and disoriented from being knocked out, but he was alive. I threw the rope to him and held tight. Soaked in feces, he dragged himself out of the muck until he was by my side. He had minor shrapnel injuries and was still disoriented from being knocked out, but otherwise he was all right.[4] Together, we crawled on our stomachs back to safety at the hill.

Morgan and I were the sole Americans on the hill, along with about a dozen Montagnards from the 883rd. After I got him back, a group of enemy soldiers charged the hill. I picked up a machine gun and dropped four or five of them—the rest retreated. There was a 60mm mortar near me, and I dropped five or six mortars into the muzzle, firing them toward the North Vietnamese positions.

With the cover from the mortar rounds, I crawled out of the foxhole and ran to Waugh again, this time with Morgan providing machine-gun cover. When I reached the buffalo rub, I tried to pick up Waugh, but the fire from the NVA positions was too intense. I told Waugh I would have to come back a third time. He handed me the AK-47 he had been firing, and I shimmied back up the hill a second time with the AK. The only way I could get Waugh was if I had more air support, and it hadn't arrived.

* * *

To our south, Tiny Aldrich tried to decipher the information he had received. An encoded message had finally reached Quy Nhon, where Major Billy Cole commanded Detachment A-121, the Special Forces command and control team that oversaw all of the camps in Binh Dinh, including ours at Bong Son. The message that reached Tiny reported on the fighting north of Bong Son, but information was sketchy and something had clearly gone wrong.[5]

Tiny immediately told Cole about the battle underway. Then he radioed Bong Son, where he probably talked to Kenny Bates and told him to send him all data in the clear, meaning not to encode it.[6] The process of encrypting and decrypting messages wasted precious time when lives were at stake.

Cole headed immediately to the airport. Because the original FAC, Bronson, was grounded with thirteen bullets in his Bird Dog, Tiny's operations sergeant, "Big John" Manthey, ordered another FAC to the battle site and called up air support. Manthey was a quiet rock, a jungle fighter and veteran of multiple combat missions, one of the original Green Berets.[7] The FAC that he sent up to the battle was an Air Force major named Charles Villa. Everyone in the command team called him "Pancho Villa."

As Cole's helicopter thundered north, he could hear the radio traffic from my PRC-10. It was about fifty-five miles from Quy Nhon to Bong Son, so he had time to monitor what was happening on the battlefield. Over the radio, he heard me tell the commo at Bong Son that we were running low on ammunition and needed resupply. One of the commos came out of the radio shack and yelled to Deis that I wanted our 105mm recoilless rifle and ammo brought up. A 105mm is a huge gun that's eleven feet long and weighs almost five hundred pounds, built to take out tanks, and requires three men to use. It would have given us a huge edge on the battlefield. Deis started to prepare to bring the 105mm to the airfield with ammo.

Cole ordered his pilot to set his chopper down at camp to pick up the gun, ammunition, and supplies. After the chopper set down near the gate, John Reinburg, Ron Wingo, and another member of the team ran ammo boxes and litters out to the airfield from camp and helped Cole load the chopper. Deis stayed behind. In the confusion, someone subbed Reinburg for Deis. Instead of bringing the 105mm, Reinburg brought a smaller M-60 machine gun, a less powerful gun that also required a crew.

As they got ready to board, another colonel charged out of the camp and stood between Cole and the chopper door, demanding to know where the helicopter was going. He was what Cole called a "Gary Trooper," all hat and no gun, who was at the camp because he had heard about the action.

"You're not taking this chopper in there until I am assured of a safe landing spot," the colonel barked. Maybe he was concerned that there would be a repeat of what had happened earlier with the slick that had come under fire.

Cole lowered the barrel of his M-16. "Sir, you are interfering with my command. Please step back out of the way," he said.

Face flushed with anger, the colonel started to push Cole's barrel aside. Then he heard a bullet being chambered. Wingo was in a crouch, pointing his rifle. The colonel paled, and then stepped backward. Finally, Cole, Reinburg, and the others took off north.

* * *

Cole and Reinburg were flying into the storm, and the firefight was only intensifying. At 10:30 A.M., four Navy A-1E Skyraiders roared over me, lighting up the North Vietnamese positions. In the South China Sea, the USS McMorris moved into position to shell the battlefield from offshore. A destroyer escort, the McMorris swung its three-inch-caliber guns toward our coordinates, and began sending over shells at about 11:30 A.M. It was the first time in the war that a Navy vessel had provided a shore bombardment for a battle on land. It didn't go well, at least at first. The mountainous terrain complicated the bombardment and the ten rounds fell short.[8]

The air support, though, was giving me the cover I needed to get back to Waugh a third time. By now, his exposed leg had taken more rounds. He wasn't talking anymore. He recounted later how a bullet wound to the head had knocked him out, and he'd been unconscious for a time. When he awoke, he had been stripped of some of his equipment and gear, including a Rolex watch. North Vietnamese soldiers had taken him for dead.[9]

I crawled out to him again across the rice paddy, keeping my head low as Morgan and the regional forces provided cover. When I reached him, I heaved his body up and across my back. At first I carried him fireman-style over my shoulders, but his shot-up foot was in agony and that position made it worse. I shifted him to a piggyback position and staggered with him toward the hill. Waugh wasn't cursing or screaming anymore. Now that I was bringing him to safety, he shut up. Slowly, I hauled him up the hill. Every so often I'd tell him that I needed to take a break, and I'd pause. He was still silent, his only sound his breath in my ear.

As I staggered toward the hill, another bullet grazed me in the back of the leg. I kept going. The blood from my wounds had dried and cracked, the constant sting of sweat reminding me of my injuries. Blood was everywhere, soaking the ground, our uniforms, and getting in our eyes.

When we reached the top of the hill, I pulled him into a bunker. I think at one point he mumbled an apology for insulting me. I didn't give a rat's ass. I just needed to get him off the battlefield, and I needed more ammunition and weapons to keep fighting.

It arrived soon enough. Soon I heard the chop-chop-chop of the helicopter from Bong Son with Cole and Reinburg aboard. The Huey set down behind us, where a smoke grenade marked a landing spot just back from the hilltop, shielded from ground-fire that the Viet Cong rained down on us from their positions to the north. The helicopter came down hard with a bump, and automatic gunfire met its landing, blowing out the glass in the chin bubble. The door gunner fell back, blood spurting from his arm.

When the helicopter came down, Reinburg jumped out, while the pilot began giving first aid to the gunner. I dragged Waugh over to the door of the helicopter under the whirling rotor blades. I got up on my knees and hoisted him high enough so that the crew chief could grab him and pull him up into the chopper and onto a litter. Waugh wasn't a big guy, but it was still tough getting him up. After he got into the chopper, he just looked at me. He said, "I'm safe now. I don't think I'll get shot in the ass."

I was relieved to see Cole was in the chopper. "God, I'm glad to see you," I told the major. I explained to him the situation on the ground, and that there were still men unaccounted for.

"I'm sending you out with the chopper," Cole shouted under the noise of the engine. "I'm here to replace you. You need medical attention."

I was stunned. There was no way I could leave in the middle of a firefight. It would destroy the morale of the company. They would never trust me again. I had to stay. "Sir, please don't do that to me," I shouted. "I'm not hurt that bad. I've got to get my guys out of this predicament. We have another air strike on the way. I refuse to go."

There was another reason, a more personal one. The night before the operation, Brown had handed out candy cigars to all of us to celebrate his baby's birth. I had a responsibility as the commander to bring everyone in. But I also had a responsibility to Brown's wife and his new baby, to make sure he got home.

Cole could see how distraught the order made me, and he backed down. "You've got it," he yelled. "Good luck and God bless you." And he got back onto the helicopter. I crouched under the rotor wash and watched the helicopter return to Bong Son.

With bullets still snapping around us, I scrambled back up to the rest of the company, who were still under heavy fire. Reinburg came behind me, carrying two metal boxes of ammunition by the handles. He was a big guy, tall and muscular, about thirty-two with a baby face and a lick of curl coming up from his forehead.

"Where do you want the ammunition?" he asked me. I told

him to put it next to me. When he stooped to put it down, two bullets ripped through his chest just above his heart. He collapsed into my arms, all two hundred pounds of him, his eyes rolling back in his head.

I staggered under his weight. One rescue had suddenly turned into two, and I was downhill from the helicopter landing site once again. I was slippery from all the sweat and blood, and it was impossible to get a grasp on Reinburg. He had fallen unconscious, so he couldn't help me. I fumbled everywhere I could to figure how to hold him, looking around for a rope or something to loop around him. I couldn't find one, so I started dragging.

We weren't too far from the helicopter landing site, but it felt like a mile. Reinburg was fatalistic. He was sure he was going to die right there on the rice paddy. At the top of my lungs, I screamed that we needed another dustoff to get Reinburg out. Partially sitting up, I held him in front of me, grabbed him under the arms, and began using my legs to push myself backward up the hill. I dug in my heels for traction, straightened my legs, and heaved myself backward a couple of inches, like a rower pulling on his oars. I talked to myself as I pushed. *Don't stop. Whatever you do, keep going. Keep going. Unless they kill you, keep going.*

I prayed, too, as I pushed and heaved up the hill with Reinburg. *We need to get this done, Lord,* I said silently. I lost my grip, and he slipped out of my hands and down the slope. I grabbed him again and kept going up and up. *Lord, not now, let me get this guy.*

After fifteen minutes of dragging his body, I finally reached the landing zone behind the hilltop. I gave Reinburg chest compressions to keep his heart beating while we waited for another medevac. Morgan took over after a moment or two while I tried to keep the men organized. The dustoff arrived a few minutes later. I hoisted Reinburg up as best I could, and a crew member tried to grab him but couldn't get a grip on his slippery uniform.

"This isn't going to work," the crew member shouted. He disappeared inside the helicopter and came back with rope. We looped it around Reinburg, and I boosted him from below as he was dragged up into the helicopter. They strapped him into a litter, and moments later the helicopter rose up over the knoll and thundered south toward Camp Bong Son and safety.

9

"NOT BEFORE ME"

Reinburg's medevac disappeared to the south. I scrambled back to the foxholes where the 883rd soldiers were still dug in. Chaos spilled around us. A hail of gunfire and mortars showered us every whichaway. There was no center of gravity to the battle. We were holding our own, but there was no clear plan or strategy to fight our way out except for creating the best possible defense. We were just trying to survive.

We had begun the day dug into the base of the hill. We had moved further uphill over the hours, closer to the crest, about thirty meters up. My goal was to claw every defensive advantage we could find. Sometimes a better defensive position was a matter of inches. The ammunition resupply bolstered my confidence that we'd be able to hold our positions.

At the top of the hill, we were in the catbird seat. We had a view of the whole area. My men—the regional soldiers—were spread out around me. Morgan was still to the rear, protecting our backs. I crawled back and forth from one dugout to another, keeping the men focused.

When I reached the men, I tried to keep my voice low and avoid shouting over the sound of the mortars and machine-gun fire. I wanted to project calm and control. An officer who yells or screams is losing control. I wanted to remain focused. I didn't think about Delores, or what burger I'd eat after I got back to Bong Son, or what I would do if I ever got the fuck out of that battle alive. When your mind wanders, the bullet finds you.

I kept up the radio traffic with Bong Son and the FAC over-head, my heart pounding in my chest. I'm not sure which FAC pilot was in the spotter plane overhead; it was probably Charles "Pancho" Villa, who Billy Cole had dispatched to the battle site. In front of me, the North Vietnamese soldiers were making a strategic retreat back toward the hamlet to the north of the battlefield. "Dammit, the Cong are running toward the village again," I shouted over the PRC-10.

A voice broke into the transmission—it was Major Cole. He identified himself and ordered Villa to mark the area with smoke for an airstrike. Two F-105s were in a holding pattern over Binh Dinh. After the spotter dropped a smoke grenade, the Thunder-chiefs dropped their entire payload of ordnance, including na-palm, onto the camp.

At MACV headquarters, the duty officer was finally gathering real-time reports about what was happening. "Mohawks made a strike at 10:00 and 4 A1Es are over the area plus Navy gunfire will support. The RF unit is presently pinned down although there is plenty of air support," he typed at 12:03 P.M. Not all the informa-tion was accurate. "Reported that 1 US possibly KIA and 1 WIA believed serious, plus 1 US received wounds in the leg and arm and was evacuated to Quy Nhon at 10:55H. A reaction force is

being organized to assist the RF company."[1] Somewhere, someone was gathering reinforcements.

* * *

Back at Bong Son, Deis had gone about his daily work on the
camp's defenses, unspooling more barbed wire on the perim-
eter, running wires out to the napalm-filled drums, setting up
Claymore mines. The battle up north made the camp uneasy.
Everyone was tense and worried. The second in command, First
Lieutenant Pierson, was strangely absent as the hours went by.
Deis didn't see him once all day.

All morning, Kenny Bates had been hunched over the radio
in the commo shack as he monitored the radio traffic from the
battle up north. A fan blew on the equipment to keep it from
overheating. Deis and the others would stick their heads into
the hut every so often to get the news and hear if there were any
developments.

Bronson's spotter plane was grounded; when the mechanic
checked over the plane, he found thirteen bullet holes in the fuselage. Over the course of the morning, choppers came and went
from the airstrip outside the gates. High-up Special Forces officers began to arrive like moths to a candle. MACV's senior advisor in Pleiku had come to the camp, and was leaning over Kenny
Bates's shoulder listening to the radio traffic so he could approve
helicopter or fire support.

When Bob Baden's crippled resupply helicopter arrived, Deis
ran out to help Hubbard. He was taken aback when he saw the
damage to the chopper. The instrument panel was a sieve of bullet holes. A round had blown out the nose bubble. Blood covered
the inside from the crew chief's spurting artery. He had almost
died from blood loss, and the pilot had been shot through the
heel. Deis knew that the situation up north had not gotten any
better.

Around noon, the medevac arrived with Waugh on board, along with the wounded gunner and Major Cole. The chopper touched down just outside the gates on the landing field. Deis and Hubbard ran out again. As the chopper landed, Cole heard my voice over the radio reporting that Reinburg had been shot, too.[2]

"Jesus," Hubbard said when he saw Waugh's foot and ankle injuries. Waugh was moaning and barely conscious, probably drugged up on morphine. Hubbard wanted to cut Waugh's boot off, but he was afraid Waugh's foot might come off with it. They patched him up as best they could right on the chopper. The gunner who had been shot in the arm was in terrible shape too, his face white and his arm dangling loosely as if held by only a strip of sinew or muscle.[3] They stabilized both men before sending them to Quy Nhon for surgery.

A few minutes later, the next dustoff thundered down from the north with Reinburg on board. Deis and Hubbard went out through the gates again. Reinburg was conscious, but in rough shape. Except for his obvious sucking chest wound, they couldn't see the extent of his injury.

Hubbard could see the entry points of the bullets, two holes about an inch apart on the front of his shoulder. The bullets had entered his body just above his artery and just barely missed his lungs before exiting through his left shoulder. Hubbard cut his shirt off. When he and Deis looked at Reinburg's back, they couldn't believe what they saw.

Reinburg was missing about a pound of meat on the outside of the shoulder blade from the two rounds. The bullets went through his scapula and punched out of his back, leaving a bloody crater of mangled tissue and muscle. A little bit down, and the bullets would have gotten his lung or his heart.

"Is it bad? Is it bad?" Reinburg kept asking. He was going into shock.

"No, no, no," Deis lied. "You're gonna be alright." He had no idea if Reinburg was going to be all right. Deis was just trying to comfort him. They gave him some shots of painkillers and patched him up as best they could. The chopper lifted off and headed to Quy Nhon. Reinburg never returned to the detachment.

Inside the camp, a senior advisor from MACV who had come to the camp for the operation dressed down Cole for ordering the airstrikes. All fire support requests were supposed to go through him, and he was livid that he hadn't been consulted.

"Major Cole, did you consider that there may have been civilians in that village you just ordered destroyed?" he asked.

"Yes, sir!" Cole answered. "But it was my decision to save my men and the 883rd company from massacre."

The advisor took Cole's explanation without comment. Then he apologized for the behavior of the colonel that Cole had leveled his gun at. "I ordered him to leave this area and never come back. I'll send a full report to MACV headquarters."

One of the commo NCOs, either Kenny Bates or Ron Wingo, ran up to Cole with a message. Tiny Aldrich was near the Bong Son camp. Tiny was bringing a company from the Twenty-Second Division of the Vietnamese army to assist me. Help was on the way.[4]

* * *

Time turned elastic for me. It felt as though this battle would never end. All of us were exhausted, thirsty, and hungry. There's no pause for a piss break when bullets are ricocheting all around you. Every sip of water to wash away the tinny taste of blood in my mouth or dampen my raging thirst had to be taken with an eye to how much was left and how many more sips remained. By early afternoon, there was some broken cloud cover to cool the air, but the sun still hammered down on us. The blood on my knees had dried so hard it felt like plaster encasing my leg.

As midafternoon approached, a new threat appeared. As I surveyed the hillside and the battle, I saw a wave of North Vietnamese soldiers in black charging our position. The attack resembled a flying wedge formation; the ones in front had their weapons at the ready, while those in the rear were keeping pace to replace the ones who fell at the front. They were trying to overrun our defenses with sheer numbers.

I had an automatic weapon—an AK-47—that I had taken off the battlefield. I stepped up out of the dugout and set my feet. Because of my mangled fingers, I put my pinkie on the trigger. I began to fire at the soldiers charging us. The attackers began to fall, but not all of them. As the ones in front went down, the ones behind kept running forward. A grenade bounced on the ground near me, and I ducked. Shrapnel sliced me with another injury. I kept firing until the soldiers were either dead or retreated. I was told that I killed at least twenty North Vietnamese soldiers in that attack alone.[5]

I still couldn't find Brown. He was out in the open somewhere but out of sight. We were running out of time. We needed to get Brown out before nightfall. The bombing run shut down the enemy activity for a time, which allowed me some time to regroup.

"Where's Brown?" someone asked me over the PRC-10.

"I don't know," I said. "I'll get right back to you." I thought I knew roughly where he was, but I couldn't see or hear him. One of our Montagnard interpreters on the knoll, a man named Jong, pointed down the hill to where he had last seen Brown.

"He alive, he alive," he said. Jong was in rough shape himself and in shock—his arm had been shot off—but he was clear about where Brown was. Morgan gave me cover, firing over me as I made my way down the hill to search.[6]

When I was down in the rice paddy, I crawled out on my hands and bloody knees. There was still heavy firing. I stayed as low as I could, close to the ground. I thrashed through the grass and mud. I came across a turtle, moving slowly across the field. Moments later, a black snake slithered in front of me. It scared the shit out of me. I waited for it to disappear into the grass before I continued.

Every so often, I called out for Brown as quietly as I could, and then would stop and listen. The minutes ticked by. Every so often, I'd hear a cough that I was pretty sure was Brown's. I kept going through the grass. I got closer to the coughs, until finally I found him, lying face up in a shallow ditch.

Brown was barely conscious when I reached his side. By that time, he had probably been lying there for ten hours in the heat. He had a head wound, with blood all over his face. His eyes were partially open. I couldn't tell the nature of the wound. He might have been shot, or he might have been hit with shrapnel, because there was a shell crater near him. He had a partial bandage on his head that one of our 883rd medics had applied before he was shot and killed.

Brown's breathing was irregular, and his arms made jerking motions. "Am I going to die?" he gasped.

"Not before me," I said, and began figuring out how to get him to safety.

We were about a hundred yards out from the hill, and farther than that from the helicopter site where a dustoff would take him out. Like Waugh, he needed to be dragged up the hill. I held him as I had Reinburg, sitting on my ass with his back to my chest. I locked my arms around him and used my legs to push myself up toward safety, heaving us backward a few inches at a time.

We had been fighting since dawn, nearly twelve hours. There were no words for my exhaustion as I inched backward toward safety with Brown. I felt like all the reserves of strength that I had had been tapped dry. To keep going, I kept reciting my poem like a mantra, like a prayer. *If I should die, think only this of me.* Brown, half-conscious, mumbled every so often, "Am I dying?

Am I going to be okay?" Sometimes just a word, a partial sentence. I knew what he meant.

"We're in this thing together," I whispered back. "Don't ask me any questions—we're in this thing together." And then I asked him a question: "Do you believe in God?"

He told me he did.

"Start praying," I said. *If I should die, think only this of me.*

Inch by inch, foot by foot, I dragged him through the grass and over shrubbery that lay in the way of the knoll. The gunfire had died down, and I stayed as quiet as I could, to avoid attracting attention in the stillness. Mostly Brown stayed quiet, conserving his energy. He had become incoherent, mumbling to his mother and his wife as if they were there at his side. He was fading. He talked to himself about the church. He was Catholic and wanted to be a good soldier. He wanted to go to heaven.

I kept dragging. Another few inches. Up and over hillocks of grass. Through the mud in the field. Around bodies. A few inches more. And then we reached the slope, and I began pulling him up the incline. Now we were more exposed, directly opposite the higher ground that the enemy held to our north. But the Mohawk air support had pushed the North Vietnamese some distance to the north and we didn't have to worry as much about a frontal assault. I kept tugging him up, ignoring my raging thirst, the stiffness of my blood-encased legs, the pain in my shredded fingers. Nothing mattered but getting him to the top of the hill.

Finally, just before 4 P.M., I was able to get him over the crest to the landing zone. The chopper had landed with an east–west orientation, so that the gunner could point the machine gun northward toward the enemy's positions. When he offered to help me get Brown up into the troop compartment, the pilot ordered him to stay with his gun and not to help. The pilot berated his gunner so loudly that if Jesus Christ was listening, he would have heard it, too.

I somehow got Brown onto the helicopter. Some of the remaining regional forces might have helped, and Morgan, too. Within a few moments, he was strapped into a gurney in the troop compartment, and I squinted against the whirling dirt as the pilot took the chopper up.

In Saigon, the MACV duty officer made another notation at 3:50 P.M. "MSGT Waugh, SPF4 Brown WIA and evacuated to Nha Trang. Capt Davis also WIA is still in action," he wrote. "No reaction force yet from 22nd Div."[7]

* * *

With the last wounded American evacuated, I went back to the spot where I had dropped my rucksack. Up on the hilltop, I had everything I needed—our PRC-10, gun placements, ammunition, foxholes. I just needed to reload to get back into the battle. When I found my rucksack, it had a sandwich and a small tin of fruit. I took a brief moment to rest and swigged a mouthful of water from my canteen.

As I drank, I felt the barrel of a pistol against my head. An NVA soldier had managed to creep through our defenses and sneak up on me. I froze. With his gun at my left temple, he pulled the trigger.

Click. The pistol misfired, or there wasn't a bullet in the chamber. Whatever on God's green earth the reason, I was still alive.

Now neither one of us had a loaded firearm. We both jumped back at the same time. I remember looking at the soldier's useless gun and realizing that for some reason, he was carrying what looked like a German Luger. He drew a knife, a long, shiny ceremonial blade. I reached down and pulled my bayonet out of my boot where I had tucked it. We circled, crouching low. We feinted and slashed at each other. I nicked him first, and he barely flinched. I cut him again.

And then he took a step back.

A memory flashed through my mind. One of my Special Forces instructors in close combat, a former Russian soldier, had taught me that a knife fighter who steps back isn't prepared to go on the offensive. I knew I had him. We circled again. I lunged, a feint to draw him off to the side. It worked. He overreached to the side, and I plunged my knife into his stomach.

With the NVA pushed back, the battlefield was quieter. More dustoffs arrived to bring out about fourteen of our wounded from the 883rd. About thirty minutes later, Tiny Aldrich's huge frame emerged from the brush with dozens of Vietnamese soldiers from the Twenty-Second ARVN Division. On their way up from Bong Son, he had left a few of them on our flank to bolster our perimeter. He brought the rest to where I was. I can't imagine what I must have looked like, my hand wrapped in a bloody bandage, my uniform stiff with dried blood and sweat, a stench of shit coming off me.

"Why the hell are you here?" I asked Tiny, confused. "I didn't ask for reinforcements."

Tiny told me that he and Major Cole had decided that they had to get us the hell out of there, and that it was time for us to go back to the camp. I didn't have a choice this time. The company from the Twenty-Second Division was going to finish what we had started. Within about two hours, they cleared the whole area of North Vietnamese. The battle was over.

We started the long march back to camp. The uninjured supported the walking wounded along the way. I doubled the distance between soldiers, to keep us from bunching up into an easy ambush target. Morgan led the company, reading the maps. Spotters up ahead watched for trouble. Every so often, Morgan would beat a false trail off to one side, to throw off pursuers. The withdrawal was as dangerous as the battle itself. Fear and adrenaline had kept us going all day with almost no food or water or rest. We had cooked through all our reserves, and we just wanted to be back inside the wire. This was the moment when we might have been the most vulnerable, when safety was within reach.

We kept as quiet as we could. We barely spoke. I was completely drained, my body aching and my wounds throbbing. While my body was exhausted, my brain was still on overdrive. I was preoccupied with the battle, turning over in my mind what had happened. I felt sick, because the things we had done hadn't gone as planned. You bring those thoughts back with you.

Every moment of the day was seared into my memory, and they ran through my mind on an endless loop as I thought about what we had survived. I could still feel Reinburg's body slumping into my arms. I could hear that son-of-a-bitch Waugh screaming insults at God and me from the rice paddy. I brooded over Brown, wondering whether he would make it home to see his wife and boy.

"What did I do wrong?" I asked Morgan quietly.

"As far as I can see, you did everything right," Morgan said.

When we left the tree line and I finally spotted the guard outside camp, I felt as though I could finally breathe a sigh of relief. I think the guard smiled when we walked in, happy that we had made it back. I didn't smile back. I didn't want to talk to anyone. I walked past Deis without saying a word. He could see from the expression on my face that I was upset.

I went to my hooch. I took a couple of minutes to pull myself together. I kept thinking about the whole ordeal—what went well and where things got fucked up. A quarter of my detachment was injured on one day, and I wasn't certain that they would all survive. All day, I had kept a lid on the pain and panic. When we got back, the airtight lid on my emotions finally cracked. I could feel the pain pushing up against my throat. If someone had said the right word, I'm sure I would have broken down sobbing.

After several minutes, I shook off my feeling of doubt. *Paris, get your ass up*, I thought to myself. We could be vulnerable to attack in the aftermath of the battle, and I needed to make sure that we didn't let our guard down and the men were taken care of.

I went looking for Hubbard. I wanted to make sure that my injured men were attended to. When I found Hubbard in the clinic, Joe the monkey was sitting up on a high perch, looking down at us.

"What the hell happened up there?" Hubbard asked me.

"Open up your hand," I told him. I reached into my pocket, pulled out the tip of my finger that had been shot off. It was sticky with blood and had stayed in there throughout the whole firefight, even when I reached into my pocket for extra shells. I dropped the fingertip into his palm. He stared down at it.

"Well, where's the rest of it?" he asked.

"That's all there is," I said.

"What the fuck am I supposed to do with it?" he asked, looking at me as if to say, *How dumb can you be?* "You want me to burn it or bury it?"

I didn't care. He got out his gauze and bandaged the finger up so thoroughly that you could see my middle finger sticking up from a mile away. He took care of the rest of my injuries right there in camp, just like he had promised he would. He checked me over, then made me strip down to make sure I didn't have any leeches on me. I did. I didn't smoke, but I lit up a cigarette and started burning them off.

Afterward, I went around the camp talking to the men who had come back, making sure that they were cleaning their weapons, and staying as sharp as they could be for the next few hours, when the risk of a counterattack was high. The time for jokes and stories about the battle was later.

That evening, Morgan and Deis sat outside the mess hall. Morgan, unfazed by what had happened that day, asked Deis to check him for leeches. Morgan stripped off his shirt. Deis stared. Morgan's back was seething with them.

Deis borrowed a cigarette and lit it. He began burning the leeches off Morgan's back, holding the cherry up to the wriggling creatures one by one. The leeches twisted and recoiled, dropping off Morgan's back to the ground as Deis and Morgan talked.

"I think Captain Davis deserves the Medal of Honor for what he did today," Morgan said matter-of-factly. It made a deep impression on Deis that someone with as much combat experience as Morgan had said that. He kept at his grim task. When he was done, he had removed eighteen leeches off Morgan's back.

Later, I joined the men gathered around a bonfire. Night had fallen, and someone had built the fire in a spot between the mess hall and Hubbard's clinic. We didn't have fires often, but this day was different. There weren't very many of us, maybe four or five members of the team. All of us were silently thinking about Waugh and Reinburg and Brown, wondering if they would pull through. I know I was.

The sparks spiraled up into the sky. We were all so fucked up from the day that I don't know what we talked about. There was one thing I told them, though, that Deis remembered decades later. I told them about the officer flying over the battle and asking for an update over the radio, and Deis and the others chuckled when I told them how he cursed at me when I refused to leave the battlefield. On any other day, I would never have talked to the men about things like that. But this wasn't any other day.

In the days that followed, more reports reached Billy Cole and Tiny Aldrich in Quy Nhon about what had happened up there on the hilltop. Some of the intelligence came from the Vietnamese army, others from eyewitnesses like Morgan. Each piece of information began to fill out a picture of what had happened. Colonel Cole completed an After Action Report, and after talking with Tiny Aldrich and other officers, he decided to recommend me for the Medal of Honor. Captain Larry O'Neal, the B-team's administrative officer, prepared the paperwork, and they sent the nomination to Fifth Special Forces Group headquarters in Nha Trang.

They never heard a word about it again.

10

AMBUSHED

SEPTEMBER 23, 1965
BINH DINH PROVINCE, VIETNAM

In the hours after we returned to the camp, the weight of what had happened began to sink in. We'd lost a quarter of our detachment, and most of the Montagnard and Nung soldiers in the 883rd were dead or injured. Any of us could have been in Waugh, Brown, or Reinburg's boots that day. We didn't know if Brown was going to make it. The night before the company marched out of camp, some of us had unwrapped and chewed up those candy cigars that he had given out to us.

When the sun came up on June 19, we awoke to meet the day as we did every other. We didn't have the luxury to mourn or lick our wounds. Hugh Hubbard had advised me to rest for a few days after the battle. Recover from my injuries. Allow my injuries to start to heal. I couldn't do that. The only way to lead is to keep moving forward and be an example. If I slowed down, I'd allow doubt or fear to creep in the way of our mission.

The thing is that what happened to Brown hit closer to home than I realized at the time. More than eight thousand miles away,

Delores was pregnant and nearing her third trimester. She was living alone in Reading, Pennsylvania, working as a speech therapist in the local school district. She knew almost no one in the city, just her boss and two friends, one of whom lived upstairs from her apartment. Even though our first child was on the way, I could only focus on what was in front of me and my soldiers: carrying out our mission and staying alive.

After all, nothing had really changed in the aftermath of the battle. The Viet Cong and the North Vietnamese still owned Binh Dinh Province. More fighters were arriving constantly from the North. They were taking advantage of every toehold they could find. We couldn't allow our disappointment to interfere with our mission. We needed to stay steadfast in trying to block them at every turn.

* * *

The war continued to change around us in that summer of 1965. The ongoing debate among President Johnson's advisors about whether it could be won continued as well. Westmoreland, Ambassador Maxwell Taylor, National Security Advisor McGeorge Bundy, and Defense Secretary Robert McNamara all had different opinions about U.S. strategy. But they all agreed on one thing: that the war was not going well.

Westmoreland's views continued to prevail, along with his belief that the key to defeating the Communists was to control the countryside where the Viet Cong and the North Vietnamese were building up troop strength and moving freely. The strategy of "pacification"—suppressing Viet Cong and NVA activity in rural areas—became more urgent than ever.

The camp that we had raised out of nothing would soon become a busy stopover and refueling station for troops operating in the area. MACV would soon decide to move the Twenty-Second Division of the Vietnamese Army—the same division that had sent soldiers to relieve us in June—near Bong Son. They set up camp across the airstrip from our gates. Caribous began to regularly ferry in conventional ground troops. The thunder of helicopters became a constant soundtrack to our work as the First Cavalry Division also began appearing on our airstrip regularly and became a permanent presence in Bong Son. Eventually, the First Cav would take over our camp altogether.

When the North Vietnamese attacked with force and numbers, the Air Force would now be permitted to cross the Nineteenth Parallel to carry out retaliatory bombings, and Navy vessels in the South China Sea, which hadn't engaged in land battles before our June 18 operation, were allowed to bombard from offshore. But there were limits. U.S. ground troops were forbidden from crossing into North Vietnam. If we did, it would constitute an invasion and potentially draw in Russia and China.

As reporters filed stories about U.S. soldiers in combat, the American public and Congress came to realize that troops were no longer limited to defensive fighting in the war; the Army had switched strategies. It was in early June, about two weeks before our battle, that the State Department quietly revealed the decision to use U.S. troops offensively. Under pressure to clearly define the U.S. military role in South Vietnam, the State Department put out a statement on June 6—which happened to be the anniversary of D-Day—acknowledging that U.S. combat troops were now permitted to attack without being fired upon first.[1]

Back in the States, protest grew. The administration anticipated that the policy change would inflame opposition to the war. During graduation exercises the day after the announcement, several U.S. officials made commencement speeches urging students to speak their minds but not to be irresponsible or excessive. Some tried to denigrate militants who grabbed headlines. "Those who are the least learned make the most noise," McGeorge Bundy told graduates at Notre Dame.[2]

About ten days after our battle in Bong Son, 120 helicopters began carrying U.S. paratroopers from the 173rd Airborne Brigade into the jungle in an area called Zone D, about twenty miles from Saigon. It was almost 650 square miles of thick forest that Communist guerrillas had used as a base since the Indo-China War against France. Westmoreland asked reporters in Saigon to hold off on reporting, but within a day or so, acknowledged that he had directed the paratroopers' participation in the joint offensive. U.S. TROOPS OPEN FIRST BIG ATTACK AGAINST VIET-CONG, *The New York Times* reported.

* * *

In Bong Son, we kept focused on our mission to maintain a presence in the countryside. We continued our nighttime patrols, and continued to come under fire. Hubbard's clinic was as busy as ever, with Montagnard villagers lined up to see him for every type of malady. We responded to bombings and sabotage, such as when the Cong blew up a rail bridge not far from the camp, dropping tons of concrete onto Highway 1, the north–south highway that went all the way down the coast to Saigon. In one blow, they had effectively stopped both rail access and road traffic. Deis, who went up to the site to help us figure out how to clear the twisted rails and piles of shattered concrete from the road, seemed amazed at the precision of the Viet Cong sappers.

New faces appeared in camp. One was Master Sergeant Danny West, who arrived not long after the battle to replace Waugh. He was a fireplug of a Special Forces soldier, short and compact and cut from the same cloth as Billy Waugh. Though he was quieter and more introspective than Waugh, he had the same appetite for combat. The older members of the team who knew him well from other detachments told us he was fearless and thrived under fire. He also didn't back down from anything.

One day not long after the battle, another Green Beret medic named James Branecki walked through the gate to replace Bobby Brown. He just showed up in camp one day unannounced. Deis was thrilled—the two had been friends in Okinawa. Branecki was just two years older than Deis, and they were both outgoing jokesters with a lot in common. They had snorkeled and gone drinking together at the VFW on the Rock.

I wanted to keep our team tight and keep out others who didn't belong. Sometimes visiting officers would come to the camp and make demands, ask for supplies and take advantage of our water and mess hall and generators. If we weren't careful, we'd soon have permanent guests in our camp who we would have to defend. It would be way too easy for us to get sideways with other companies and create confusion when we needed clarity.

Sure enough, when other outfits tried to take advantage of our camp, confusion resulted. In late 1964, the U.S. command, MACV, had created a reconnaissance operation based out of Nha Trang called Project Delta, officially called Detachment B-52.[3] A tough Special Forces officer, Major Charlie Beckwith, was in charge. Beckwith vetted the soldiers based on his experience as an exchange officer with the British SAS.[4]

Project Delta had some similarities to our patrol structure. A Project Delta team was a four-man unit with one Green Beret sergeant and three Nung soldiers. First Cav choppers would fly teams of paratroopers deep into the jungle and drop them on high-priority missions. While it was mostly a reconnaissance and intelligence gathering operation, the teams also planned and directed air strikes, attacked concealed NVA positions, recovered POWs, mined transportation routes, and carried out other risky missions.

Sooner or later, I knew we would come into conflict with them. Sure enough, we did. One morning, I was on a patrol returning to camp at dawn and we encountered a Project Delta team that included Charlie Beckwith himself. As we crossed paths in the bush, he said to me, "I'm out here and we're on a mission, and since I've seen you and I outrank you, you're my reserve now." That meant that I would now have to drop our mission, take orders from him, and dedicate our resources and manpower to his mission.

"Like hell I am," I said. "I'm not your fucking reserve."

He looked at me like I had two heads. "You don't understand. I can report you for disobeying an officer."

"You know I don't give a rat's ass what you do," I told him. "We're leaving. We're on a mission ourselves." And off we went, marching back toward camp. After a short distance, I ordered the men to stop and rest to make sure that Beckwith didn't cross our paths a second time.

Sometimes I would allow other outfits to use my men, but sparingly. When another team needed a demolitions expert for a search-and-destroy mission, for example, I loaned Deis to them. The target was a distant valley that intelligence indicated had been infiltrated by the Viet Cong.

Deis marched with regular Vietnamese soldiers deep into the jungle. They reached a village. When they arrived, the Vietnamese Army troops didn't encounter any hostile fire. But the soldiers opened fire on the villagers' livestock, killing all of their ducks, pigs, and water buffalo used to plow the rice fields. The goal was to deprive the Viet Cong and the North Vietnamese of food. Instead, they were threatening the villagers with starvation.

In the middle of the village was a Buddhist pagoda. It was small, delicate, and beautiful, with elegant stained-glass windows. The MACV advisor approached Deis and said that a tunnel had been found under the pagoda, indicating it was probably being used by the Cong or the North Vietnamese. The reason they had requested an explosives expert was to blow up the pagoda. That was exactly what Deis did, blasting the religious house to pieces. Deis began to doubt whether the U.S. was actually doing any good in Vietnam. *This ain't gonna work*, he thought.

In a way, these episodes showed how the U.S. mission had become a goat fuck. Different parts of the military were at cross-purposes with others. Our goals in the camp—to build relationships with the rural villagers and provide an alternative to the Communists—wasn't shared uniformly. We were no longer all reading from the same sheet of music. It was becoming clear to us that the Army was turning toward pacifying the population with heavy armaments, force, and sheer numbers. We were even bringing in weapons that didn't belong in the jungle, like tanks.

We heard more and more about the opposition to the war brewing back home. Reports about American casualties and deaths were making their way into the newspapers and nightly newscasts at home, and more and more independent news organizations were arriving to report what was happening on the ground. Sometimes in Quy Nhon or Nha Trang, they would troll for comment from unsuspecting service members. Often they had preconceived notions of the war and what American troops were doing, and it didn't really matter what people said to them— the stories would come out the same.

We sometimes heard about protests back home on Voice of America radio. The network didn't report bad things about U.S. troops, but what they did report was honest and fair. We could hear Hanoi Hannah's voice too on Voice of Vietnam, taunting and mocking us. *Your wives would like for you to be home taking care of the families that you love*, she crooned. She would play the Animals' "We Gotta Get Out of This Place," which came out in August, while reading the names and hometowns of U.S. casualties listed in *Stars and Stripes*.[5] *Wouldn't it just be better if you all just went home?* she asked.

* * *

Because of all the North Vietnamese activity in our area, Major Cole and I decided that we should have a satellite outpost to track the enemy's movement. We were concerned about Highway 1, the north–south highway which the Cong had blocked when it blew up the rail bridge. It was a heavily travelled road, and it wasn't just farmers and villagers using it. We had intelligence assets throughout the area, but we needed our own eyes and ears on the ground, and fortifications to spot and prevent the enemy's use of the road.

We chose a spot for an operating base about three miles southeast of our camp, in an area known as the Phu Cu Pass. The outpost was a more traditional configuration: star-shaped and mostly underground. Two Green Berets were stationed there, and about 130 members of the 731st Regional Force Company, watching the highway and reporting on any enemy movements that they saw. In the middle of the night, we would often hear Kenny Bates or Ron Wingo in the commo shack, talking to the outpost in the darkness.

By September, our daily intelligence reports showed a buildup of NVA forces in our province, as well as in neighboring Kontum Province. The Ho Chi Minh Trail wasn't a trail anymore; it was a highway with fresh troops streaming out of the North into rural provinces. The U.S. now had some 185,000 combat troops in the country. The overall mission remained the same: to assist ARVN in countering North Vietnamese activity in the South and to provide security for pacification efforts.

Our intelligence found that three North Vietnamese regiments were repositioning around Bong Son. Something was about to happen, but we didn't know what. The movement prompted the First Cavalry Division to begin to lay groundwork for new operations. And then, on the damp, chilly morning of September 23, we learned what the North Vietnamese had been planning.

* * *

The attack began at about 2:45 A.M. A large North Vietnamese force—two or three companies—attacked our outpost at Phu
Cu Pass, far outnumbering the camp's defenders.[6] Our commos
crouched over the camp radio as the defenders in the outpost yelled
over the sound of gunfire and mortars for several hours. I directed
mortar fire from our camp, while Major Cole flew up from Quy
Nhon in a spotter plane with a FAC to call in air support.[7]

The shooting suddenly stopped at dawn for an hour, yielding
to an eerie calm. Just like that, an hour later, the firing resumed,
just as F-105s streaked over the outpost, showering ordnance
onto the attackers.

As the F-105s flew away, the outpost alerted us that they were
about to execute an emergency breakout plan to elude the NVA
attackers. Inside the outpost, they blew underground explosives
to create an escape route. As our men fled, the North Vietnamese breached the barbed wire perimeter and streamed into the
compound. Overhead, Cole called up a C-130 strike. These were
specially outfitted planes nicknamed "Puff the Magic Dragon"
because of their heavy armaments. With the Viet Cong teem-
ing through the compound, the plane roared overhead, Gatling
guns blazing, and strafed the North Vietnamese with a blizzard
of machine-gun fire. The C-130 stayed over for about ten minutes,
making run after run over the outpost and showering it with lead
with each pass. When the plane finally left, nothing was moving.[8]

In late morning, I left the gate of the camp with David Morgan and an interpreter to head to the site by helicopter to see
what was left. It was a short flight, less than five minutes. As our
Huey approached the Phu Cu Pass southeast of our camp, so
many corpses in NVA uniforms lay on the ground below that I
couldn't see the grass for the bodies.

Off to one side, men in our uniforms waved the pilot toward
the landing zone. I saw what looked like a white flag, a signal

that it was safe for us to approach. We knew the soldiers were ours because they all wore the red bandanas around their necks that were a signature of the regional forces we trained. The Huey touched down, and Morgan and I jumped to the ground, the rotors still spinning. We started to look around at the bodies, trying to get a sense of what happened in the battle. Morgan was a little farther away from the helicopter than I was when the soldiers opened fire.

The uniforms were a ruse. The soldiers who had waved us in had stripped the regional soldiers killed in the attack and dressed as friendlies to ambush us. I couldn't tell how many directions the incoming fire was coming from, but we were being attacked from at least two sides, and at least one of them carried a machine gun.[9] Morgan and I were still a distance apart, and we opened fire in opposite directions. I killed several of the attackers—I don't know exactly how many—as I laid down cover fire.

We sprinted for the chopper, ducking the rotor wash as the blades whirled over our heads. I jumped into the cabin as the pilot started to pull up. I reached down to pull Morgan into the compartment with me and gripped his hand in mine when I saw a flash. Gunfire ripped through the helicopter. Morgan slipped from my grasp as the bullets lifted me up and threw me across the cabin. I landed against the gunner, who was killed. If he hadn't been blocking the door, I would have gone right out the other side onto the ground.

The chopper was still on its way up, but the pilot was injured and the copilot had been shot dead with a bullet in his head. "Is there any-fucking-body alive on this aircraft?" the pilot yelled.

"Yeah," I said.

"Well, get the fuck up here and pull back on the stick," he shouted. Even though I was bleeding from multiple gunshot wounds, I reached up in the cockpit and pulled back on the stick as he asked. With the pilot and me flying the aircraft together, we took off again toward Bong Son, leaving Morgan and the interpreter behind.

We touched down in Bong Son, but I wasn't there long. The pilot called ahead to let the camp know that he was incoming with wounded. As the chopper came down, Deis and Hubbard rushed to the helicopter. I was still conscious as Hubbard cut off my shirt from the collar to the waist. The fabric held in place a huge blob of congealed blood that Deis peeled off my back so that Hubbard could examine my injuries. He cleaned me up and slapped a patch on the wound, and then sent the chopper off to a field hospital at Quy Nhon.

Afterward, one of the nurses who was there for my surgery told me that she didn't know how many times I had been shot. As the doctor pulled the bullets out of me, she said she stopped counting and started crying.

11

RECOVERY

Bright lights above. Hazy shapes, blurred by painkillers. Rumbling wheels. A man's voice: *"One-two-three."* Airborne between a gurney and a bed. I sink. Cold clutches my body. A blanket settles over me. Warmth. A voice asks where the pain is. I can't answer. The pain is everywhere. Shapes by the bedside. Lean in. Lights on. Off again. I close my eyes. I sleep.

In my fog of painkillers, I barely remember my hospital stay. I can't recall exactly how long I was bedridden at the busy evacuation hospital in Quy Nhon.[1] I had a private room, and every half hour or so nurses or doctors came to check on me. IV tubes and wires looped all around my body. I remember one visitor clearly. Not long after I was hospitalized, a long, familiar frame appeared at my bedside. Dark eyebrows, a sculpted face and a chin like a ship's prow. General Westmoreland. He was with another man, I think a U.S. congressman from South Carolina.

The congressman asked the doctor at my bedside why I was in

the hospital, and the doctor described what happened at Phu Cu Pass. Amazed, the congressman said that I should get the Congressional Medal of Honor. Westmoreland wanted to give me a Distinguished Service Cross right on the spot. They tried to drum up a photographer, but they couldn't find one. "Whenever you need those goddamn people they're never around," the congressman grumbled. Eventually, they found one, and he snapped a picture as Westmoreland laid a medal on the blanket on top of me.

"You're a credit to your race," the congressman said before they left.[2] I'm still not sure if it was the DSC, the Distinguished Flying Cross, or a different medal. I'll never know. After Westmoreland left, I fell asleep with the medal still on my blanket where he had put it. When I woke up, the medal was gone.

There were other visitors, too. I'm sure that Elmer Monger came to visit. He's likely the one who brought the news from back home that Delores had delivered our first baby, Stephanie. I admit I had secretly been hoping for a boy. Without me there, Delores had asked a friend to take her to the hospital after going into labor.

She delivered Stephanie alone, she later told me, with only a physician at her bedside. While she was recovering from the birth, the nurses fussed over her and brought her flowers. They were a little surprised that this dark-skinned mother had given birth to such a fair-skinned baby.

The news about my injuries reached her through her boss in the school district. I had wired him money for flowers and told him what had happened. He brought the bouquet to her in the hospital and gently broke the news about my injuries.

"He's going to be all right," he told her. She cried, unsure of what it meant and how bad the injuries were. But she was the daughter of a pastor, and she had been around plenty of death and illness, and this gave her some comfort. She resolved to be strong because I would be coming home soon.

I found out later I had other visitors in those hazy first few days. On the same day that I arrived in the field hospital, Tiny Aldrich came to check on me. A day or so later, Major Billy Cole stopped by. He told me that he had helped recover David Morgan's body from the ambush site. With our detachment close to the end of its six-month temporary duty, I had selected Morgan before the battle to go to Nha Trang to begin the post-mission clearance for our team. Instead, every member of the command detachment went to the morgue to pay their respects before his body was evacuated.[3]

* * *

A day or so after the battle, I learned, Major Cole had gone up on a chopper with Wingo, Hubbard, and six Montagnards to find Morgan's body. Two gunships escorted them in case there were still enemies in the area. The outpost was so close to our camp that the chopper couldn't have been in the air more than a minute or two before the carnage came into view.

Bodies of dead North Vietnamese soldiers spread in every direction. On the western side of the site, corpses lay atop corpses, sometimes four or five deep where the attackers had been shot dead as they clawed over their fallen comrades. As the chopper got closer, Cole could see that many of the North Vietnamese were young, in their late teens or early twenties. Many had new gear, indicating that they had come down from the North well equipped for fighting. In one spot alone, he counted two hundred bodies. He estimated 1,400 dead North Vietnamese in all.

The pilot set the chopper down in the middle of the sea of bodies. The nauseating stench of decaying flesh washed over them. The Gatling guns from the Magic Dragon had shredded meat and bone. Napalm had seared soldiers into charred statues. In the tropical climate, the bodies were falling apart. Skin sagged off bones, bodies bloated in the heat. Flies rose and droned in clouds over the carpet of mangled bodies.

They searched that hellscape for Morgan for an hour. Finally, they spotted a pair of U.S. jungle boots protruding from the bushes. Fearing a booby trap, Wingo gingerly tied a long rope to Morgan's ankle. They retreated about fifteen yards, playing the rope out as they went, and took cover. Then they carefully pulled Morgan's body from the undergrowth. Inch by inch, they tugged out his body. Fortunately, his corpse hadn't been rigged.

Wingo tied another rope to Morgan's arm and turned his body over. Insects had already eaten away the flesh of his face and arms, which still clutched his grenade launcher. Cole wept like a baby. Wingo broke down in sobs as well as he knelt beside Morgan's body. Cole radioed back to Bong Son to send another chopper with a litter to bring out his body. Hubbard zipped him into a body bag to prepare him for his last flight back to Bong Son.[4]

Morgan had a fiancée back in Okinawa whom he was supposed to marry at the end of his temporary duty in Vietnam. He would have been home in about two weeks, ready to walk down the aisle with her and start a new life together. Instead, we were sending him back to the Rock in a body bag. At the camp, Wingo, Rat, Deis, and Hubbard sat together to decide who was going to be the one to break the news. They decided on Wingo.

Deis took Morgan's death particularly hard. They had been close, and spent a lot of time talking and joking together. He went up to the battle site a few days later to see where Morgan had died, bringing his camera. What he saw never left him: the sight of bodies falling apart, flesh falling off bone, consumed by insects and maggots. He stopped to take a picture of an NVA officer propped against a tree. The man's flesh had slid off his face like a wax mask, his scalp sloughing off the skull.

As the end of our six-month temporary duty in Bong Son

got closer, the team spent the next few weeks getting ready to transfer control of the camp to a new detachment after our team was gone. Then it was time for the men to leave. Cole flew into Bong Son on the Caribou that would take them away from Binh Dinh. After loading the men, the plane took off with the rear loading ramp open. Cole, Deis, Hubbard, Wingo, and the rest of the men could see out the back of the aircraft as it gained altitude. Moments after takeoff, the plane roared over Phu Cu Pass, where Morgan had met his end. Mountains gave way to beach and ocean. Bong Son disappeared from sight.[5]

Ron Deis couldn't wait to get back to the States. The demolitions man wanted nothing to do with demolitions anymore. He never wanted to hear "Let's kill some Cong" first thing every morning. He wanted the death and misery behind him. He didn't want to dwell anymore on the carnage he'd seen. He'd planned to meet a friend in San Francisco. He never called the friend, going straight home to Dayton. On his flight home in his crisp uniform and beret, a stewardess flirted with him and asked if he would have dinner with her after they landed. Deis said no. He just wanted to be home.

* * *

As for me, my three-month recovery felt like an eternity. At first, the nurses and doctors would just ask me to wiggle my fingers and toes, to make sure that everything was working. The doctor cautioned me not to exert myself. One time I worked a little too hard moving my legs, and I must have torn some stitches because when they checked on me, the sheets were bloody. The doctor, whose bedside manner left something to be desired, was annoyed. "Goddammit, I told you not to move around," he said. *I wish I was strong enough. I would kick your ass right now,* I thought.

About three weeks after I was injured, Lieutenant Colonel

Monger wrote to Delores to update her on my condition and congratulate her on Stephanie's birth. He also passed on praise from Westmoreland. "Paris' accomplishments are well known not only here, but all over South Vietnam as well," he wrote. "One of his first questions of me was, 'What will I be doing when I get out of the hospital?'"[6]

News about our work in Binh Dinh went beyond just the Army. A grizzled war correspondent named Charlie Black, a former Marine who wrote for the *Columbus Enquirer*, had been a regular visitor at our camp, and reported for readers back in the States. In a strange coincidence, an article he wrote about me came out the day before I was injured, calling me "one of the most famous Special Forces officers in Viet Nam."

In the article, Major Cole described the June battle at Bong Son. How I had carried three men to safety and kept the Cong and NVA at bay. How he had nominated me for the Medal of Honor.[7]

"They clobbered the Viet Cong," Cole said. "We're proud of that man, not only because of the job that he's done and because of the kind of man he is, but as much because of the fact that he has showed as much cold courage as any human I've ever heard of."

After I was injured, Black wrote about me again, calling me "one of the officers I admired more than almost anyone who has been on duty in Viet Nam." This time he reported on my wounds. "The wounds suffered by Captain Davis. . . . were the fifth, sixth and seventh wounds received in a single six-month tour in Viet Nam," he wrote.[8]

Day and night, I could hear the thunder of medevacs arriving and departing from the hospital helipad. I didn't know this at the time, but my hospitalization was another signal of the war's rapid escalation. In January of 1965, the Eighth Field Hospital in Nha Trang was the sole American field hospital in Vietnam, with just one hundred beds, and there were only 164 medical evacuations in the whole country. By the end of 1965, there were over 1,600 beds countrywide and in November, the month I left the hospital,[9] there were 2,361 wounded soldiers evacuated. [10]

As my body healed and my wounds knitted back together, I worked on rebuilding my strength. Before too long, I was walking again, slowly at first and then more quickly. I'm sure that because I kept fit and healthy before I was injured, my recovery was shortened. Eventually, I was back to jogging, and I developed a rigorous daily physical conditioning regimen to regain my strength and endurance that weeks in bed had sapped.

By Thanksgiving, I was back in Okinawa for convalescence leave. On December 15, I joined fifty-six other Green Berets from Binh Dinh detachments who were still in Okinawa for an awards ceremony. Colonel Francis John Kelly, the commander of Fifth Special Forces Group, handed out 250 decorations as the group adjutant read the citations. Kelly pinned an interim Silver Star to my uniform.[11] I was proud to wear it.

* * *

The war was not going well. The number of North Vietnamese flooding into the South on the Ho Chi Minh Trail was staggering. U.S. intelligence estimates put the number at about 35,000 in 1965. By late 1967, it was 150,000.[12] Retaliatory American airstrikes over North Vietnam hadn't weakened the Communists' resolve; it appeared to have had the opposite effect.

It also fanned opposition to the war at home. In April 1965, Students for a Democratic Society had held the first mass protest against the war in Washington, DC, and in cities around the country. About fifteen to twenty thousand protestors participated.[13] In October, the International Days of Protest brought as many as a hundred thousand protestors in the streets in the U.S. and Europe.[14] In early November, two American war opponents set themselves on fire in protest.

I had my own experience with opponents of the war. On one of my trips stateside from Asia, my flight went through Travis Air Force Base, halfway between San Francisco and Sacramento, California. Anti-war protestors often gathered there to greet the soldiers disembarking from Vietnam. It was also where the war dead returned to the United States for burial.

I had gotten off a flight with my bags and was outside the base, where I encountered some protesters. One, a young woman in a long dress, eyed me with anger and asked, "How many babies did you kill today?"

I started to answer her. She didn't wait for me to say anything. She puckered up and spat right into my open mouth. The thing about that is that when people made up their minds that you kill people, they don't know what you were, or what you did in the military, or who you saved and how you helped. This young woman had made up her mind about me, and there was no way I was going to change it.

I put down my bag. "Ma'am, if you do that again, there's gonna be some problems here," I said.

A couple of men, also anti-war demonstrators, came up behind her. "Says who?" they said to me.

Fortunately, a couple of soldiers nearby saw what had happened and hurried over to back me up. The protestors backed off, outnumbered. As they walked away, they yelled back a series of well-worn epithets, calling us baby killers and so forth. They kept it up until I got in a taxi and drove off.[15]

Three days after I received my Silver Star in December, President Johnson convened a multiday meeting in the White House cabinet room. His advisors were pressing for a new strategy to provide a diplomatic off-ramp for the North Vietnamese. The top proposal was to pause bombing of North Vietnam, to create an opening for talks with the North Vietnamese. At the White House meeting, Secretary of Defense Robert McNamara openly voiced doubts about the existing Vietnam strategy for the first time. He estimated that the U.S. had, at best, a 50 percent chance of winning militarily.

"What you're saying is that no matter what we do militarily, there is no sure victory," Johnson said.

"That's right," McNamara replied. Military force alone would not succeed. "We need to explore other means." Many of Johnson's other advisors agreed, but not all. Johnson himself admitted that he was baffled by what to do. He didn't understand what Ho Chi Minh wanted or believed, he said. On the second day of debate, Johnson made a sudden decision, following his gut. "We'll take the pause," he said, and left the room with his advisors still sitting around the table.[16]

By January 1966, I was ready for a new assignment. I couldn't have dreamed up what came next. First Special Forces was preparing to send a detachment for Ski and Cold Weather Training School in Hokkaido, Japan's northernmost prefecture and second-largest island. It's just a few miles south of the Russian-occupied Sakhalin Island. It was a technically and physically demanding course, but also politically delicate. It included counterinsurgency training for forces in the Japanese Area Northern Command. The presence of U.S. Special Forces in a country that the U.S. had defeated and dropped nuclear bombs on twenty years earlier risked inciting political unrest. It was both prestigious and risky.

I was tentatively chosen to lead the training school. The officers, though, worried that I hadn't completely recovered from my wounds. I told the skeptical commander, Major James Asente, that I was fit and prepared for the assignment. Reluctantly, I think, he allowed me to proceed.

We prepared in Okinawa with daily physical training, classroom lectures, skiing instruction in boots and skis on a straw-covered incline, language classes, and equipment training. We boarded planes for Hokkaido on February 12. Amazingly, our preparation in tropical Okinawa prepared us well. Not only did the detachment excel in brutal midwinter conditions, but I also impressed my superiors with how well I worked with my Japanese counterparts. I was later told that I'd left a favorable impression with the Japanese Area Northern Command, as something of a goodwill ambassador. At the end of the training, we held a ski competition with the Japanese. We lost, partly because I reinjured myself in the race. Our team was angry, but I'm sure the Japanese skiers were overjoyed.

* * *

I finally had some leave and was able to go home to see Delores and our new baby, Stephanie. Delores was still living in Reading, Pennsylvania. She had the support of her friends, but otherwise she was all alone with Stephanie. One of her friends minded the baby each day while she was at work. She knew I was coming home. When I knocked on the door of the apartment, she was shocked to see how much weight I'd lost because of my injuries.

I held her tight and we kissed. "Where's the baby?" I asked. She brought me into the bedroom where Stephanie was asleep in the middle of the bed. I picked her up as Delores coached me on how to support her head and neck.

We stayed in Reading through the end of the school year, when Delores's job ended. Then the three of us moved to Fort Gordon in Georgia, where I took a counterinsurgency training course. The transition wasn't easy. Six months earlier, I had been in near-daily combat in Vietnam, a detachment commander living under constant threat of enemy fire with responsibility for the lives of my men and the prosecution of a war.

Now I spent my days in a classroom in Georgia, poring over books and trying to focus on lectures, memorizing statistics and operating procedures, all while living in a small apartment with a six-month-old baby and my young wife I hadn't seen in over a year. I struggled. When a soldier comes home injured or is killed, there's obvious grief and pain. But the long absences, the distance between soldiers and their families—those take a toll as well that takes time and work to bridge.

At night, I lay awake with thoughts about Vietnam turning over and over in my mind. And I'd later learn that I wasn't the only one struggling to recover from this experience. Billy Cole would have to recuperate in Okinawa after leaving Vietnam. He was an emotional and physical wreck after his high-pressure command in Binh Dinh. On top of that, he had to wean himself off the amphetamines that had kept him going during his stressful B-team command. Tiny Aldrich had troubles of his own. He had been threatened with a court martial for disobeying a sentry in Quy Nhon, but Westmoreland had rejected the court martial recommendation and sent the documents to Cole to toss out. He gave them to Tiny as a memento of Binh Dinh.

In August, I began preparing paratroopers for deployment to Vietnam. When I arrived, morale in the 230-man unit was the lowest of any company in the battalion. Unlike my group, these guys had been subjected to daily media coverage of a war that wasn't going well, and of soldiers coming home in body bags. I was able to turn the company around by giving them a sense of agency and preparedness, drawing on my combat experience to teach them the latest techniques and tactics. I took under my wing a soldier who had spent five months in the stockade and was considered one of the worst soldiers imaginable. I challenged him to not just behave but to lead by example. By the time I left, I had turned him into a decent infantryman and the company was considered one of the best in the brigade.[17]

Those men would be needed for the war. The brief Christmas pause at the end of 1965 and early 1966 had done nothing to nudge Ho Chi Minh to negotiate. By mid-1966, the Joint Chiefs of Staff estimated that U.S. force levels in Vietnam would have to increase again, to five hundred thousand by the end of 1967.[18] Johnson wasn't yet ready to call up reserves, so the administration approved more bombing of North Vietnam instead. The North Vietnamese invited American reporters into the country to chronicle the impact of the aerial bombardments, including a *New York Times* editor.[19] The reporting enraged the administration and stirred up more opposition to the war. In April 1967, Martin Luther King Jr. condemned the war in a speech at Riverside Church, saying that "my conscience leaves me no other choice."[20]

I was stateside long enough for Delores to become pregnant **again**. She gave birth to our son, Paris Davis III, in May 1967. When I returned overseas three months later in August, it wasn't to Vietnam—at least not at first. Not long after he returned to Okinawa, Cole had been handed a plum new assignment. Colonel Francis John Kelly, the commander of Fifth Special Forces Group, called Cole to his office, where they talked for a half an hour about the operations in Binh Dinh Province. Then he asked Cole to head a top-secret, unconventional warfare operation in Thailand. When Kelly asked Cole for recommendations for personnel on the mission, he gave him ten names. Mine was one of them.[21]

The State Department strongly opposed the operation. Diplomats feared that organizing guerrilla forces in Thailand, potentially for unconventional warfare missions into North Vietnam, would be seen as a provocation that would lead to further escalation.[22] The operation was cancelled, but I went to Thailand anyway in a more conventional role. Now Major Davis—I had been promoted in September—I began my tour on October 30, just ten days after the largest anti-war march in U.S. history, the March on the Pentagon.

My role was to assist and advise the Thai government in

preventing what had happened in South Vietnam. The U.S. government and the Thai monarchy had long been deeply concerned about Communist infiltration because of its shared borders with Burma, Laos, and Cambodia. In 1953, the U.S. and Thailand had set up a security arrangement called the Joint United States Military Advisory Group for U.S. Special Forces training of Thai troops. I was put in charge of a B-team detachment with four subordinate A-teams to organize, train, and direct soldiers in the Royal Thai Army Volunteer Force in unconventional warfare tactics and counterinsurgency operations.[23]

I was based in Lopburi, and never wore a uniform; I wore jeans and civilian clothes, with a .45 tucked in the waistband of my Levis. During my entire thirteen-month assignment in Thailand, I never fired a shot.

I had been in Thailand for about five months and was reaching the end of my first tour when I flew to Vietnam in January 1968. I'd been invited to meet with Major Charles "Chuck" Allen, who had taken command of Project Delta, Charlie Beckwith's search-and-destroy detachment that had caused me headaches in Bong Son. I had known Allen, or "the big 'un," as Westmoreland called him, since Airborne School. He was burly as an oak tree with a neck to match, with thick black eyebrows that always made him look a little surprised.

I had learned valuable leadership lessons from Allen. He taught me not to yell or berate subordinate officers who were angry or upset; instead, use their first names and speak to them softly enough that no one else could hear. It was a calming tactic that never failed me with junior officers or enlisted men.

Allen had asked me to come to Fifth Special Forces headquarters in Nha Trang. He wanted me to take over Project Delta. His tour was up later in the year, and he wanted someone he trusted to assume command. When I arrived, I told him I wasn't interested. I envisioned the job would be a difficult command. He was disappointed, but he understood. He was a little distracted when I was there, with his hands full dealing with intelligence reports that something was about to happen in Nha Trang. That night, I retired to the quarters that Allen had offered up to me during my stay. As it turned out, I ended up being useful in Nha Trang for a completely different reason than Allen had in mind, one that no one could have expected.

* * *

Just after midnight on January 30, gunfire rang out and mortars began to fall near the MACV Recondo School,[24] an offshoot of Project Delta that trained soldiers in reconnaissance techniques such as scuba, high altitude–low opening parachuting, escape and evasion, and other skills.[25] The gunfire and mortars stopped, but then restarted again about two hours later. A few minutes later, a MACV advisory team reported over the radio that they were under attack with small arms and mortars. A mobile strike force—what we called a MIKE force—was dispatched.

At almost the same time, the advisory team inside reported that a Viet Cong force had seized the compound, and a North Vietnamese battalion was on its way with reinforcements. Just before dawn, another battle broke out between a North Vietnamese battalion and a Special Forces detachment west of the city.[26]

The attack on Nha Trang was one of the first attacks in the Tet Offensive, one of the most important turning points in the war. The North Vietnamese saw coastal Nha Trang as a crucial target, and Fifth Special Forces was at the center of the bullseye. There had been some intelligence rumors that the North Vietnamese and the Viet Cong were about to launch a major offensive, but everyone assumed that it would happen after the Lunar New Year, which was the reason for the sacred celebration known in Vietnam as Tet.[27] The NVA had explicitly pledged a truce during the holiday.

We didn't realize it immediately, but the scope of the offensive was vast. Within two days, the Viet Cong and the NVA would launch hundreds of attacks around the country from the northernmost districts at the DMZ down to the southernmost tip in the South China Sea. It was the largest and broadest attack on American and South Vietnamese forces in the war so far. Major targets came under attack on January 30, while a second wave of attacks on smaller cities came the next day. Invading forces attacked thirteen of the country's sixteen provincial capitals. Rockets rained down on the American base at Camranh Bay. The most brazen attacks would be around Saigon, where the U.S. embassy was attacked on the morning of January 31.

When I heard the fighting break out, I jumped onto a chopper without a gun or a weapon of any kind and flew toward the action. A radio station manned by U.S. Signal Corps advisors with Vietnamese staff was also under attack. The MIKE force company had arrived—headed by one of Major Cole's Fifth Special Forces commanders, Captain Larry O'Neal—but neither the MIKE force nor the NVA were able to advance. A housing area lay to the north of the radio compound, with a commercial area to the east, a prison to the south, and rice paddies to the west. The Viet Cong and North Vietnamese forces were holed up in the housing area, and the MIKE force couldn't sneak around the flanks. So the two sides just shot back and forth at each other from their cover. It was a stalemate.

In the meantime, civilians had arrived to watch the action, including soup vendors trying to make a buck off the crowds. At the same time, dozens of non-combat soldiers with Fifth Special Forces—clerks and typists who had volunteered, then been diverted to desk jobs—had shown up and jumped into the action.[28] The situation was a goat fuck.

Still weaponless, I landed at Fifth SFG headquarters and began to help organize cooks, drivers, and clerks to join the battle.

We needed to get guns into the hands of anyone who was sober and willing to come out and fight and to get this thing done. One of the Green Beret officers managed to get all the civilians out of the compound. Without the human shields in our way, we were able to fight our way in, drive out the Viet Cong, and kill those who didn't retreat.

Off in a mountainous region where the Laotian, Cambodian, and Vietnamese borders intersected, another Green Beret named Willie Merkerson was monitoring radio traffic countrywide. He already knew my name from the battle in Bong Son. As he tuned in to the Nha Trang radio traffic, he recognized my name and listened over the radio as I coaxed and coached this impromptu squad into the battle.

The battle lasted all day. Early in the morning on January 31, the Viet Cong and North Vietnamese began to break off contact and pull back into the hills west of the city. Though the siege at Nha Trang had ended, on February 1 I boarded a command and control chopper as a MIKE force company below hunted for Viet Cong and North Vietnamese troops to mop up. I was in the air for almost eight hours directing search-and-clear operations. When the door gunner was wounded, I gave him first aid and then took his place at the open doorway, firing tracer rounds at sniper positions for the MIKE force below us to identify.

At one point, the helicopter dove in low. I leaned out the door of the helicopter, firing as I hung over the ground, bullets flying around me. Our helicopter was so persistent and accurate that the Viet Cong stopped firing at our soldiers on the ground and instead fired up at me, trying to shoot us out of the sky.

As the chopper circled, we got a report from the ground commander that one of our men on the ground had been wounded. I got the location and ordered the pilot to bring the chopper to the spot to get him. I told him to come in with the gunner door broadside to the enemy fire, so that I could lay down cover fire as the man was retrieved. With the door facing the enemy fire, we came in with the gun blazing as we settled next to the wounded man. The crew and I hopped to the ground, loaded him into the chopper, and the pilot brought us all back up as I kept firing.[29]

The fighting continued through the next day as well, with running gun battles all around the city. In the early afternoon of February 2, I led a reaction force of twenty-five Nung fighters on a clear-and-destroy operation. Realizing that snipers had pinned down a MIKE force company, I organized the Nung soldiers to draw the sniper fire toward their emplacements and counterfire on the sniper positions. I dashed from one Nung placement to another, distributing ammunition and distracting the snipers. At some point I laid down some cover fire and dashed out to drag in a seriously wounded man lying exposed to the enemy gunmen. For all of these actions, I would later receive an Air Medal for Heroism and an Army Commendation Medal for Heroism.

I went back to Thailand soon after. The attacks continued over many months in 1968. The offensive was a tactical failure because the U.S. response destroyed the Viet Cong nationwide. After Tet, the war became almost exclusively a battle between the North Vietnamese and the Americans.

But strategically, the outcome was very different. At the daily afternoon briefing in Saigon—the "five o'clock follies"— Westmoreland touted the American and ARVN response as a massive victory over a failed offensive. But Tet captured the front pages of American newspapers and led television coverage back home, leaving the impression with the American public that we had been caught flatfooted, and that the victors were the North Vietnamese.

No one could forget the searing scenes from Tet: the bodies outside the U.S. embassy in Saigon, smoking and ruined villages, bloodied refugees fleeing the fighting, and bandaged American soldiers. One of the most unforgettable images of Tet came out of Saigon when General Nguyen Ngoc Loan put a pistol to the head of a handcuffed prisoner named Nguyen Van Lem, led him through the debris-filled streets, and shot him in the temple. An Associated Press photographer captured the summary execution, as well as an NBC cameraman who filmed the killing and the prisoner's body falling to the pavement as blood spurted from his skull.

After the offensive, *CBS Evening News* anchor Walter Cronkite went to Vietnam to report, and would end his broadcasts with personal commentary. "It is increasingly clear to this reporter that the only rational way out then will be to negotiate, not as victors, but as honorable people who lived up to their pledge to defend democracy, and did the best they could," he said on February 27. It became conventional wisdom of the war that when Johnson lost Cronkite, he lost the support of the American public, too. Not long after, Johnson removed Westmoreland as commander and replaced him with General Creighton Abrams. Westmoreland returned to Washington as Army Chief of Staff. When I heard the news that he had been relieved, I cried for him because he didn't deserve to be tossed aside like that.

* * *

Just before Christmas of 1968, I returned home to the family, and met our second daughter who had been born in October. Delores and I chose a name from literature: Regan, the second daughter in Shakespeare's *King Lear*. Then I was stateside for a while after that, assigned as a squadron leader at Fort Meade in Maryland.

The following July, I loaded the car and buckled the three kids into the back seat, and Delores and I drove out to Cleveland. I hadn't been home since college. Delores had still never met anyone in my family so she'd finally get to meet my relatives, and they could meet Steph, Paris, and Regan. When we arrived, Delores warmly greeted my dad, Barney Sr., and my Uncle P.D.—my mother had died while I was overseas. We introduced the three kids to their grandfather and great-uncle and brought the bags into the house where I grew up.

I didn't stay long in Cleveland. I would have liked to have spent more time with the family, but I had to fly to Dayton to see Ron Deis and Bobby Brown. I had been invited to appear on a TV special about the war called *Vietnam: One Story*. The host, Phil Donahue, also had a popular daytime show that would soon go into national syndication and turn him into a household name everywhere in America.

After my flight landed in Dayton, I took a taxi to the Statler Hilton Inn. That evening, I had dinner with Deis. The last time I had seen him, he had helped strip off my blood-soaked blouse before the chopper flew me to the field hospital in Quy Nhon.

He was a civilian now, living back in Dayton where he grew up. He had married. He looked trim and healthy, and had gained back the weight he had lost in Bong Son. His hair was brushed into a careful part above his thick-rimmed eyeglasses. He still had a dimple in his chin. He looked like the same Deis that I knew from Vietnam, but the war had changed him. He didn't have the taste for combat that some of his team members had. He had trouble forgetting the sight of bodies shredded by automatic weapons, and falling to pieces in the heat.

Deis and I had a good visit over dinner in the hotel. We talked about old times. I told him how I had been since I had left Vietnam. He told me about his life now. And then we said goodnight, because we would see each other again the next day.

In the morning, I got up and dressed in my service charlies—khaki trousers and a short-sleeve shirt—to go to the VA hospital. The Dayton VA was about five miles west of downtown. When my taxi turned into the gates, I drove past rolling lawns, gardens, ponds, and paths on our way to the newest hospital building on the campus. It was an enormous institution, one of the nation's original three hospitals for wounded soldiers.

At the front desk, I asked where I could find Robert Dennis Brown. A nurse sent me upstairs. I took the elevator to an upper floor to his room. He was in bed, as he had been for the four years since the battle. When I entered, he was facing in the other direction. "Bobby, it's Paris," I said softly. He turned his head and his eyes locked on mine. He looked emaciated and shrunken, a shadow of the sunny, smiling man I remembered. He didn't say anything because he couldn't talk. I think he was trying to move his lips. I think he wanted to say something to me.

I hadn't seen Brown since I had pulled him off the battlefield in 1965 and loaded him onto a medevac. He had lain in the sun for half a day while a firefight raged around him. I preferred to think of him as I had seen him the night before he was wounded, when he was happy and proud as he handed out candy cigars to celebrate the birth of his baby boy. Now he was curled in bed, unable to talk.

I sat with Bobby for a while. After about twenty minutes, it was time for me to go. I had another appointment in the afternoon. I took a taxi from the hospital to a Dayton suburb. The cab drove me to the television station, WLWD, where Phil Donahue worked.

Deis was there, too. Producers brought us to the set and sat us on yellow chairs around a small hexagonal table. A floor-to-ceiling map of Vietnam hung behind us, next to a chalkboard with a sketch of the battlefield in Bong Son. Usually Donahue's show had a live studio audience. For this special, there was no audience. Donahue joined us. He was thirty-five then, tall and lanky with a mop of brown hair combed into a wave. He sat hunched across from us in a dark green suit and a red tie.

Donahue asked me about visiting with Brown. "He looked

real good," I said. "He looks like he's doing a lot better from the initial prognosis that I heard."

Then Donahue asked Deis and me about the battle. Donahue had constructed a diorama of the battlefield, using toy soldiers. In the miniature scene, plastic greenery covered a hill that represented where I had been pinned down. Below it, a light green expanse represented a rice paddy where Brown, Waugh, and Morgan had fallen. Donahue had scatted plastic figurines across the green area to represent the Montagnards killed by the North Vietnamese.

He asked me to describe what happened. I stood up with a piece of chalk in my hand and went to the chalkboard. I walked through what had happened that day, how I dragged Billy Waugh up the hill to a medevac landing zone, and how I got David Morgan out of the pit where he was stuck. I told him about Reinburg and the officer who tried to order me off the battlefield.

"I just disobeyed the order," I said. "I was real psyched up and I said some words that I don't care to repeat right here. I did do a little swearing. I think it was due to the intensity of the situation."

After I sat back down, Donahue pressed us about the impact of the war on us. "What has the war done to you?" he asked Deis.

"Well, it's taken a lot of the glory out of war that I may have had before," Deis said.

Donahue asked me the same question. "I sort of agree with Ron here. It's one of these things that you're committed to by virtue of being an American citizen, and when you're called, I think you have to go," I said.

"What do you think of kids who don't go?" Donahue asked me.

"I think they have a right to dissent," I said. "I want to be real clear here, however. I think there are other ways—there are many soldiers over in Vietnam, I would say the majority of them—who don't wholeheartedly agree with the war or don't understand it. But yet they still go. They do their solemn duty as American citizens."

Then he asked me about being a Black officer. "Here in this country, we're in the throes of one of the most serious domestic crises in the history of our nation. Black and white. You're a Black man who was in a command position of an all-white outfit. And you risked your life and your career when you refused that order. That could have been the ball game, couldn't it?"

"It sure could have," I said, nodding.

"Do you understand why I would raise that point?" Donahue asked, and then continued before I could answer. "Do you *mind* that I raise the point?"

"Not really, it's something you're aware of all the time—Black, white, the race problem, domestic issues," I said. "In the dark, brown is just as Black or white as anyone else. We're human beings. We're akin—not ethnically, but by virtue of being American citizens."[30]

When the interview was finished, Donahue took Deis, Paula Brown, and me out to dinner. A producer told Deis that it was the first time that he had ever done that.

Sitting around that table in the studio, it was strange to be relating what had happened that day in 1965, so many years later. I had been in so many battles. I described to Donahue what happened in almost clinical terms, as if giving a lecture. The fact is that I never talked about the battle. Years later, some of my closest friends had no idea what happened that day. I never talked about other parts of Vietnam, either, like my fights with Billy Waugh. Like how the pilot who ditched near our camp, who we brought to safety before the Cong captured him, had crossed the street when he saw me in Quy Nhon so that he didn't have to introduce his girlfriend to a Black man.

It had been four years since Billy Cole had put me up for the Medal of Honor. Medals are important to soldiers for their symbolic value and prestige, and because they can hasten a promotion or a command. And the Medal of Honor, the nation's highest award for military valor in action, stands above all other recognition for bravery, sacrifice, integrity, and patriotism. But though I was certainly ambitious and proud of the medals I had won, I hadn't given it much thought to that point. Cole had thought about it, though. Specifically, he wondered why it hadn't moved forward. And so he asked for an inquiry into what happened to his packet. The inquiry found no record of the 1965 nomination. Cole created a new Medal of Honor nomination packet from the surviving records. This second nomination vanished as well, either destroyed or lost. It was as if it had never happened.

12

THE PENTAGON

JUNE 13, 1971

FORT LEAVENWORTH, KANSAS

In the scorching summer heat of 1970, the family had come with me from Fort Meade to Fort Leavenworth for a yearlong command and general staff officer course. We lived in a single-family house, and we were the only Black family in our neighborhood. We socialized regularly with some of the other officers' families, and Delores was thrilled to learn that the wife of one of the officers was also from Baton Rouge. We stayed in touch for years afterward.

As the course came to an end, an article appeared in *The New York Times* that rocketed across Fort Leavenworth and the country. PENTAGON STUDY TRACES 3 DECADES OF GROWING U. S. INVOLVEMENT, headlined the paper's front page. The article was the first installment in what would be called "the Pentagon Papers." A man named Daniel Ellsberg, one of its many authors, had leaked the Pentagon's classified history of U.S. involvement in Vietnam. The article described the behind-the-scenes decision-making over four administrations that guaranteed deepening U.S. commitment.

The Nixon administration did everything it could to prevent newspapers from publishing articles about the report. The attorney general got an injunction to shut down the reporting. The *Times* paused publication, but *The Washington Post* published its own stories and refused to stop. The Supreme Court sided with the press after a trial, ruling that it was in the public interest to publish the papers.

The papers revealed that one administration after another deepened U.S. involvement but didn't tell the public. It didn't change my opinion of the war. But it did make me furious that the information had been leaked and published. It bothered me that the press cherry-picked information to publish from the reports. I also did not like that it turned the press into martyrs.

At Fort Leavenworth, everyone I knew agreed on one thing: Ellsberg deserved to go to prison. We agreed on one other thing: not to talk about this outside of military circles—that would only cause problems. Reporters circled everywhere for reactions to what the *Times* had published.

I didn't bring those conversations home with me. We didn't talk about military affairs over the dinner table.

After the general staff officer course finished, I received new orders. My appointment was at the Pentagon working for Lieutenant Colonel Charlie Norton, the Army's deputy chief of staff for military operations. I was happy for the assignment. A Pentagon staff job was an advancement on the Army career path, and it was a step that I needed to take. But I didn't want to climb the ladder just for the sake of it. Working at the Pentagon meant that I would rub shoulders with Army top brass. I had to do that if I eventually wanted to reach my goal: a command of my own.

* * *

Delores and I packed the kids in the car and drove east. She was used to moving by now, but that familiarity didn't make the upheaval of relocating any easier. I found us a little brick ranch house about ten miles south of the Pentagon, in a quiet neighborhood. The house was less than a mile from the local elementary school, so the kids could walk to school as they grew up.

I could see that my constant travel in recent years had been tough on the children. I was often gone for long stretches. I'd return home on leave, and then I'd have to disappear overseas again. There was a rhythm to their lives when I was away, and when I came back, that sense of consistency disappeared when I re-entered their lives. One time when Regan was very young, she showed that to me clearly. One summer when I returned home on leave, Delores and I decided I'd surprise the children when they were visiting their maternal grandparents in Baton Rouge.

Regan still remembers how she was playing on the screened-in front porch when I appeared around the corner of the garage. She hadn't missed me until that moment, but seeing me set off a flood of emotions. She knew me; she just hadn't realized that I had been gone. She began to cry and scream hysterically. I picked her up and tried to calm her, holding her tight to soothe her, but she just clung to me and sobbed in my arms. Finally, Delores carried her to her bedroom and put her to bed, where she cried herself to sleep, exhausted.

Now we would all be together, and the children wouldn't have to go without their father, though they would have to get used to him being around, and working odd hours. I got up in darkness at 5:30 A.M., showered and dressed, and walked to the curb. My carpool would pull up and I'd squeeze in. If I was driving that week, I'd drive from house to house in my Buick and pick up the other officers at their homes. Everyone tried to be on time. We didn't want to honk in the darkness and wake up the neighbors.

The carpool would arrive at the Pentagon before 6:30 A.M. The building was already humming with activity as I made my walk to the special operations division. My office, a cramped suite on one of the inner rings of the building, had a view of the five-acre central courtyard, complete with hot dog stand in the middle. Because of the highly classified nature of our special operations work, the door to the reception area had a sign asking visitors to knock before entering.

Just past the receptionist's desk was a door to the office of my boss, Colonel Norton. Norton was tall and trim with neatly parted hair. He dressed immaculately, his uniform neatly pressed and his gig line perfectly straight. In contrast to his clean appearance, Norton had a dirty sense of humor, joking about the busty secretaries next door in a booming voice that could be heard everywhere in our office. He had been in Tenth Special Forces Group (Airborne) in Germany and Korea. We had first met in Vietnam when he visited the camp at Bong Son. We got along well.

It was a very different job from what I was used to. Rather than having my operations coordinated from Washington, I would be part of the team doing the coordinating. As a staff action officer, I had responsibility for supervising Special Forces across the globe, monitoring and coordinating operations wherever it was needed. I managed a lot of red tape as well: logistics, budgeting, force structure, and doctrine. I was the point man on prisoner-of-war rescues and operations for soldiers missing in action. But I was still the most junior person in the division, which meant that I was the one who took our special operations plans around the building for generals to sign off on.

A strange thing happened when I started bringing paperwork upstairs for the generals to sign. When I appeared, they would grill me about Vietnam, peppering me with questions about this battle or that rescue. *What happened when you saved that guy in the fuel truck?* I would get their signature, and by the time I got to the next office, the next general knew I was coming and started in with the same questions. I saw that there was an endless hunger to get the details of battles fought on the other side of the world.

But there was something more to these questions. I realized that the generals would let the others know that I was coming, and they would compare notes afterward on what I told them. I'm not sure they believed what I was telling them. Some weren't convinced that I had been in Vietnam at all. Many of the mostly white career officers in the Pentagon had never been to Vietnam, let alone in combat. Here I was, a decorated Black Special Forces officer with more than one Purple Heart and more combat medals than they would ever have. Their mind couldn't get around this fact. When I showed up, it was like a Black swan had flown in the window.

I can't say that it didn't get under my skin to have my experience doubted. And for this reason, I began to think about the mysterious case of my "lost" Medal of Honor file. If I had gotten the Medal of Honor, there would have been no confusion—I would have been military royalty.

When I was still at Fort Leavenworth in 1970, I had written to the Army personnel office to ask about my awards. A lieutenant colonel wrote back with a record of the citations and medals I had earned. The Medal of Honor wasn't one of them, the lieutenant colonel wrote, and no other awards were pending. He included a note from the adjutant general's office that snuffed any flicker of hope about the nomination, even after Billy Cole resubmitted it in 1969. "Search of records on file at this HQ failed to reveal a rec for MOH" for the battle in June 1965.[1]

Even in the corridors of the Pentagon, there were plenty of firefights—though ideological ones. It turned out that the skepticism about Special Forces that I'd experienced earlier— sometimes Regular Army officers called us "Special Feces"— extended to the top military brass. When Nixon announced the "Vietnamization" of the war—shifting responsibility for the war from U.S. troops and advisors to the South Vietnamese Army we had been training for a decade—there was finger-pointing everywhere. The troop increases, bombing, and offensive actions came too late, the argument went. In trying to win over hearts and minds using Special Forces, the U.S. had lost the war.

At that time, I believed that we were winning the war. Every time we had a battle with the NVA or the Cong, we usually won. But now that I was stateside, I could see how the war was playing out on TV screens and in the newspapers. A small anti-war wire service based out of Saigon called Dispatch News Service had published Seymour Hersh's reporting about U.S. troops massacring civilians in the Vietnamese village of My Lai. The story confirmed every criticism of the war and made every U.S. soldier into a monster.

I'd observed the declining media coverage in the months leading up to my appointment. In early May, there had been massive protests all around Washington, including outside the Pentagon. Then in June, *The New York Times* dropped the bomb that was the Pentagon Papers. I could see how the stories and images were influencing public opinion. I think the press had turned firmly against the war. I could see it in how the news was reported every night.

After I started the new job, it wasn't unusual to see demonstrations outside the building and groups of protestors, sometimes entire families, with signs and bullhorns. They'd leave all their crap on the curb at the end of the day for us to clean up. Sometimes we were told that we could come to work in civilian clothes, to avoid attracting attention as soldiers.

Occasionally a protestor would come to me as a Black man. Getting on or off the bus or going about my business in uniform, I'd get comments like, *Why are you doing the white man's work?* In their questions I observed a subtle racism—an assumption that I was sharpening pencils for white officers rather than being an active participant. I never gave them the satisfaction of a response.

At the same time that I faced comments for being Black outside the building, I had to bat down petty racism inside. At our morning meetings, I was the most junior officer. I usually had some duty beforehand, like picking up the doughnuts for the meeting. That meant every day, I would enter the meeting room with my arms loaded with pastries or coffee. To make matters worse, there would be no seat for me. It wasn't because the room was full. It was because the staff would put that morning's classified binders on every chair in the room for the incoming officers, who were almost exclusively white and often from the South.

It took me a while to catch on. At first, I'd just nonchalantly move a briefing book and then sit. But the next morning the same thing would happen. This went on for months. Finally, I realized they were trying to make me look stupid. They wanted to let me know who was in charge and who wasn't. *Paris Davis, you have to be the dumbest person there*, I thought. *You have got to do something about that.*

I decided to stop playing their racist musical chairs. One day, I just stood. As all the officers filed into the room to find a chair, pick up the red binder, and sit, I just stood in the way and didn't move. I made it inconvenient as hell. A Naval captain ran the meetings. That day, I stood right in his path as he entered the room and had to walk around me to reach his seat.

The captain looked at me with an irritated expression. "Why the hell are you standing here?" he asked.

"Well, every time I come here, I do all the things that I'm supposed to do, and then when I try to find a seat, there's always books on every seat."

He pulled me away and walked me to the back room. "Davis, what's going on?" he asked. "Why didn't you say something to me?"

"I thought you told them to do this," I said point-blank.

"What?" he said again, looking shocked. He was livid. "I'm going to do something, and don't say a damn thing. Step outside. I'll be back with you in minute."

I stepped outside the room and could hear him dressing down his staff. Then he called me back in. "Okay, take a seat." Now there was an empty seat next to some colonel from Mississippi or some damn place. When I sat down next to him, he acted like I was covered with bugs. "We're going to end this right now," the officer said. "You'll see the results of this meeting right here on your OERs." OERs are officer efficiency reports, the performance evaluations that can make or break an ambitious officer's military career.

Then he added the kicker that really must have gotten under the skin of all those officers. "One other thing," he said. "From now on the only person that can answer the red phone is Major Davis." The red phone was the direct line to the Oval Office. I never did get to answer the red phone, but I was happy to know that I would have been the person President Nixon talked to.

I continued to work hard, refusing to allow the politics of the Pentagon to bother me. In August 1972, I moved to a different position working for the Joint Chiefs of Staff. The position was similar—I was an action officer for special operations and unconventional warfare, coordinating between Pentagon departments while reviewing operations, programs, and budgeting.

At the same time, I was studying for two master's degrees, in political science and business. Sometimes I worked seven days a week, leaving before sunup and returning after sundown. I moved on from the master's programs to a PhD program. At the same time, I was leading a Boy Scout troop, coaching youth basketball, and volunteering for charities.[2]

It's hard to convey how different the magnitude of the operations I helped plan at the Pentagon were compared to when I was in Vietnam. Much of is still classified, but not all. In March

1973, I helped plan and then participated in an operation called High Heels. It was a five-day worldwide simulation of a nuclear war to test plans and procedures if diplomacy collapsed between nuclear powers and someone launched a warhead.

The number of agencies and offices involved was mind-boggling. The Department of State, the Office of the Secretary of Defense, the Office of the Joint Chiefs of Staff, the Office of Emergency Preparedness, the CIA, the National Security Agency, the Federal Aviation Agency, and more than a dozen other military commands. The Army Operations Center was in full operation twenty-four hours a day between March 7 and March 13. Around the country, soldiers went into bunkers and didn't come out for weeks.[3] While I wasn't one of those, I didn't see much of the family during those five days.[4]

My work didn't go unnoticed. In one evaluation, my rater reported, "Major Davis did everything so well that it is difficult to single out a specific area. In view of the many projects and off-duty study efforts in which he was involved, organization of work effort had to be near perfection to get it all done."[5]

"Major Davis' performance has been truly outstanding," another of my evaluators wrote. "He worked effortless and tirelessly and without error in establishing himself as an extraordinary Joint Staff officer."[6]

"His performance is totally superior to that of his contemporaries, and he is, at his experience level, the finest, most effectively productive officer I have known," another wrote.[7]

Something new had begun appearing in my officer evaluations. Beginning in 1971, my rating officers consistently recommended what was my big ambition, that I receive an appointment to a Special Forces battalion command. If I had eleven soldiers in my A-team in Vietnam, I would command hundreds at the head of a battalion. It became a repeated refrain from review to review. "He should be given command of a battalion-sized unit," one read.[8] "Major Davis should be assigned to command a battalion size unit," the next rater wrote.[9] "Major Davis should be selected for command of a battalion-sized unit and attendance at a senior service college ahead of his contemporaries," wrote the one after that.[10]

Heading a battalion was the brass ring for Special Forces. If you looked at the number of soldiers in Special Forces and the tiny number of command positions, it was a huge honor. There were guys who would give their left nut just to be considered for a command slot, and I was certainly one of them. Green Berets worked their whole career for their number to come up.

And then in 1975, it was my turn.

13

COMMAND

In mid-August of 1975, I turned our Pontiac station wagon off Route 2 in central Massachusetts and rolled up to a brick guard house. The sentry checked me in. "Welcome to Fort Devens, commander," he said, and waved us through the gate.

We drove past a golf course and basic housing for enlisted men, and turned into curving, tree-lined streets where the officers lived. Our new home was a duplex we'd share with another family. We let the dog out of the stuffed car, and the children spilled out, ready to explore.

I had been promoted to lieutenant colonel on June 1. My dream had finally come true—I'd been appointed to command the men of Second Battalion, Tenth Special Forces Group at Fort Devens. It was a prestigious appointment because Tenth SFG had an important mission that was unique among the Special Forces groups: assisting and training our allies in Europe against a common adversary, the Soviet Union.

Three months earlier, I had watched in disbelief the scenes

from Saigon as the city fell to the North Vietnamese. Desperate Vietnamese families packed the U.S. embassy grounds, helicopters landed in the courtyard and on the roofs of nearby buildings. Tanks and equipment lay abandoned in the streets. Looters pillaged stores and businesses. South Vietnamese pilots threw themselves out of their helicopters as they ditched into the ocean. American sailors pushed ARVN choppers into the sea to make room for incoming American ones. Then came the trucks packed with waving North Vietnamese soldiers rolling into the city, flying the red-and-blue flags of the Communist Provisional Revolutionary Government.

I could not accept the fact that we had lost. When I was with other officers and talk turned to the war's humiliating end, they usually coped by getting drinks—lots of them. Though I still didn't drink, at that moment, I wished I did because I would have gotten drunk right along with them.

With the end of the war, the whole military was realigning and cutting back. We would turn our attention from Southeast Asia to other hot spots around the world, though containing communism would still be a major priority. Our biggest global adversary was still the Soviet Union and would be for years to come.

At Fort Devens, we settled into our new home, enrolled the children in school for the fall, and Delores started work as a speech pathologist in the public schools in nearby Ayer. Delores learned that being married to a commander required a lot more entertaining than she was used to. We hosted potlucks and parties and ceremonies, and she befriended many of the other officers' wives. I stayed fit and even managed to win the Fort Devens handball championship one year.[1]

Our family grew some more. We adopted another son, Chris. He was biracial and barely spoke English because he had been living with his Italian-speaking grandparents. Regan still remembers it as being one of the best days of her life when we brought him home.

Though we were together, I still had to travel frequently for overseas training missions, leaving Delores with the kids as they grew. The Tenth Special Forces Group was the oldest Special Forces group, and it was active all over the world. It had been the subject of one of the first articles in *The New York Times* about Special Forces, describing it as a "liberation force" populated by a mix of Americans and former Eastern Bloc natives.[2]

By the time I got there, it was still true that many members of the detachments spoke Russian. Many of our operations centered on Eastern Europe and Soviet Bloc countries. Just as when Tenth SFG had been based in Germany, we worked closely with the U.S. European Command—EUCOM—training forces in countries bordering the Soviet Bloc. We were also training for deployment in unconventional warfare missions, from sabotage to guerrilla warfare. We had a HALO—high altitude, low opening—team trained in radar-evading parachute jumps. Dropped anywhere from fifteen to thirty-five thousand feet up, the paratroopers opened their chutes just before hitting the ground. Radar never saw them.

Winter training was critical to our mission, and central Massachusetts was perfect for that reason. New England had it all—snowy mountains, coastline, dense forest. The harsh winters were one of the biggest benefits, though, because mastery of cold-weather warfare survival, winter weapons training and tactical maneuvers, climbing and rappelling all required heavy snowfall and long winters.[3] In addition, Fort Devens was only about two hundred miles from West Point and forty miles from Boston.

The Tenth had been at Fort Devens since 1968, when the group reorganized and most of its battalions relocated from Germany. We had an unusual relationship with Fort Devens.

Though Tenth SFG called Fort Devens home, Special Forces was outside the regular Army chain of command. Fort Devens was like a landlord to Tenth SFG. As a result, the fort commander had little authority with the group or leverage over it. Our operations were classified and top secret, and our detachments came and went in secrecy, just like in Okinawa. The fort commander was in the dark as to our missions, or even how many of our men were on the base at any time. It was a unique arrangement. Sometimes it was an uneasy relationship, but I did my best to be a good tenant, and it was generally amicable.

I now commanded about three hundred men in Second Battalion, spread across three companies and eighteen operational detachments in all. My work as commander required constant attention. After I arrived, I shook up and reorganized the battalion. Winter warfare training was one of the primary tasks of my first year. Every year, we had five weeks of intensive winter warfare training. It was usually planned for the first Monday of the new year. I planned out the exercise, and several detachments from my battalion boarded planes for Europe to master cross-country skiing, mountaineering, and weapons training in extreme environments. I slept in snow holes with them, skied every day, seven days a week, teaching them how to fire a rifle in subzero weather, survive in the snow, and climb ice-covered peaks. By the time the men boarded planes for home, they could ski backwards and turn 360 degrees as they went downhill.

Just like in Bong Son, I invited my men to speak up and make suggestions for our work. Once a week, I had afternoon office hours when anyone could come in to discuss the work of the group and what we could be doing better. Most of the time, the men wanted to talk about the battalion, but sometimes they came to me with personal issues. The constant overseas travel and the need for complete secrecy of classified missions were hard on families, and sometimes the men came to me with their problems at home. I tried to be sympathetic and even helpful. Sometimes wives would come to talk to me, too. I warned them they shouldn't bring me personal problems that they wouldn't want others in the battalion to know. I didn't want to be in a position of keeping anyone's secrets and then be accused of running my mouth if the secrets got out.

One of my detachment leaders was a captain named Dan Vannatter. When he returned from Norway at the end of winter warfare training, he came to see me in my office. He needed to go see his wife in Washington, he told me. They were having marital problems and she had moved out of Fort Devens while he was gone. I told him that he could take some time off to get his personal situation straightened out.

He flew down to Washington and knocked on the door of his wife's place down there. She was home. She told Vannatter she was leaving him, and things almost turned ugly. But he took the keys to their car and went to his in-laws' house, where he got drunk and passed out for the night. The next day, he got in the car and drove back to Massachusetts.

The 1970s weren't an easy time to be in Special Forces. Force cuts hit Special Forces particularly hard. For Tenth SFG, that meant a reduction in the number and frequency of operational deployments for detachments.[4] We weren't completely starved for money, though, because our obligations to NATO required us to continue training and missions with our European allies.

We were insulated from most cutbacks, but not completely. Budget cuts in 1977 meant that we wouldn't get funding for our winter ski training. So I did something unheard of: I asked the men in the Second Battalion to pay their own way. Most of them did. We went up to New Hampshire and stayed with local residents who filled us with pie and home cooking. We didn't even have to pay for the lift tickets; the ski area where we trained let

us ski for free as long as we wore our green berets. Girls flocked
to the slopes to watch us.

As commander, I constantly had my eye out for particularly
talented, steady, and dependable men. One such man was Sergeant Tommy Shook, commander of the HALO paratrooper
team.

When a detachment deployed to Europe for training, we'd
launch the mission at an operating base in England. Sometimes,
when the men were loading a plane at 2 A.M. to prepare for a
nighttime departure for Norway or Germany, I'd stand in the
back of the hangar, watching silently just as Monger had with
me. Tommy was one of the men I was watching. I stopped him in
the street one day. "When I make full colonel," I said, "I'm either
going to command an armored cavalry regiment or a special
forces group. You're going to be my command sergeant major."
In other words, he would be my number two if I got a group
command. He probably didn't believe me, but I'm sure he nodded and said, "Yes, sir."

In 1977, the Army gave me a new assignment. This position
was in Germany, as Operations Center Director in the Operations Directorate of U.S. European Command, or EUCOM, in
Stuttgart-Vaihingen, Germany. I wouldn't leave the family behind this time; they would all move to Germany with me.

On the afternoon of March 1, I found my seat on a podium
in the sports arena in Fort Devens as I faced my battalion for
a change of ceremony identical to the one held for me when I
arrived. This time I was passing the command to my replacement, Lieutenant Colonel Tom Bridgewater. I faced my battalion
standing at parade rest in their fatigues and berets, M-16s at their
sides and pistols on their belts, combat boots polished. The commander of troops faced the men.

"Present arms!" he said, as the men raised their rifles to their
chests. "Sir, the battalion is formed," he said to the reviewing

officer. After the presentation, the review officer inspected the troops, and the Army band played "The Ballad of the Green Berets" and the national anthem.

I stood and faced Bridgewater with the Tenth Group commander, Colonel Othar Shalikashvili, between us. A sergeant major handed our battalion pennant—called a guidon—to me. I handed it to Shalikashvili. He handed it to Bridgewater. He passed it back to the sergeant major. The commander of troops barked, "Parade, rest!" After a few speeches, the ceremony was over. The band played "The Army Song," and the ceremony ended. My command was over.[5]

* * *

A short term later, the family flew in a noisy military transport to join me in Stuttgart-Vaihingen. Our apartment was in the Patch Barracks on the base, in a neighborhood called "White Village." It was a small apartment, but different from any other place we had lived. It was spread across two floors, with tall plate glass windows in the stairwell that allowed us to look over the base.

We were in Germany for about two years. It was heaven for the kids. They went to school on base with other Americans, and made friends with the other officers' kids. There was an apple orchard, and the kids would climb the trunks and eat the fruit right off the tree. A high fence encircled the base, but the kids found a place where they would squirm underneath. They'd run to the town to look in the windows of the shops and buy candy.

In the winter, Delores put them on buses for ski trips to the Swiss Alps, and in the summer we travelled to Austria, Italy, and Holland, where we bought the girls wooden clogs in which they clomped around the apartment. I bought Delores a present too: a Morgan roadster, sleek and beautiful and fast, a trophy to bring back to the U.S.

My job was to review the readiness level of U.S. forces in

Europe and evaluate intelligence data, operational reports, and press.[6] The commander in chief of EUCOM was General Alexander M. Haig,[7] who oversaw more than three hundred thousand Americans from all branches of the military stationed throughout Europe, with areas of responsibility extending from Western Europe through the Mediterranean, the Middle East, and North Africa.[8]

My immediate boss was Haig's deputy, General Robert Huyser. He had been drafted in 1943, became a pilot in 1944, flew B-29 bombing missions in the Pacific in World War II, B-52 missions during Korea and Vietnam, and had arrived in Stuttgart around the same time as I did.[9] His wife was recovering from hip surgery at the time, so I picked up extra responsibilities as he attended to his family. Sometimes when he was in a bad mood, he would take a plane up and fly around until he had calmed down. He kept a pearl-handled pistol in the car. He warned me never to touch it because it had a perfectly calibrated hair trigger.

It was a tense time to be stationed in Germany. During the 1970s, terrorist groups targeted U.S. facilities and personnel with bombings, kidnappings, and assassinations. In the late 1970s, the Soviet Union developed and deployed new generations of ballistic missiles to Eastern countries in the Soviet Bloc, including mobile intercontinental missiles capable of reaching the United States.[10] To reassure our allies in NATO, we had an ongoing operation called REFORGER to increase U.S. troop commitments in Europe. When I was at Fort Devens, I helped plan the Tenth SFG participation in REFORGER.[11]

I still wondered sometimes about the medals I never received, among them the one that General Westmoreland had given me as I lay in my hospital bed in 1965, shot up with painkillers from my wounds at the Phu Cu Pass. Right before Thanksgiving of 1977, I wrote to Westmoreland asking if he had any memory of the hospital visit that would improve my likelihood of officially receiving the Distinguished Service Cross. "Sir, if you can recall the action I would be most appreciative," I wrote. "If you do recall the action, I still desire that you present the award."[12]

He responded about two weeks later. "I have searched my memory after reading your letter and the clippings, and regretfully, I only vaguely remember the incident. Although your recollection is probably accurate it is not sufficient to support an award," Westmoreland wrote. I tucked that letter away, too.[13]

* * *

After our family celebrated Independence Day in 1979, we got on a plane to return to the United States. I had gotten word a few months earlier that I would be temporarily promoted to fullbird colonel even though I was what the Army called "below the zone." That meant I wasn't technically eligible—because I hadn't been a lieutenant colonel long enough—but was getting my promotion earlier because of consistently exceptional performance.

I had applied to attend the Army Research Associates Program, a training program with the Department of Energy. The program places officers at DOE laboratories to conduct research on nuclear weapons, and to develop expertise in weapon design and production.[14] I was turned down for the program, though, and instead given a slot in the Naval War College in Newport, Rhode Island. I was disappointed, but I agreed to attend.[15]

I threw myself into my studies at the Naval War College. I was studying national security organization and process, individual behavior, and contemporary Middle Eastern problems. I worked hard at school and out of it, coaching basketball and soccer in the fall and spring, and agreed to be in charge of the ceremony marking the 205th birthday of the Army, which thirteen thousand people attended. Even with the extracurricular activities, I still impressed my reviewers. "He is an exceptionally intelligent officer who continuously sought to expand his competence in areas of joint operations," one reviewer wrote. "He is forceful yet sensitive and compassionate, perceptive and insightful—all those elements one seeks in a successful combat leader."[16]

I was still at the Naval War College in mid-1980 when I got a call about a new assignment. The commander of Tenth Special Forces Group, Colonel Edward Cutolo, had been killed in a car accident while he was in Europe with a detachment.[17] I would be his replacement. I had finally reached one of the pinnacles of a career in Special Forces: I would have command of an entire group. And not just any group. Tenth Special Forces conducted some of the most crucial operations in the Cold War, training for a Soviet invasion of Europe and preparing for unconventional warfare behind the Iron Curtain.

After I got the news, I called Tommy Shook, my former HALO commander. He was with the First Ranger Battalion. Though he was rarely in his office, he happened to be at his desk that day. "This is Paris Davis," I said. "We have the Tenth Group."

"Congratulations, sir," Tommy said. "I'm so happy for you."

"You're not listening to me," I said. "*We* have the Tenth Group." I fully intended to make him my command sergeant major. But I wasn't able to pull that off, and he stayed where he was. It was probably for the best, I soon found out.

* * *

I moved the family to Fort Devens for a second time. We were assigned a big colonial house that looked out on the parade ground in the center of the fort. Delores entertained even more than before. She was one of the rare officers' wives who worked full time and still made fast friends with the other wives, and impressed visitors—and there were a lot of them—with her warmth and hospitality.

Things had changed at Fort Devens while I had been gone. The fort command had gone to another officer, Colonel Richard J.

Kattar. He was a deeply conservative man from Lawrence, Massachusetts, an old mill town on the New Hampshire border. He had served two tours in Vietnam. Though we were both colonels, he had slight seniority over me and was older.

I reported to his office and waited outside while his aide went in to announce I had arrived.

"Well, let that nigger just stay out there for a while," I heard a voice say in the office. I sat. Eventually, the aide showed me in.

"I heard someone use the word nigger," I said to Kattar.

"Oh no, we never use language like that," he said. I heard snickers behind me.

This was just a taste of what was to come. After twenty years in the Army, during which my race had only very occasionally been a significant problem, I would have a racist boss. To make matters worse, I learned that the uneasy relationship of Tenth SFG to the Fort Devens command had turned into a kind of cold war under Kattar. Kattar seemed to take the arm's-length relationship between Tenth SFG and the fort as a personal slight, and chafed at not being privy to the group's classified activities.

To some officers who served in Tenth Special Forces Group, one thing seemed obvious: Kattar hated Special Forces. He openly ridiculed us in front of troops and had a fundamentally different view of Tenth SFG's purpose. Rather than a unique unit wired into security concerns in Europe, he saw the group as more like a conventional infantry unit, and one that should have been under his control.[18]

One time, he'd dropped in unannounced to a class for company commanders. About thirty minutes into the class, he interrupted the instructor and launched into a monologue riddled with criticism of the group. The tirade lasted for two hours. At the end, the instructor cancelled the rest of class. As a parting shot, Kattar warned the company commanders not to repeat anything he had said over the previous two hours. If anything came back to him, he said, he "would know where it came from."[19]

He seemed to be obsessed with road rules and speed limits. When two members of Tenth Group were caught going five or ten miles over the posted speed limit, Kattar demanded their driver's licenses and tore them into pieces. One of those times, he brought the shreds of license and dumped them on the desk of my predecessor. "The Post Commander is the most ego-centric individual I have ever encountered," the officer observed.[20]

His outbursts were ludicrous and sometimes childish, and his reputation went far beyond central Massachusetts—a friend of mine serving in Iran had heard tales of Kattar. He berated Tenth SFG officers for any transgression, however slight, whether real or perceived. One time, he had an officer handcuffed and brought to the Military Police office because his ID card was chipped. Another time, he sent MPs to bring in an NCO at 1 A.M. because the officer's dog had gotten loose.[21] He complained that the deputy commanding officer of the group didn't mow his lawn frequently enough.[22]

He would explode in furious tirades in front of troops, and then threaten to throw them out of Tenth SFG if anyone repeated what he said in the room. He told one officer that he probably would have relieved my predecessor of his command if he hadn't been killed in Europe. When an officer missed a meeting at post headquarters, Kattar dressed down the group's executive officer in front of group soldiers. "One more failure to have your staff at post meetings and you are relieved," he screamed at the top of his lungs. "I hold you personally responsible for everything your staff does. If one of them makes a mistake you are gone."[23]

More than once, he ordered me to divulge classified information about missions. I refused, which infuriated him even more.[24] He regularly tried to exert authority over the group and our missions. Some of my staff would groan when they arrived at group headquarters, because his car would be idling outside. He would leave his driver in the car, even in freezing winter weather, to spend half a day in the group headquarters demanding information about upcoming operations.[25]

I tried to placate him and make every effort that I could to keep him satisfied. But my relationship with Kattar never improved. Instead, it only got worse over time. I tried not to let the open antagonism get in the way of the work. Our work was too important.

One of our biggest responsibilities was a joint training exercise in Europe called Operation Flintlock. It was an annual exercise held in early summer. The group would fly to England and set up an operational base. The A-teams conducting the exercise would go into isolation for a week or so just to study and prepare for the mission. Then they'd be flown to a NATO country and infiltrate—maybe by HALO jumps, maybe by ship if it was a coastal country—to carry out a mission meant to simulate operations that might be necessary in the event of a Soviet invasion.[26]

The missions varied. Sometimes it was strategic reconnaissance. Sometimes it was mock unconventional warfare, meeting up with guerrilla fighters to train, advise, and assist them in fighting occupying Soviet troops. Sometimes the mission was sabotage. Our HALO detachments were what we called "Green Light Teams." These were Special Forces units trained to parachute into occupied territory carrying small nuclear bombs called Special Atomic Demolition Munitions. They were backpack nukes that could blow up critical infrastructure like bridges, ports, and dams. At the end of the mission, we would come in and exfiltrate them again, and we'd all head home. Some of Tenth Special Forces' top-secret missions wouldn't come to light for decades.

Throughout, Kattar constantly tried to interfere with my command, and my staff watched in dismay as the friction grew. It was clear that I was in a no-win situation—there was no way to make Kattar happy if I was effectively commanding the group. I don't think there was really any doubt that he would eventually relieve me, as he had with other staff and had threatened to do with the previous group commander. He made no secret that he wanted me gone, and directly threatened to relieve me in January 1981, when he dressed me down in his office for two hours. Afterward, he wrote a memorandum that he never showed me and I never saw: "Col. Kattar formally indicated that should Col. Davis ever be called in again under these circumstances that it would be for relief of his command."[27]

In fall of 1981, that's what happened. Kattar used the flimsiest of excuses to relieve me of command, and I left Fort Devens after less than two years. I appealed the relief of command, arguing that I had been falsely accused and railroaded out of my position. But the Army took Kattar's word over mine, accepting the judgment of a white officer of the same rank as me, an officer who had never seen combat and seethed with resentment and jealousy toward me.

In the aftermath of my dismissal, many officers I had worked with over the years, both subordinate and superior, wrote letters of protest and support, pointing out the corrosive relationship at the fort. Many wrote that a grave injustice had been committed, and asked for my relief to be reversed.

"Colonel Paris Davis is, without doubt, one of the very best commanders I have ever known in twenty years of service. His total dedication to accomplishment of the mission and acceptance of responsibility for the welfare of his men and their families are without equal in my experience," one letter read. "My observation of Col. Davis has led me to the conclusion that he has general officer potential," a three-star general wrote on my behalf.[28]

One of the letters came from Tiny Aldrich, who had retired

and was president of a company in Maine. He talked about my service record and my nomination for the Medal of Honor. Over thirty years, "I have never met a man of the caliber of Col. Paris D. Davis, his honest, forthright manner, coupled with an extraordinary ability to react positively while under great stress has continually placed him a notch above the norm," Tiny wrote. "I would have to say that any individual questioning, or indicating in any manner or deed that Col. Davis's integrity was anything but above reproach, would do so only to discredit Col. Davis for their own special needs or gain."[29]

I don't know if Kattar's fury toward me had anything to do with jealousy over my Vietnam experience, which I never talked about and which my closest friends from that period knew nothing about. I do know, though, that one of the strangest ironies about this period was that in 1981, Billy Waugh—for reasons I'll never know—took it upon himself to write an affidavit in support of my Medal of Honor nomination for the 1965 battle. I hadn't seen him since I put him on the medevac, and yet despite all the friction between us, he wrote a powerful letter in support of me.

"I only have to close my eyes to vividly recall the gallantry of this individual who, through physical strength and complete disregard for himself killed and destroyed thirty-nine armed North Vietnamese, saved a group of friendly infantry soldiers and was instrumental in disrupting a complete NVA takeover of 11 Corps in June," he wrote.[30]

None of it mattered. Despite years of dedication and sterling performance reports year after year, I never regained my command. Instead, I received a new posting back at Fort Bragg, North Carolina, as head of the Directorate of Combat and Doctrine Development. The family uprooted at the end of the school year and moved back to Virginia. I remained at Fort Bragg until 1984, the year I found myself back in the hospital again.

14

"THIS JUST CAME UP"

JULY 30, 1985

ARLINGTON, VIRGINIA

The doctors at Walter Reed weren't sure what was wrong with me. In 1983, I had joined a classified training operation at Fort Bragg that included a jump from an airplane. I had done hundreds of jumps—close to three hundred of them—but this time something went wrong. The altimeter that was supposed to show me when the chute should open malfunctioned, and the chute opened prematurely. My whole body snapped in the air, and I felt a crushing sensation in my back. I landed in agony. A teammate helped me gather my things, and I continued with the mission, which lasted another five or six days.

It was obvious that I was injured. When I went into the hospital around Christmas 1983, the doctors told me that I had to have surgery because I had ruptured a disk in my back. I underwent surgery in February, but it didn't solve my problems—it made them worse. Something had gone wrong as a result of the surgery. The pain in my lower back became excruciating, and I could only sit for ten to fifteen minutes at a time before I had to get up. I developed shooting pains in my right leg, and my right toe was numb all the time. I could only walk about three hundred yards before I had to rest, and I had to steel myself whenever I felt a sneeze or a cough coming, because it would send waves of pain through my body. My right knee would sometimes suddenly give out, and I lost about 50 percent of the sensation in my right leg when I was pricked with a needle. A back brace didn't help. The only way for me get relief from the pain at night was to curl up in a fetal position.

I could barely fulfill my job duties at Fort Bragg, and that July, Walter Reed admitted me as a patient. I was in and out of the hospital as the doctors puzzled over my condition. It was clear that I needed to hang up my uniform, and I submitted my retirement paperwork. But the Army's Physical Evaluation Board recommended that I receive only 20 percent disability, which far underestimated the extent of my injuries. I appealed, asking for 60 percent disability. After some additional testing, the board had a hearing on my physical evaluation in February 1985.[1] They settled on 40 percent disability.

In mid-July, the Army sent me an official letter relieving me of duty because of physical disability. On July 31, I officially retired after twenty-five years, eight months, and twenty-four days in the Army.[2] My health wasn't the only reason for leaving the military. The situation at home was bad. Delores had been diagnosed with cancer. I wanted to help her, but she had been so used to living independently for so many years as a military spouse that she just wanted to fight the battle on her own. We had been apart far more than we had been together during our marriage and she was tired of moving. She wanted to heal without me. We separated, though we stayed under the same roof. I wanted to stay close so I could help her and be with the kids. I moved to the basement, and Delores had the upstairs.

After all those years in the Army, I wasn't sure what to do.

Vietnam had been over for a decade. The Cold War would soon be over with the fall of the Berlin Wall in 1989. The collapse of the Soviet Union would come two years later. Steph was in college, and Paris III and Regan were in high school. Chris was ten but was growing up fast. My life as a soldier was behind me. I was a civilian, and for the first time in my adult life, no one was telling me what to do.

More than anything, I wanted to make sure that my family was taken care of and prepared for life. I would tell the kids that because we were Black, they had to work at least twice as hard as everyone else. I remember telling Stephanie one day as I drove her to school, "You are Black, and you are a woman, and you're going to always have to work ten times harder than other people." It wasn't fair, it's just the way it was. It was like that for me in the Army, too. I had aimed to be a general one day. Even though I worked as hard as anyone around me, I never did get those stars.

I almost never talked about my service. The people I worked with late in my career didn't know about the battles I had been in and the scrapes I'd gotten out of. Neither did the family. Sometimes they'd ask, though. Once when Stephanie was little, she asked me loudly in church what had happened to the middle finger on my right hand, the one that the grenade blew up on June 18, 1965. At the sound of her loud question, everyone in the pews around us turned to look at us. I whispered to her that I had been hurt once, but I was fine now.

* * *

It took some time for me to find my footing. For a time, I had a business partner, a guy named Preston Royster. We tried to start a couple of business ventures together. We bought a juice company that sold fruit drinks and concentrates out of a storefront in Alexandria. We incorporated a company for a medical research business, and another as a cleaning business. And so on. But we didn't see eye to eye, so we went our separate ways.

I decided to start a newspaper. At the time, there were no papers in Northern Virginia geared toward Black readers, so I started one that would contribute to our community and highlight our achievements. There was a practical reason for this. Writing was one of the few things I could do that didn't require a lot of physical exertion. Even if I was in the hospital, I could write articles.

I named the paper *The Metro Chronicle*, which I changed to *The Metro Herald* in the 1990s. The first edition came out right before Election Day of 1986. The election was a huge win for Democrats, who took a 55–45 margin in the U.S. Senate, and was seen as a rebuke to President Reagan and his conservatism. I saw something else: the power of the Black vote.

"This past Tuesday, the fourth of November, Black Americans voted for change. They were saying to Mr. Reagan, enough of your big defense spending and enough of your domestic cuts and enough to all the insensitivities of your administration that have taken [their] toll on Blacks and other minorities," the editorial read that week. "This past election also said to the white political structures throughout this great land of ours: that you ought not to take Black folks for granted."

Maybe those who knew me in the military would have been surprised by my take on the president. He was a Cold Warrior, a defender of U.S. interests overseas, and a believer in strength through power. It's probably safe to assume that a former Special Forces colonel would like that.

But Reagan said other things that made me angry. The way he talked about Black people, for example, people who looked like me and my family. When he ran for the Republican nomination in 1976, he talked at almost every campaign stop about a "welfare queen" in New York who was on public assistance, but supposedly owned a Cadillac, used eighty aliases and had four

Social Security numbers, and collected $150,000 a year, including veterans' benefits for four deceased husbands she never had. Of course, she was Black.

It didn't matter that most of the welfare queen story was untrue.[3] The story managed to make Black people everywhere into scapegoats for everything that was wrong with the government. Anyone who was poor and Black was automatically suspected of being a grifter, a thief, living high on the hog while on the public teat. He was blowing a racist dog whistle to white voters. That whistle is still blowing loud and clear today.

Every week, I wrote about what I thought was important for the Black community. The Howard Beach riot in New York, Reagan's budget cuts, apartheid in South Africa, police brutality in Prince George's County, Maryland. We published political cartoons opposing aid to the Contras in Nicaragua. We ran editorials from public figures like Marion Wright Edelman, president of the Children's Defense Fund.

The paper's parent company, Davis Communications Group, had a four-room office suite on North Washington Street in Alexandria, just south of Washington along the Potomac River. I filled the space with plants that I'd water once a week. As the years went by, the paper won awards for its coverage of the Black community, and for journalism in general. I'd frame the awards and citations and hang them in my office. We also hung the pages of the paper, showing off editions we were proud of.

My office had a big window overlooking the street. Just like in the Army, I had an open-door policy. Pretty much anyone could drop in any time to pitch a story idea, ask about taking out ads, or print posters for an event. There was always a steady stream of people coming in and out of the office, and the phone rang constantly. Every so often, someone I served with would call or ask to drop by, and we'd talk about old times. When they did, I'd close the door so that I could talk without anyone hearing us.

The paper did well. My main writer and editor was a woman named P. J. Robinson. She was an old-school reporter who had worked with CNN anchor Bernard Shaw. She would come into the office and slide into a chair in my office to talk about a story she wanted to do. Once I'd signed off, she'd go into the workroom, light a cigarette, pour a glass of port, and start pounding away on her keyboard.

For a time, I had a receptionist named Tina Blanchard. Tina also worked for a talent agency that recruited contestants for pageants. After she offered to help find candidates, she convinced Regan to try out for the Miss World Virginia pageant. She'd never tried out for a pageant, and to everyone's surprise—including Regan's—she won.

For a couple of years in the mid-1990s, Stephanie worked for me in the office and helped me redesign the paper. We put the paper to bed on Thursday nights, and Stephanie would stay until early Friday morning, when it would go to the printers. Sometimes, she'd go to IHOP after the paper was done. Chris would help me out with the paper as well. Sometimes I'd bring Chris's son, my grandson CJ, to the office, and he'd toddle around while I worked.

We were a small operation. Most of the responsibility was on my shoulders. When the papers came back from the printers, I would load them into the car and take them around Virginia, the District, and Maryland, dropping them off at the distribution spots. When we decided to try to expand south to Richmond, I would drive them down, leave the papers, and then return with an empty trunk. We pushed to grow over the years. In 1999, we started a paper in Baltimore called the *Baltimore Press*, hiring some local reporters.[4]

In a way, the newspaper helped me find my voice. Often I wrote the page one news articles or shared a byline with one of the reporters, but I also wrote the paper's editorials. It's a fact that if you're in the military, you can't talk politics. You can't write politics. My voice was always there, even when I was in the military. But once I got out, I had the freedom to use it in a way that I couldn't before. And the place where those thoughts came out was in the pages of my newspaper.

* * *

Though the paper was doing well, my home situation didn't improve. For four years, Delores and I lived under the same roof. She lived upstairs and I lived downstairs. Stephanie and Regan graduated from college and moved away, leaving Chris, Paris III, Delores, and me in the house. It wasn't comfortable, but we all learned to live with it.

After our divorce went through in 1989, we had to sell a lot of things—she sold the Morgan and a vintage Model T Ford that her father had left her. We had bought a plot of land a little to the south intending to build a house on it; we sold that, too. She got the house and then sold it to our son Paris III a few years later, so I was able to stay there for a while. She moved to South Carolina, and both Regan and Steph were gone. For a time, it was just me and my two sons.

And then things took a turn. Chris got into trouble and needed money, and tried selling drugs for some cash. He sold to an undercover police officer and ended up in jail. My son's troubles took a toll on me. I withdrew into myself and stopped talking to anyone in the house. Paris III and I would pass each other silently in the hallways. Eventually, it was too much for him and he asked me to find somewhere else to live. Years would go by before we spoke again.

When I moved out, I also had to get rid of the stuff that I was storing in the basement. There was so much crap. It was years' worth of documents, furniture, and junk I didn't even know I had. It was every whichaway. Boxes filled with clothes. Tools and furniture, pictures, and knickknacks. Towers of papers spilling into other piles of paper that I had kept since Christ was a corporal.

I brought down a bottle of Coke, rigged up a seat for myself, and got to work sorting through my things, deciding what to keep and what to throw away. I'd take a swig of soda, pick up a pile of papers to look through, and put it in a pile to keep or throw away. It felt like it was going to take forever.

I'm not sure where I found the slim stack of stapled papers—probably sandwiched in with some unrelated documents—but I barely looked at the pages as I tossed them into the trash pile. The staple wasn't flush against the paper, and the sharp point scraped a knuckle and drew a little blood.

I wouldn't have given it a second thought, but for some reason the scratch made me go back to look at the contents. When I picked up the papers, I saw the date at the top: 22 July 1981. Below that, it read, EYEWITNESS RECOMMENDATION FOR THE MEDAL OF HONOR FOR CAPT. PARIS D. DAVIS, COMMANDING OFFICER, DETACHMENT A-321.

I sat back down on the board and read the five typewritten pages. I had forgotten all about Waugh's affidavit that he had written sixteen years after the battle in which I saved his life. It wasn't on my hit parade. As I read his words, I was surprised by the amount of detail that Waugh had included. How I had used the butt of my rifle as a club. How I had dragged him to safety. How I had disobeyed Cole. *Wow*, I thought to myself.

After all these years, I wasn't sure what to do with it. I packed it up and brought it with me to the small apartment I rented for myself in Alexandria. It was a nice place, and I got a good price for it. Most of my belongings went into a storage locker on Telegraph Road. But Billy Waugh's pages went with me to my office. I held on tight to that relic of my Army life, a record of the old Green Beret I once was.

* * *

In fall of 2011, my old buddy from Korea, Ambrose Brennan, dropped in to see me at the newspaper. He was retired, too, living in North Carolina a couple of hours west of Fort Bragg. Ever the West Pointer, he was headed to upstate New York for a football game at his alma mater. I still had that open-door policy that I had when I was in command at Fort Devens. Ambrose decided to stop in Alexandria and catch up.

He came up to the newspaper offices, and we chatted for a while, and had a few laughs. As we were talking, I showed him Billy Waugh's statement about the battle in Bong Son.

"This just came up," I told him, or something like that. He took it from me and glanced at the heading. *Well, that's interesting,* he thought. We kept talking for a while before it was time for him to get on the road again.

We said goodbye, and he took a copy of Waugh's statement with him as headed out the door and downstairs. When he reached the car, he put it beside him on the passenger seat. Then he started the engine and drove off. When he came to a red light, he picked up the papers and started reading. He was still reading when the light changed.

He put it down and kept driving. At the next red light, he picked it up again. He couldn't believe what he was reading. On the second or third page, he had already read descriptions of battle that would have earned a Medal of Honor, and he was only partway through. He was still reading when the light changed again. *Somebody's got to do something with this,* he thought. *That's you Ambrose, baby.*

* * *

In my retirement, I tried to stay in touch with some of my old Army friends. I had stayed in touch with one of my officers at Second Battalion, Rod Azama, and even had him writing articles for the newspaper for a time. Around 2010, I reconnected with Dan Vannatter from Second Battalion. After his divorce from his first wife, he gone to Seventh Special Forces Group at Fort Bragg, where I had relocated as well after I was relieved at Fort Devens. Now remarried and retired like me, he lived near me in the Washington, DC, area. Our friendship deepened in retirement. He would drop by the newspaper every so often, and we started going to Cracker Barrel every Saturday for breakfast. Pretty soon we knew every waiter and waitress in the restaurant. That tradition lasted for years.

Around 2012, another one of my fellow Green Berets returned to Washington: my old friend and former HALO team commander Tommy Shook. He was between stints in Iraq and Afghanistan, where he had been working security for the State Department. During his time in the capital, he was staying in a hotel near the Pentagon. I asked him if I could drop by his hotel and show him a copy of Waugh's nomination. "You sure can, sir," he told me in his North Carolina accent. "Come on over."

Shook was an incredible man—a soldier's soldier. I knew he wouldn't bullshit me. When I got to his hotel that evening, I handed him Waugh's nomination. Even though we'd known each other for years, he had no idea that I had been nominated for the medal. I had never discussed it with him. He read through the sheets of paper and spent a few minutes studying them.

"I'll take care of it," he said.

When I showed Waugh's statement to Shook, he didn't know what to think. He had known Medal of Honor recipients who had earned the medal with only a single act of bravery. Just like Brennan, he was struck by how unusual this was. Capturing enemy soldiers. Carrying out a successful mission. Setting up the defense on the hill. Rescuing three Americans under fire. Refusing to be evacuated. "Cpt. Paris D. Davis' actions and total disregard for his own personal safety during the above-mentioned period of combat against the enemy in the Republic of Vietnam were of the highest degree of heroism," it read.[6] Shook knew me, but still wasn't sure if what he was reading could have actually happened. Shook brought the eyewitness statement to a high-ranking official at the State Department, who had also been in Tenth Special Forces Group. The official agreed to help, typed up a nomination, and submitted it. Shook returned to Iraq for eighteen months. He emailed back and forth with the official. Very little happened. Shook's contact grew disinterested and gave up. Once again, it seemed to be going nowhere.

* * *

In spring 2012, Ron Deis was going through the day's mail when he came across a letter with an unfamiliar name. The name on the envelope was Ambrose Brennan, from a North Carolina address.

Deis had married and moved to Alaska years before. He still had his boxes full of photos from Bong Son, but like me he rarely thought about his time in Vietnam.

Deis opened up the letter. Brennan introduced himself and wrote that he had learned of my lost Medal of Honor nomination, and wanted to try again. The byzantine requirements of the medal nomination required eyewitness statements, and there weren't many members of the detachment alive anymore. Deis was one of them. Another was Waugh, who had agreed to update and notarize the affidavit that he had written in 1981.

Brennan and Deis spoke by phone in the spring of 2012, and Deis agreed to provide a statement to support a Medal of Honor recommendation. Then months went by. Brennan wrote back in November. "Sometimes it's just hard to get started on a project like this," he wrote. "I am hopeful that you are still interested in providing such a statement. Sometimes we do get busy in our lives and some items get deferred."

About a year later, in November 2013, a notary public in Anchorage stamped Deis's affidavit. Brennan put together an enormous packet, several inches thick, packed with details about what happened on June 18, 1965. There were MACV duty officer logs; weather reports; declassified daily reports from the camp; and affidavits from Waugh, the FAC pilot Bronson, Tiny Aldrich, and Billy Cole. And of course it included Ron Deis's affidavit, which ended with the sentence: "Sgt. Morgan, who had an incredible amount of combat experience, told me that evening that Captain Davis deserved the Medal of Honor for his actions that day."

Deis agreed to be the nominator for Ambrose's packet. There are two ways to nominate someone for a Medal of Honor. The first is through the chain of command, with a commanding officer making the recommendation. But that must happen within three years of the act that the nomination is made for. The other way is through a member of Congress, who forwards the nomination to the secretary of the Army, Navy, or Air Force—whichever branch the nominee served in. If the nomination goes up through the Secretary of Defense, the House Armed Services Committee is notified and can ask for a waiver of the three-year time limit from the senator or congressman.

Deis took the massive packet to downtown Anchorage and dropped it off at the office of U.S. Senator Lisa Murkowski. In Washington, Ambrose brought copies to members of Congress on Capitol Hill. They didn't hear anything for a long time.

* * *

When Tommy Shook came back from Iraq, almost two years had gone by since he had enlisted the help of the former Tenth Special Forces officer to get the nomination back on track. The effort seemed dead. But Shook still had one lead—he had been in contact, on my behalf, with an Army veteran and researcher named Neil Thorne. Thorne had been working on medals and awards for various Special Forces officers affiliated with Military Assistance Command, Vietnam-Studies and Observations Group, the special operations unit established in Okinawa in 1964 to conduct clandestine operations in North and South Vietnam, Laos, and Cambodia. He knew all the ins and outs of the military award process.

They talked by phone. Thorne was hesitant about getting involved, saying his focus was the Studies and Observations Group in Okinawa, but agreed to help out in an advisory role. Then in 2014, Shook went down to Eglin Air Force Base near Pensacola, Florida, for a Distinguished Service Cross ceremony for another soldier who Thorne had worked with. It was a multiday event, with various presentations and ceremonies in different locations. Partway through, he climbed into a six-van convoy headed to one of the events. A friend and Special Forces legend named Mike Nelson was in the van with Shook. As the convoy sped down the base road in perfect intervals, driven by Seventh Special Forces support soldiers, the van abruptly braked and stopped. The van door slid open, and to Shook's surprise, Neil Thorne climbed in with his wife, Molly.

Both Shook and Thorne knew the DSC recipient, MSG Patrick N. Watkins, and Thorne had come with his wife to help plan and coordinate the ceremony. At the guard station, the sentry told them to get out of and leave the electric blue Mustang convertible they rented and jump into the van convoy. He just happened to get into the same vehicle as Tommy Shook. In the van, the two of them talked at great length about the nomination.

Thorne, who had already spent some time on my case in his advisory role, threw himself into the effort, and put together a team to work on the nomination. There were Thorne and Shook, of course, and Dan Vannatter. Tiny Aldrich was part of the crew, along with two retired lieutenant colonels and a full-bird colonel, Mac Dorsey. In late 2020, a former JAG and retired lieutenant colonel named Robert "Al" Broadbent, a Trump appointee in the Pentagon, joined the team and advocated for the nomination from inside the administration. They enlisted Rob Graham, a talented video game designer from England who specialized in Vietnam, to create visual images depicting what happened in Bong Son.

Thorne made a crucial connection when he had lunch with an attorney named Jim Moriarty. Ostensibly, they were meeting about Moriarty's effort to upgrade a medal for an officer named Captain Gary Michael Rose. Moriarty was a retired Marine who had served three tours in Vietnam before becoming a lawyer. He had debunked a bullshit story in 1998 about the U.S. Army using sarin gas against civilians on a secret mission in Laos called Operation Tailwind and forced a retraction. Rose had been a medic on that mission, and Moriarty and a team of volunteer experts he assembled had helped upgrade Rose's Distinguished Service Cross into a Medal of Honor. The moment Thorne told Moriarty about my case over lunch, the lawyer was all in. As Rose's case gained momentum, *New York Times* military reporter David Philipps learned of my case, and stayed in contact with the team for years about their efforts.

For a time, they worked with Brennan. After he had submitted his packet, they continued on and put together a new, separate nomination package that would upgrade my Silver Star to the Medal of Honor. The result was an updated awards package composed of Army files, after-action reports, new and old affidavits and interviews, and long-lost news reports. Billy Waugh's eyewitness statement was central, along with Ron Deis's statement. Tiny Aldrich ended up being the nominator for that packet.

On March 16, 2016, I put on a tie and went up to Capitol Hill. I met Tommy Shook, Neil Thorne, Jim Moriarty, Dan Vannatter, and four other members of the team. Together, we delivered the packet to Senators Tim Kaine and Mark Warner, as well as my congressman, Representative Don Beyer. We were confident that this time, everything would go right.

* * *

But we again hit roadblock after roadblock. The packet got mired in impenetrable bureaucracy. High up in the Pentagon, an official kicked the resubmitted packet back to Neil repeatedly, always claiming that something was missing or seeking new documentation, pointing to decades-old contradictions in the accounts of the 1965 battle. Meanwhile, after a couple of years of work by Thorne and the volunteer team, Mike Rose got his Medal of Honor in 2017. Yet, my nomination seemed to be going nowhere, as far as I knew.

But behind the scenes, Thorne and Moriarty intensified their efforts and brought more volunteers in beyond the core group to include researchers, a computer expert, and a communications advisor, Erin Powers. It was a dream team. "I don't think there's anything this team couldn't do," Moriarty said.

Eventually, there were sixteen veterans and volunteers working on my case. Some of these volunteers worked on my case for a decade, each one contributing in ways that I was amazed to find out about years later. For example, an investigator on the team named Ellen Cousins located the long-lost 1969 Phil Donahue interview and found witnesses that helped breathe new life into the nomination. Erin Powers and Rob Graham created public relations and digital communications plans. Others contributed database, research, and administrative skills. The group made hundreds of calls to military, political, and veterans' leaders and news media contacts. They even built support with the leadership of my alma mater, Southern University. Their efforts went on for several years, almost all of it without my knowledge. The group had weekly video conference calls—more than seventy in all—to report on their progress, sometimes just to encourage each other to keep on going, they told me later.

We got extra wind in our sails when Secretary of Defense Lloyd Austin ordered new reviews of Black and Native American Distinguished Service Cross recipients for possible upgrade to the Medal of Honor.

Then, in mid-2021, the group introduced me to David Philipps, the *New York Times* military reporter who broke the news of the Rose case, and Catherine Herridge, a national security reporter then with CBS News. Catherine pushed the Army hard for answers. She met with the secretary of the Army, among others. Through their efforts, David and Catherine first shared my story—and the questions it raised—with the American public.

Our team kept the story in front of high-level decision makers. As their efforts continued, the Pentagon began to send quiet, encouraging signals that the nomination had new momentum. Neil and I agreed that if he got word that the secretary of defense had signed off on the nomination, he would tell me to break out the champagne.

* * *

As the years went by, my health situation deteriorated. I moved in with Regan, her husband Dale, and their two sons in 2020, when the country started shutting down because of Covid. I was a little bit of a medical mystery. I was iron deficient, and the doctors couldn't figure out why. I had been around plenty of Agent Orange in Vietnam. Sometimes on a clear blue day we'd feel droplets on our faces, a fine mist of chemical defoliant. I'm sure I drank it when we were out on patrol and filled our canteens with rainwater. On top of that, I had travelled to every corner of the globe on classified missions that I still can't discuss to this day. I've been so many places in the world, the doctors had trouble assessing what might have been making me sick. "Where *haven't* you been?" one doctor asked me.

One day, as I was coming home from lunch with Dan Vannatter, Regan and Dale rushed out of the house to greet me. Regan was holding her phone in her hand. I leaned on the car door as she held up the phone so we could both hear. It was Neil Thorne.

"Hey, Colonel Davis. I got a message about you," Thorne said.

"Uh-oh," I said with a chuckle. "I'm already in jail. But go ahead."

"Your Medal of Honor nomination packet has been endorsed by Secretary of Defense Austin, and it's headed to the White House."

"I don't believe you. Have you been drinking?" I asked. Regan broke out into giddy laughter next to me. "Neil, you know how close I am to you. Thank you very much."

"It's an honor, sir," Thorne said. "This is the time to crack open that champagne."

"I tell you, if I do, it's going to be over your head," I said.

"At this point, I am so giddy, I'd never feel it," Thorne said with a laugh.

"I'll tell you this never would have happened if it hadn't been for you. You guys—the group and all that, you made it happen."

"We've had a hell of a team. A hell of a team," he said.

"I don't understand it though—it only took you fifty years," I said. We all laughed again.

* * *

A few weeks after Thorne's call, I sat expectantly at my desk, staring at the phone. I knew a call was coming. Even so, the ringing phone startled me. When I picked up, a young woman's voice on the other end of the phone asked me if I had a few minutes to speak with the president of the United States.

"I sure do," I answered.

"Okay, thanks so much. I'll put you through," she told me. The phone went quiet. I sat back with my legs crossed. I couldn't calm the butterflies in my stomach. I had known that the president was going to call, but I didn't completely believe it was going to happen. I took off my green baseball cap and placed it carefully on the desk in front of me. I glanced at the mementos scattered across my desk. A Special Forces mug. A coaster with the Green Beret motto, *De Oppresso Liber*. A notepad that read "Brave" on the bottom.

The phone came back to life. "Is this Colonel Paris Davis?" a different woman's voice asked.

"Yes, I am," I said.

A familiar voice came on the line. "Colonel, this is Joe Biden. President Biden," the president said to me.

"Good afternoon," I said.

"I want to tell you that on the recommendation of the secretary of the Army, the secretary of defense, for your courageous actions based on June 17 and 18 in 1965 during Vietnam, I've approved the awarding of the Medal of Honor, and it's overdue, sir."

"Thank you very much," I said, and smiled.

"Thank you. I'll tell you what. It's my great honor. Your story is remarkable. You saved lives. You've changed the lives of so many families back home in doing so and your willingness to put your life on the line for your fellow service members and your actions saved lives and are an inspiration to demonstrate the kind of selflessness and sacrifice, and I really look forward to meeting you and hosting you and your family here at the White House for the medal presentation," he said.

We chatted for a few minutes. He cracked that I already had so many medals, they'd never fit on my uniform. I smiled at the joke. "You're everything that our generation should have been," he said.

Even after President Biden told me that the nomination had been approved, he couldn't quite believe himself all the things that had happened in 1965. He called me back later to double check.

"Did you really do all these things?" President Biden asked me.

"Yes, sir," I told him. "I sure did."

15

THE WHITE HOUSE

MARCH 3, 2023
WASHINGTON, DC

I awoke before dawn in an unfamiliar hotel bed. It was early morning on Friday, March 3, 2023. I felt a little disoriented. I hadn't slept well because the room was so cold. I had called the front desk in the middle of the night to send up blankets. Then I lay awake in the darkness thinking about the day ahead.

Outside the wide picture window, the sky was still dark. In the near distance, lights lit up the Pentagon where I had gone to work before sunup each day in the early 1970s. To the left I could see the neat white headstones of Arlington National Cemetery. Across the Potomac River, the floodlights illuminated the Washington Monument pointing toward the sky. Just north of the monument I could just make out the White House. Later that day, I would be going there to finally receive the Medal of Honor I had been nominated for so many years earlier.

It had been a dizzying few days. On Wednesday, a black Pentagon minibus had pulled up in front of Regan's house. The sound of roaring engines filled the cul-de-sac as Arlington police motorcycles thundered down the street and parked at the curb alongside the van. It was my escort to the hotel, where my family and I would spend the next few days. I wore jeans and sneakers and a Special Forces fleece with a ball cap pulled down over my dark glasses as I walked out the front door. I posed with my escort on the front lawn before I climbed in with Regan.

Regan rode in the front passenger seat next to the driver. A young woman from the Pentagon sat to my right, briefing me about what to expect when we arrived at the hotel. The Pentagon City Sheraton would be our base of operations. There would be a welcoming party in the lobby when we arrived, she told me. The motorcade wound through the neighborhood, sirens blaring, and neighbors came out to see what all the noise was about. The police in front stopped traffic at each intersection so that we could roll right through without slowing down for red lights or stop signs.

When we reached the hotel, we made quite a scene as the motorcade pulled into the driveway and I got out of the van. A three-star general with graying temples, Lieutenant General Walter Piatt, met me at the door and clasped my hand. I went upstairs for a Veterans Administration benefits briefing. When I went to my room, I discovered I had a whole suite to myself with the windows looking out over Washington. The family had rooms of their own nearby.

The next day—Thursday—we had media training after breakfast to prepare me for the day ahead. The Pentagon public affairs team offered their talking points and their experts previewed the whirlwind day of news interviews ahead. Regan and I then had a whole day of back-to-back interviews—about fourteen in all, I think. Lester Holt from NBC was one of the first, and the major networks outlets followed—ABC, CBS, Fox, CNN. There were print reporters from the Associated Press, the *Army Times*, *The Washington Post*, and *Stars and Stripes*. By the end of the day,

I'd talked to more reporters than I had in my entire life. Erin Powers, the communications strategist on our team, told me later that Pentagon research estimated that the news reports were seen by more than 500 million people around the world, including 120 million in the U.S. What happened at Bong Son and afterward was no secret anymore.

That night we had the first of two parties where I got to see many of the friends—old and new—who had either helped me along the way or had a sudden new interest. The Congressional Medal of Honor Society hosted a large group that first night.

By the time I went to bed that night, I had a lot on my mind. I had to be up early to get ready for Friday's ceremony. After my restless night, I was happy to be awake. Regan knocked on the door to make sure I was up. When the Army had brought my bags, they also delivered my dress uniform in a suit bag, cleaned and pressed. A Pentagon minder came to my room to help me get ready for the ceremony.

While I was in the shower, he laid out my uniform on the bed, along with my shirt and tie. I wanted everything just right. My uniform had to be immaculate. I wanted my shoes so polished that I could see my reflection. My gig line needed to be perfect. I made sure that I had respectable socks, in case my trouser legs lifted to show my ankles when I sat.

I examined myself carefully in the mirror. I looked at all the badges and medals and service ribbons. That jacket displayed my entire career. I had a badge or a bar for almost every step of the almost twenty-six years I had served. My left sleeve showed my Special Forces long tab and my Ranger and Airborne patches. The full-bird eagles I earned as a colonel were pinned to my shoulders. Above my heart, I wore my Silver Star service bar, with the Bronze Star and Soldier's Medal below it, then my Purple Heart and my Meritorious Service bar, with more service bars below.

The battles, the postings overseas and at home, the scars I carried on my body—emblems of all of them were pinned or sewn to my uniform. All but the one that the president would hang around my neck later that morning. The one that had eluded me for fifty-eight years.

I didn't have much time to admire my uniform. Everyone had to be downstairs by 7 A.M. Regan came back to the room to make sure that I was ready. We went downstairs together in the elevator. Our guests for the ceremony milled in the hotel lobby, where the Army had set up a Covid testing station and security screening stations for everyone.

As I looked around, I could see so many who had played a role in resubmitting my nomination—Neil Thorne, Jim Moriarity, Tommy Shook, and many of the members of their team. Ambrose Brennan had come, and Ron Deis had arrived from Alaska with his wife, Pat. Bobby Brown's widow, Paula, and son Troy were there. I could see Robert Braden, the crew chief on the resupply helo that tossed ammo to us. As Regan and I walked out of the elevator doors, a crowd of well-wishers swarmed me, shaking my hand and clapping me on the back. The people who weren't there, the ones who had passed on like Tiny Aldrich and Billy Cole—I felt as though they were there with us too, even if we couldn't see them.

Pentagon minders hustled us through the Covid test line, and then sent us through a mobile metal detector so that we didn't have to when we arrived at the White House. My family and I left before the rest of the group, piling into a black van just like the one that had picked us up at home on Wednesday. I sat by the window in the second row, behind the driver. Regan and Dale were behind me, with their two boys Mason and Keyden in the back row. Fifteen Pentagon police motorcycles raced out ahead of us, lights whirling and sirens blaring, before we pulled out behind them. Three charter busloads of family, friends, and other guests settled in behind us for the escorted trip to the White House.

We took the freeway past the Pentagon and crossed the Potomac River over the Fourteenth Street Bridge. I didn't talk much along the way. Everything was so overwhelming it was hard to know what to think or say. I just looked out the front of the van as we crossed the river, curved around the Thomas Jefferson Memorial and the Tidal Basin, and then headed north across the Mall. Heads swiveled to look, traffic came to a standstill, and then the motorcade turned into one of the rear entrances to the White House, as if a foreign president was coming to meet with the president.

Marines ushered us upstairs and into one of the formal rooms that had an enormous portrait of President Abraham Lincoln. The room was chilly, and we waited for a long time. We paced and looked out the window at the view of the Washington Monument. The ornate marble fireplace was carved with a quote from John Adams: "I Pray Heaven To Bestow The Best Of Blessings On This House And All that shall hereafter Inhabit it. May none but Honest and Wise Men ever rule under This Roof."

After what felt like hours, our escorts led us out one of the doors and into the Blue Room. It was oval-shaped, with a high ceiling and a fireplace and tall windows overlooking the National Mall. A small wooden table had been set in the very center of the room with the presidential seal in front.

A few moments after we got there, President Biden walked in with a wide smile, wearing a blue suit with a shirt the color of a robin's egg, a red tie, and an American flag pin on his lapel. He came straight for me. We chatted for a few minutes, our faces close together and our right hands clasped and our left gripping each other's shoulders. After a few minutes, he met everyone in the family one by one, shaking hands with my grandsons Mason and Keyden, chatting with Regan, Steph, and Paris, before he sat down at the table to sign the certificate.

"This is to certify that the President of the United States authorized by act of Congress on March 3, 1863, has awarded in the name of Congress The Medal of Honor to Captain Paris D. Davis," it read. When he was done signing, he handed the pen to me with a wide smile.

Escorts came for my children, and the rest of the family, and led them down the long hallway to the East Room. The rest of the group were already there in their assigned seats. Ron Deis had come to Washington expecting to be just a bump on a log during the events. Instead, when the vans from the hotel reached the White House, a military liaison met him outside. "I've been waiting for you, Mr. Deis," she said. "Please come with me." To his surprise, she escorted him to a seat in the second row, right behind Regan, Dale, Stephanie, and my son Paris.

I stood to the president's right as we walked down the red carpet in the Cross Hall. Marines stood at attention as we passed. When I stepped into the East Room, "Hail to the Chief" filled my ears. Camera shutters whirred as I walked past photographers stationed around the doorway, and up to a dais at the front of the hall. Everyone in the packed room was on their feet, holding their cellphones over their heads to take pictures.

I stood to the president's side at the front of the room as a chaplain read a prayer. "Praise be to the Lord, my rock, who trains my hands for war, my fingers for battle. He is my loving God and my fortress, my stronghold, my deliverer, my shield in whom I take refuge," the chaplain said.

When he was done, I sat down in a gold chair reserved for me on the stage. I sat there all by myself, between an American flag and a framed Medal of Honor flag. Holding my hands in my lap, I looked out at Regan and her family, along with Steph and Paris, in the front row. I locked eyes with Ron Deis behind them. His eyes were full of tears, and we nodded silently to one another. To my left, Secretary of Defense Lloyd Austin faced me from the front row. He was a trailblazer, too: a Black man now in charge of all the nation's armed services. Five previous medal recipients sat on the far left of the stage.

The president stood at the podium. "I have to say at the outset— and I've had the great honor—and we have other Medal of Honor recipients here—and that I've been able to give one of those medals. And we have five here. But this, Mr. Secretary, may be the most consequential day since I've been president," he said, referring to Secretary Austin. "This is an incredible man."

One hundred and fifty-eight years earlier, President Biden said, President Lincoln had been finishing his second inaugural address in the White House where we sat. "And he wrote, 'Let us strive to finish the work we are in, to bind up the nation's wounds, and care for him who shall have borne the battle.' Today, fifty-eight years after he bore the battle, we honor a true hero of our nation: Colonel Paris Davis."

Then the president recounted the story of Bong Son, describing that day almost fifty-eight years ago. He acknowledged Deis, who stood smiling, as the audience applauded. As I sat there on the stage, the sound of that bugle rang in my memory as he described the counterattack that began after our raid. He described each moment of that day. He talked about how I rejected orders to leave the battlefield. He described how I crossed the rice paddy to rescue Waugh, Morgan, Reinburg, and finally Brown. "Captain Davis was going to give him a chance to see his baby boy," the president said.

I listened as he told the story about how when I got back, soldiers would sometimes cross the street when they saw me in uniform to avoid talking with a Black soldier. "Paris, you are everything this medal means. I mean *everything* this medal means," he said.

I stood and faced forward beside the president. A lieutenant colonel read the language of the citation, and a Marine handed the medal to President Biden. I turned slightly as he hung it around my neck. As I felt the weight of the medal on my chest, I silently recited the words of the poem that I said to myself each time I went into battle:

If I should die, think only this of me
That there's some corner of a foreign field
That is forever America.

When the president was done, he turned me ever so gently with one hand and shook my hand with his other. The room broke out in applause.

Two days after the ceremony, the Army held an induction ceremony for me at the Pentagon. There was a reception afterward. A parade of generals came through, shaking my hand and having a word. There were so many of them, I didn't know them from Shinola. As I was sitting there in the chair, one of the generals leaned over and whispered in my ear. "We sure screwed you, didn't we?" he asked, smiling and laughing a little.

"Yes, sir, you really did," I replied, but I didn't smile back.

EPILOGUE

When my grandfather used to tell us, "The truth never moves," I believed him. Over all those years, I almost never talked about what happened in Bong Son. Soldiers and officers who worked alongside me for years knew nothing about that battle. But I knew the truth. As I listened to the president in the East Room, I remembered each moment of that day in 1965. I can still smell the blood and the reek of feces. I remember the sting of my shredded finger and the burning bullet wounds. I can still hear the bugle, and the whine of artillery and the explosions of mortars. I remember how heavy Brown's body was as I dragged him toward the chopper, and how much I wanted to get him home to his baby.

Public opinion turned against the war. Our soldiers came home. We buried our dead. We buried our memories. The country moved on. I moved on.

In the weeks and months after I received the medal, people would come up to me and ask what the hell happened with the nomination. How could such a thing come to pass? I always said that I didn't know. We may never truly know what happened to my nomination all those years ago, but plenty of people believe that only racial prejudice could have been the reason that medal never made it around my neck until 2023. Ron Deis believes that it was because I'm Black. "It just disappeared. How can you explain that? I mean, the only explanation is that somebody discarded it, because he was Black," he said.

Tommy Shook was once at a Ranger Hall of Fame event and ran into a major general he knew, one of the many influential officers that Tommy knew. They got to talking about my case. The major general told Tommy point-blank that only racial prejudice could have explained what had happened to me and my nomination. "I don't mean in Special Forces," the two-star told Tommy. "I mean, the three- and four-star level." In other words, when the nomination got sent up the chain of command, it undoubtedly stalled on the desk of an officer in Okinawa or in Pacific Command in Hawai'i who didn't want a Black man to get the Medal of Honor.

Al Broadbent, who beat his head against the wall pushing for my packet to be approved from inside the Pentagon, goes a step further. The intentionally opaque bureaucracy around valor medals makes it virtually impossible to gauge what's happened to a nomination, but he believes that my files were intentionally and systematically destroyed not once, but twice. "Someone went through the files and destroyed all that," he said.

He may be right. Perhaps some vindictive person made sure my nomination never saw the light of day. Or maybe it was something less sinister, a casualty of bumbling bureaucrats or mountains of Army red tape. I'll probably never really know. What I do know is I'm not bitter, and I'm not angry. I'm just grateful— grateful to be alive and for the men who were there with me in Bong Son. This is Paris Davis talking when I say that there was plenty of bravery to go around on that day in the mountains of Vietnam.

That day in March 2023 proved one truth that had been with

me all those years. The fact that, as a Black man, I had never been fully recognized for what happened that day always told me that Black soldiers at that time weren't held in the same esteem, or given the same value, as white soldiers. I was reminded of that fact all through my military career. Even when I was in the Naval War College and I overhead classmates snickering that they'd better not fight with Black soldiers or sailors, or else they wouldn't get out safely. My medal shows that this Black man fought as hard and with as much heart as every other soldier in Vietnam. And that truth will never move.

NOTE ON SOURCES

When this book is published, it will have been almost exactly sixty years since the bullets first began to fly as the sun rose on June 18, 1965. As with the war itself, memories fade over the years and decades. Even for those alive today who were there on that day in Binh Dinh Province—and there aren't many of us left—it has been a challenge to reliably chronicle that day, and those of my life that came before and after. This book represents the best effort of a dedicated team to recreate what happened that day with as much accuracy and documentation as possible. That goes as well for the days of my life before and after that battle.

Much of this account relies on my memory. But that's not all it rests on. We also relied on the recollections of those still with us who were with me in Bong Son that day. Those include Ron Deis, whose account was crucial to the campaign to revive my nomination, and Robert Baden, who flew the first resupply helicopter to the battle site. Whenever possible, we looked for and used additional documentation to substantiate and confirm events that have grown hazy with the years. The Phil Donahue interview was critical in that respect, as was Billy Waugh's affidavit from 1981. The incredible team that put together the packet to upgrade my Silver Star to the Medal of Honor also gathered records from the National Archives, publicly available sources, and interviews to substantiate parts of the story that have grown hazy or have been lost to memory. Ambrose Brennan was able to collect voluminous records to fill gaps in surprising ways. He was the one who compiled the MACV duty logs from that day, which documented events in real time as they were reported to the duty officer. He collected the weather reports from that day. He found the classified daily intelligence reports from our camp.

For the broader context of the war, we leaned heavily on Stanley Karnow's masterful *Vietnam: A History*, which helped anchor the conflict and our activities in Binh Dinh in the political and military machinations around the war's escalation. We also used contemporaneous reporting from *The New York Times* and other news sources to create the backdrop for the battle that day, and the progression of the war.

Writing about one's own life is a humbling experience. Who perfectly remembers the name of their special elementary school teacher? Or remembers without flaw where they were or what they said on the most important day of their childhood? Or the name of the family friend who put you up in college? We hunted for every scrap of information we could to complete this portrait. The holdings of the archives at Southern University and A&M College helped in that regard to remind me of my extracurricular activities, my fraternity involvement, and other long-ago elements of my life on campus.

As with any history from the battlefield, *Every Weapon I Had* is not a perfect history and nor does it pretend to be. But it's the one that I lived, flaws and all. That's my story, and I'm sticking to it.

ACKNOWLEDGMENTS

No one wins a battle by themselves, and no one writes a book alone. This is Paris Davis talking when I say that this is an "us" book, not a "me" book. A long list of people has helped me to make this book into the work that you are holding in your hands. I'm not sure how to thank them all, but I am certain that I'll leave someone out. If I do, I hope they give me hell.

The only way to begin is to thank the group that I call "the gang." These were men and women who worked tirelessly over more than a decade to put together a new nomination for the Medal of Honor to replace the nomination packets that were lost. There are sixteen members of the gang in all. They periodically met and often had video calls, sometimes weekly, for years on end, delegating tasks, updating with developments, and delivering pep talks. Like soldiers in a battle rhythm, each one had a role. Each one lent their talents in a different way.

I call Jim Moriarty "the chairman of the board" for keeping this group together. Neil Thorne was as steady as a locomotive pulling this thing through. Ambrose Brennan was there from the start, reading Billy Waugh's affidavit at a traffic light, and Tommy Shook was the master sergeant I always wanted who saw what needed to be done and did it. Ron Deis gave the ten-thousand-foot view that we needed, just as he did over Bong Son in June 1965, and Rob Graham turned it all into images to help a new generation see what I saw that day. Ellen Cousins worked research magic to find sources and records. Erin Powers worked tirelessly to bring this story to producers, reporters, and broadcasters who could put my story in front of the American people and the decision makers at the Pentagon.

Al Broadbent, Carlos Campbell, Robin Joseph-Hochman, Sarah Kline, Lee Ann O'Neal, Will Porter, and Cal Rollins were there every step of the way. And Dan Vannatter has been as loyal a friend as he was an aide to me in Tenth Special Forces Group so many years ago, and I look forward to many more Saturday morning breakfasts at Cracker Barrel. Rod Azama has been a steadfast friend, too. Someday maybe he'll forgive me for asking him to write a business column for my newspaper.

I appreciate the Southern University leadership, including Director of Alumni Affairs Robyn Merrick. I'm also grateful to the university archivist Angela Proctor and her assistant Cyntoria Kirkendol, who scoured *The Jaguar* and *The Digest* for articles about me. I was proud to have graduated from the school in 1959, and just as proud to return in 2023 to talk about my experience with a new generation of young men and women.

Many Special Forces veterans and historians, official and unofficial, helped me reconstruct what was happening in Vietnam in 1965, and find people from that era. Steve Sherman, the unofficial historian of Special Forces, helped time and again with historical information, and contact information for members of my own detachment. Willie Merkerson, who is in line for the Medal of Honor as well, added his recollections of Tet 1968, as did Jim Morris with his vivid writings about the attack on Fifth Special Forces in Nha Trang.

I also have to thank those Green Berets who are no longer with us but who fought with me and did their duty during the war. I'll always be grateful to Billy Waugh. We had our differences and we didn't always get along, but the affidavit he wrote in 1981 and signed again in 2015 gave my nomination the thrust it needed to get across the finish line. Colonel Billy Cole was an amazing leader, commander, and man. Even in death, his words with their insights and observations have lived on to help tell my story. I watched his daughter Carol grow up and turn into the keeper of his legacy and the custodian of his memoir. Tiny Aldrich, too, was an incredible soldier, and even after his retirement came to my defense when I was unfairly relieved of my command of the Tenth Special Forces Group. That goes too for the many men who wrote to the Army to protest how I was treated at Fort Devens in 1981. They called the shots as they saw them and didn't back down. I am proud to have led you and will be forever grateful that you rallied to my side.

Decades after my nomination disappeared, a new generation of leaders finally took note of my story because of all the hard work of the people I've named. I'll never forget the kind words of President Biden that he delivered both privately over the phone and publicly in the White House. Secretary of Defense Lloyd Austin got behind the push for upgrades of military medals and represents excellence in military leadership. I'm also grateful to former Joint Chiefs of Staff Chairman General Mark Milley, former Secretary of the Army Christine Wormuth, former Acting Secretary of Defense Christopher Miller, the Special Forces Charitable Trust, and Catherine Herridge of CBS News.

To my agent Gail Ross at William Morris Endeavor—your belief in me from the start breathed life into this book. My editor at St. Martin's Press, Tim Bartlett, and his assistant, Kevin Reilly, gave legs to my story, and your patience and quiet persistence over many months shaped and molded this chronicle into what it is today. To my collaborator Theo Emery—I smile every time we talk. Make sure your boy keeps his hands on the handlebars.

Family is everything to me, so I leave my last words to them. Thank you, Dee, for putting up with me and helping correct the record. To my children—I'm not sure I have the words. To Stephanie, my oldest child, you've been a pillar to me throughout your life, whether you were helping to raise your brother and sister, or helping out with the newspaper after college. Paris—I'm proud of all you've done and can't wait to sample more of your home-cooked meals. To Chris—I miss you.

Finally, to Regan: you put the lifeblood of your being into my heart and soul. You and Dale took me into your home, and have helped me through every difficult step. There's no way to thank you, and there's no way to repay you. When Mason and Keyden read this book, I hope it makes them as proud of me as I am of them.

NOTES

1. Bristol Avenue

1. "Industrial/Manufacturing," Ohio History Connection, 2022, https://www
.ohiohistory.org/wp-content/uploads/2022/01/9_Industrial_Manufactur
ing.pdf.

2. Sharon Broussard, "Black Heritage Began in 1809," *The Plain Dealer* (Cleveland, OH), Sunday, December 31, 1995, https://teachingcleveland.org/black
-heritage-began-in-1809-from-the-plain-dealer/.

3. "Burglar Kills Heights Patrolman," *The Plain Dealer* (Cleveland, OH), Feb.
20, 1948.

4. "3 to Face Charges in Heights Slaying," *The Plain Dealer* (Cleveland, OH),
Feb. 24, 1948.

5. "Mother-Son Scene in Court Is Rapped at Murder Trial," *The Plain Dealer*
(Cleveland, OH), June 23, 1948.

6. "Cop Killer 5th Doomed in 1948," *The Plain Dealer* (Cleveland, OH), June
25, 1948.

7. "Officer's Slayer Remains Calm During Execution," *Springfield Daily News*
(Springfield, OH), June 24, 1949.

8. "News of Policeman's Death Made Killer Gloat, Jury Told," *The Plain
Dealer* (Cleveland, OH), June 22, 1948.

9. Christopher Roy, "Kinsman (Neighborhood)," Encyclopedia of Cleveland

History, Case Western Reserve University, revised May 6, 2020, https://case
.edu/ech/articles/k/kinsman-neighborhood.

10. "Cleveland Designated Landmarks," Cleveland Landmarks Commission,
City of Cleveland, accessed Sept. 17, 2024, https://planning.clevelandohio.gov
/landmark/listDetail.php?identity=69.

2. Into the Army

1. "Executive Order 9981, Desegregating the Military," National Park Service,
updated Aug. 21, 2023, https://www.nps.gov/articles/000/executive-order
-9981.htm.

2. "Battalion History," Southern University and A&M College, accessed Sept.
17, 2024, https://www.subr.edu/page/452.

3. Bob Fehringer, "African-Americans in the U.S. Military Timeline," United
States Transportation Command, Jan. 30, 2013, https://www.ustranscom.mil
/cmd/panewsreader.cfm?ID=2889B154-5056-A127-59D9E5697B66C1EC
&yr=2013.

4. Fred Kaplan, "1959: Sex, Jazz, and Datsuns," *New York Magazine*, May 29,
2009, https://nymag.com/news/features/57058/.

5. Major General John M. Wright Jr., "A Brief History of Fort Benning," https://
www.moore.army.mil/, U.S. Army. Online excerpt from article by same au-
thor in *Infantry*, September–October 1968, accessed Sept. 17, 2024, https://
www.moore.army.mil/infantry/magazine/issues/2018/Jul-Sep/PDF/12
/BenningHistory_txt.pdf.

6. "Fort Benning, 1960s," Virtual Vault, Vanishing Georgia, Georgia Archives,
University System of Georgia Digital Collection, accessed Sept. 17, 2024,
https://vault.georgiaarchives.org/digital/collection/vg2/id/10358/.

7. Paris D. Davis Academic Report, Form DA-1059, Feb. 3, 1960, Paris Davis
Papers.

8. Clayborne Carson, *In Struggle: SNCC and the Black Awakening of the 1960s*
(Cambridge, MA: Harvard University Press, 1981), 9.

3. Special Forces

1. Colonel Francis J. Kelly, *Vietnam Studies, U.S. Army Special Forces 1961–1971*
(Washington, DC: Department of the Army, 2004), 4.

2. Kelly, *Vietnam Studies*, 5.

3. "Fort Dix, NJ History," accessed Sept. 17, 2024, https://www.fortdixhousing
.com/history.

4. "The New Fort Dix," *The New York Times*, Nov. 12, 1959.

5. Paris D. Davis Officer Efficiency Report, Oct. 3, 1960, Paris Davis Papers.

6. "Kennedy Called Soft on Communism," *The New York Times*, Oct. 26, 1960.

7. Stanley Karnow, *Vietnam: A History* (New York: Penguin, 1983), 264.

8. "South Korea Rule Seized as Armed Forces Revolt; U.S. Opposes Junta Coup," *The New York Times*, May 16, 1961.

9. "President Urges Missile Build-Up: Budget Is Raised," *The New York Times*, March 29, 1961.

10. "President Kennedy's Special Message to the Congress on Urgent National Needs," May 25, 1961, JFK Presidential Library and Museum, accessed Sept. 17, 2024, https://www.jfklibrary.org/archives/other-resources/john-f-kennedy-speeches/united-states-congress-special-message-19610525.

11. "Story of the Green Beret," Chapter LX, Special Forces Association, accessed Dec. 18, 2024, https://specialforces.org/story-of-the-green-beret/.

12. "Story of the Green Beret."

13. Paris D. Davis Officer Efficiency Report, Dec. 27, 1961, Paris Davis Papers.

14. Karnow, *Vietnam*, 271.

15. Karnow, *Vietnam*, 272.

16. Karnow, *Vietnam*, 276.

17. Paris D. Davis Officer Efficiency Report, March 6, 1966, Paris Davis Papers.

18. "Research Memorandum from the Deputy Director of the Bureau of Intelligence and Research (Denney) to the Acting Secretary of State (1961–1963, Volume III, Vietnam, January–August 1963)," Office of the Historian, U.S. Department of State, accessed Sept. 17, 2024, https://history.state.gov/historicaldocuments/frus1961-63v03/d197.

19. Paris D. Davis Officer Efficiency Report, March 6, 1966, Paris Davis Papers.

20. "Vietnamese Program Chronology," Defense Language Institute Archives, Defense Language Institute, Monterrey, California.

21. Capt. Pauline Merrill to Paris Davis, "Notification of Unsatisfactory Academic Progress," May 4, 1964, Paris Davis Papers.

22. **Karnow, *Vietnam*, 386.**

23. Karnow, *Vietnam*, 387.

24. Lyndon Johnson, "Gulf of Tonkin Incident," U.S. Diplomatic Mission to Germany, U.S. Department of State, August 4, 1964, accessed Sept. 17, 2024, https://usa.usembassy.de/etexts/speeches/rhetoric/lbjgulf.htm.

25. "U.S. Planes Attack North Vietnam Bases," *The New York Times*, Aug. 5, 1964.

26. "U.S. Involvement in the Vietnam War: The Gulf of Tonkin and Escalation, 1964," Office of the Historian, U.S. Department of State, accessed Sept. 17, 2024, https://history.state.gov/milestones/1961-1968/gulf-of-tonkin.

27. "F.B.I. Finds 3 Bodies Believed to be Rights Workers," *The New York Times*, Aug. 5, 1964, p. 1.

4. The Rock

1. "Kadena Air Base 1963–1967," Remembering Okinawa History, accessed Sept. 17, 2024, https://www.rememberingokinawa.com/page/1963–67_kadena_1.

2. Robert W. Jones Jr., "A Team Effort: Special Forces in Vietnam, June–December 1964," History Office, U.S. Army Special Operations Command. Reprinted from *Veritas* 3, no. 1, 2007, accessed Sept. 17, 2024, https://arsof-history.org/articles/v3n1_team_effort_page_1.html.

3. "Green Berets: Toth, William Charles," Special Forces Roll of Honour, edited Jan. 22, 2011, https://www.specialforcesroh.com/index.php?threads/toth-william-charles.8529/.

4. Stanley Karnow, *Vietnam: A History* (New York: Penguin, 1983), 411.

5. Karnow, *Vietnam*, 415.

6. Paris D. Davis Officer Efficiency Report, Feb. 18, 1965, Paris Davis Papers.

7. Karnow, *Vietnam*, 425.

8. Karnow, *Vietnam*, 427.

9. Paris D. Davis Officer Efficiency Report, April 10, 1965, Paris Davis Papers.

10. Colonel Francis J. Kelly, *Vietnam Studies, U.S. Army Special Forces 1961–1971* (Washington, DC: Department of the Army, 2004), 5.

11. Karnow, *Vietnam*, 255.

12. Eugene G. Piasecki, "The 77th SFG Mission to South Vietnam," History Office, U.S. Army Special Operations Command. Reprinted from *Veritas* 5, no. 3, 2009, accessed Sept. 17, 2024, https://arsof-history.org/articles/v5n3_77th_south_vietnam_page_1.html.

13. Piasecki, "The 77th SFG Mission to South Vietnam."

14. "Tri-State Service Notes," *Argus Leader* (Sioux Falls, SD), Sept. 16, 1964.

15. Rupert Brooke, "The Soldier," *Poetry*, April 1915, accessed Sept. 17, 2024,

https://www.poetryfoundation.org/poetrymagazine/poems/13076/the
-soldier.
16. Karnow, *Vietnam*, 430.
17. Karnow, *Vietnam*, 432.
18. Karnow, *Vietnam*, 433.
19. Eugene G. Piasecki, "The 77th SFG Mission to South Vietnam," n5.
20. Col. (Ret.) Billy Cole, "The Mission Is . . ." (unpublished manuscript, n.d.), 231.
21. "57 Are Injured at Selma as Troopers Break Up Rights Walk in Montgom-
    ery," *The New York Times*, March 8, 1965.
22. "Dr. King Leads March at Selma," *The New York Times*, March 10, 1965.
23. Cole, "The Mission Is," 178.

5. Bong Son
1. Col. (Ret.) Billy Cole, "The Mission Is . . ." (unpublished manuscript,
   n.d.), 223.
2. Cole, "The Mission Is," 231.
3. Cole, "The Mission Is," 229.
4. Robert W. Jones Jr., "A Team Effort: Special Forces in Vietnam,
   June–December 1964," History Office, U.S. Army Special Operations
   Command. Reprinted from *Veritas* 3, no. 1, 2007, accessed Sept. 17, 2024,
   https://arsof-history.org/articles/v3n1_team_effort_page_1.html.
5. "Paris D. Davis Soldier's Medal Citation," Hall of Valor, *Military Times*, accessed June 21, 2024, https://valor.militarytimes.com/hero/142527.
6. Cole, "The Mission Is," 225.
7. Cole, "The Mission Is," 233.
8. "Five Americans Die in Major Attack by Vietnam Reds," *The New York
   Times*, May 11, 1965.
9. "Saigon's Premier Resigns," *The New York Times*, June 12, 1965.
10. Karnow, *Vietnam*, 437.
11. Karnow, *Vietnam*, 437.
12. Cole, "The Mission Is," 246

6. Bugles
1. Ambrose Brennan, "Recommendation for the Award of the Medal of
   Honor to Col. (Ret) Paris D. Davis (Final)," Addendum A, "Narrative Justi-
   fication for Valor," Tab A, "Weather Computation for Action Area Vic (inity)

Bong Son," 5–6, Extract of 17–18 June of Quy Nhon USAF Weather Observations, June 1965.

2. Billy Waugh, *Hunting the Jackal* (New York: William Morrow, 2004), 10.

3. Waugh, *Hunting the Jackal*, 10.

4. Waugh, *Hunting the Jackal*, 10.

5. Sergeant Major (Ret.) William D. Waugh, Letter to Commanding Officer, Headquarters U.S. Army Military Personnel Center, "Eyewitness Recommendation for the Medal of Honor for Captain Paris D. Davis," July 22, 1981, Paris D. Davis Papers, 3.

6. Waugh affidavit, 4.

7. Waugh, *Hunting the Jackal*, 12.

8. Waugh, *Hunting the Jackal*, 14.

9. Waugh, *Hunting the Jackal*, 13.

7. The Knoll

1. "Cessna L-19 'Bird Dog,'" Planes of Fame Air Museum, accessed Sept. 17, 2024, https://planesoffame.org/aircraft/plane-L-19.

2. "Forward Air Controllers," Air Operations Vietnam, accessed Sept. 17, 2024, https://sites.cc.gatech.edu/fac/Thomas.Pilsch/AirOps/facs.html.

3. Billy Waugh, *Hunting the Jackal* (New York: William Morrow, 2004), 16.

4. Colonel Francis J. Kelly, *Vietnam Studies, U.S. Army Special Forces 1961–1971* (Washington, DC: Department of the Army, 2004), 9; Col. (Ret.) Billy Cole, "The Mission Is . . ." (unpublished manuscript, n.d.), 248; Paris Davis Papers.

8. "I Refuse to Go"

1. Rob Savage interview with Bob Baden.

2. Billy Waugh, *Hunting the Jackal* (New York: William Morrow, 2004), 15.

3. Colonel Francis J. Kelly, *Vietnam Studies, U.S. Army Special Forces 1961–1971* (Washington, DC: Department of the Army, 2004), 94.

4. Phil Donahue Show, *Vietnam: One Story*, July 1969, Walter J. Brown Media Archives, June 5, 2018, https://kaltura.uga.edu/media/t/1_b8scjjbw/33785631.

5. Claire E. Aldrich, Letter to Commanding Officer, Headquarters U.S. Army Military Personnel Center, "Authenticity of data contained in a recommendation for the awarding of the Medal of Honor to Col. (then Captain) Paris D. Davis, Commanding Officer, Detachment A-321, A Co., 1st Special Forces Group (Abn)," TDY to Hqs. 5th Special Forces Group (Abn.), Nov.

11, 2011, Lost Medal of Honor Nomination Packet of Colonel (then Captain) Paris Darius Davis, U.S. Army Special Forces, Bong Son, RVN, 17–18 June 1965.

6. Aldrich affidavit.

7. Col. (Ret.) Billy Cole, "The Mission Is . . ." (unpublished manuscript, n.d.), 178.

8. MACV Duty officer's log, June 18, 1965, p. 16. Ambrose Brennan Medal of Honor recommendation packet.

9. Waugh, *Hunting the Jackal*, 22.

9. "Not Before Me"

1. MACV duty officer's log, June 18, 1965, p. 10, Ambrose Brennan Medal of Honor recommendation packet.

2. Col. (Ret.) Billy Cole, "The Mission Is . . ." (unpublished manuscript, n.d.), 249.

3. Cole, "The Mission Is," 249.

4. Cole, "The Mission Is," 249.

5. Sergeant Major (Ret.) William D. Waugh, Letter to Commanding Officer, Headquarters U.S. Army Military Personnel Center, "Eyewitness Recommendation for the Medal of Honor for Captain Paris D. Davis," July 22, 1981, Paris D. Davis Papers, 4.

6. Phil Donahue Show, *Vietnam: One Story*, July 1969, 31:59, Walter J. Brown Media Archives, June 5, 2018, https://kaltura.uga.edu/media/t/1 _b8scjjbw/33785631.

7. MACV duty officer's log, 17.

10. Ambushed

1. "Active U.S. Combat Role in Vietnam Acknowledged," *The New York Times*, June 6, 1965.

2. "Students Urged to Use Restraint," *The New York Times*, June 7, 1965.

3. "Project Delta: 5th Special Forces Detachment B-52," Military Assistance Command, Vietnam Studies and Observation Group, accessed Dec. 18, 2024, https://www.macvsog.cc/special_projects.htm.

4. "Colonel Charles A. Beckwith, Distinguished Member of the Special Forces Regiment," United States Army John. F. Kennedy Special Warfare Center and School, https://www.swcs.mil/Portals/111/sf_beckwith.pdf.

5. "The Mystery of Hanoi Hannah," *The New York Times*, Feb. 8, 2018.

6. "Reds in Vietnam Storm Outpost," *The New York Times*, Sept. 25, 1965.

7. Col. (Ret.) Billy Cole, "The Mission Is . . ." (unpublished manuscript, n.d.), 274.

8. Cole, "The Mission Is," 275.

9. Cole, "The Mission Is," 275; Paris Davis to General William C. Westmoreland, Nov. 15, 1977, Paris Davis Papers.

11. Recovery

1. Paris D. Davis to Westmoreland, Nov. 15, 1977, Paris Davis Papers.

2. Paris D. Davis to Westmoreland, Nov. 15, 1977.

3. Col. (Ret.) Billy Cole, "The Mission Is . . ." (unpublished manuscript, n.d.), 276.

4. Cole, "The Mission Is," 276.

5. Cole, "The Mission Is," 280.

6. Elmer Monger to Delores Davis, Oct. 15, 1965, Paris Davis Papers.

7. Charlie Black, "Special Forces Officer Stops Reds," *Columbus Enquirer* (Columbus, Georgia), Sept. 26, 1965.

8. Charlie Black, "Radio Relay Mission is Wearying Flight," *Columbus Enquirer* (Columbus, Georgia), Nov. 24, 1965.

9. Paris D. Davis Officer Efficiency Report, March 10, 1966, Paris Davis Papers.

10. Major General Spurgeon Neel, "IV. Hospitalization and Evacuation," in *Vietnam Studies: Medical Support of the U.S. Army in Vietnam, 1965–1970* (Washington, DC: Department of the Army), 1991, AMEDD Center of History & Heritage, accessed Sept. 17, 2024, https://achh.army.mil/history/book -vietnam-medicalsupport-chapter4.

11. Silver Star award citation, Dec. 15, 1965; Cole, "The Mission Is," 152.

12. Stanley Karnow, *Vietnam: A History* (New York: Penguin, 1983), 469.

13. "March on Washington to End the War in Vietnam (April 17, 1965)," Resistance and Revolution: The Anti-Vietnam War Movement at the University of Michigan, 1965–1972, accessed Dec. 18, 2024, https://michiganintheworld .history.lsa.umich.edu/antivietnamwar/exhibits/show/exhibit/the_teach _ins/national_teach_in_1965.

14. "International Days of Protest, October 15, 1965–October 16, 1965," The United States of America Vietnam War Commemoration, accessed Dec. 18, 2024, https://www.vietnamwar50th.com/1965_stemming_the_tide/International -Days-of-Protest/.

15. Rob Graham Interview with Paris Davis, "Paris Davis Medal of Honor: The Incredible Battle of Bong Son," Aug. 16, 2022.

16. Karnow, *Vietnam*, 496.

17. Paris D. Davis Officer Efficiency Report, Jan. 30, 1967, Paris Davis Papers.

18. Karnow, *Vietnam*, 511.

19. "Hanoi Inviting Westerners to Inspect Bomb Damage," *The New York Times*, Jan. 11, 1967.

20. "Beyond Vietnam," The Martin Luther King, Jr. Research and Education Institute, Stanford University, accessed Sept. 17, 2024, https://kinginstitute .stanford.edu/encyclopedia/beyond-vietnam.

21. Cole, "The Mission Is," 152.

22. Cole, "The Mission Is," 157.

23. Paris D. Davis Officer Efficiency Report, May 22, 1968, Paris Davis Papers.

24. Tet After Action report (Nha Trang), Feb. 5, 1968. Courtesy of Steve Sherman.

25. Kenn Miller, "Recondo School," History of MACV-SOG, accessed Sept. 17, 2024, https://sogsite.com/recondo-school/.

26. Tet After Action report (Nha Trang). Courtesy of Steve Sherman.

27. Jim Morris, *Indochina in the Year of the Monkey—1968* (Houston: Radix Press, 2017), 111.

28. Morris, *Indochina*, 112.

29. Citation for Award of Air Medal for Heroism, Department of the Army, HQ, 5th Special Forces Group (Airborne), 1st Special Forces, General Order 25, November 25, 1969, No. 1920.

30. Phil Donahue Show, *Vietnam: One Story*, July 1969, Walter J. Brown Media Archives, June 5, 2018, https://kaltura.uga.edu/media/t/1_b8scjjbw/33785631.

12. The Pentagon

1. Lt. Col. Wilson Wooley to Paris D. Davis, June 26, 1970, and enclosure, Paris Davis Papers.

2. Paris D. Davis Officer Efficiency Report, January 2, 1974, Paris Davis Papers.

3. "Six Selected to Join Crawford County Veterans Hall of Fame," *Telegraph-Forum* (Bucyrus, OH), Oct. 27, 2020, https://www.bucyrustelegraphforum .com/story/news/2020/10/27/crawford-county-veterans-hall-fame -inductees-2020/6038441002/.

4. William Gardner Bell and Karl E. Cocke, ed. "II: Operational Forces," in *Department of the Army Historical Summary Fiscal Year 1973* (Washington, DC:

Center of Military History, United States Army), 1977, p. 17, accessed Aug. 26, 2024, https://history.army.mil/books/DAHSUM/1973/chII.htm.

5. Paris D. Davis Officer Efficiency Report, Feb. 8, 1973, Paris Davis Papers.

6. Paris D. Davis Officer Efficiency Report, Feb. 8, 1973, Paris Davis Papers.

7. Paris D. Davis Officer Efficiency Report, Jan. 2, 1973, Paris Davis Papers.

8. Paris D. Davis Officer Efficiency Report, Feb. 8, 1973, Paris Davis Papers.

9. Paris D. Davis Officer Efficiency Report, Aug. 31, 1973, Paris Davis Papers.

10. Paris D. Davis Officer Efficiency Report, Jan. 2, 1973, Paris Davis Papers.

13. Command

1. "'75 Champ Wins Again," *The Dispatch* (Fort Devens, MA), 1976, Paris Davis Papers.

2. "Army Trains 'Liberation' Force to Fight Behind Enemy's Lines," *The New York Times*, Aug. 30, 1955.

3. Memorandum for Record, Subject: Impact of Mission Performance Due to Relocation, July 15, 1976, Paris Davis Papers.

4. "The History of the 10th Special Forces Group (Airborne)," U.S. Army Special Operations Command, accessed Sept. 17, 2024, https://web.archive.org/web/20090920094659/http://www.soc.mil/SF/history.pdf.

5. Change of command memo, Feb. 23, 1977, Paris Davis Papers.

6. Paris D. Davis Officer Efficiency Report, July 26, 1978, Paris Davis Papers.

7. "May: EUCOM in Command," U.S. European Command, accessed Sept 17, 2024, https://www.eucom.mil/moments-in-eucoms-history-a-countdown-to-the-70th-anniversary/may-eucom-in-command.

8. "History of USEUCOM," U.S. European Command, accessed Sept. 17, 2024, https://www.eucom.mil/about-the-command/history-of-useucom.

9. "General Robert E. Huyer," U.S. Air Force, accessed Sept. 17, 2024, https://www.af.mil/About-Us/Biographies/Display/Article/106693/general-robert-e-huyser/.

10. "Soviet Deploying 2 New Missiles," *The New York Times*, Jan. 15, 1975.

11. Paris Davis Officer Efficiency Report, July 28, 1977, Paris Davis Papers.

12. Paris D. Davis to William C. Westmoreland, November 15, 1977, Paris Davis Papers.

13. William C. Westmoreland to Paris Davis, November 30, 1977, Paris Davis Papers.

14. *Department of the Army Pamphlet 600-3-52, Functional Area 52: Nuclear Weapons* (Washington, DC: Department of the Army, 1987), p. 7, accessed Aug. 26, 2024, https://www.govinfo.gov/content/pkg/GOVPUB-D101-PURL -LPS65989/pdf/GOVPUB-D101-PURL-LPS65989.pdf.

15. Col. Nathan A. Offield to Paris Davis, May 9, 1979, Paris Davis Papers.

16. Senior Service College Academic Evaluation Report, Aug. 1, 1980, Paris Davis Papers.

17. Dr. Ed Cutolo Jr. and Jack Galvin, "Edward P. Cutolo '54," Grip Hands, United States Military Academy, Class of 1954, accessed Dec. 13, 2024, https:// www.usma1954.org/grip_hands/memorials/20153epc.htm.

18. Master Sergeant John Frye, support letter, undated, Paris Davis Papers.

19. Major Neil Pearce to "To Whom it May Concern," undated, Paris Davis Papers.

20. Col. John Crerar, letter, Oct 4, 1982, Paris Davis Papers.

21. Col. John Crerar.

22. Thomas Fierke to "To Whom it May Concern," Oct. 1, 1982, Paris Davis Papers.

23. Clayton Pratt, statement, undated, Paris Davis Papers.

24. Major Steven J. Abdalla, statement, undated, Paris Davis Papers.

25. USAF Captain Charles L. Weinert, letter, to Capt. Young, Fort Devens, MA, subject "Conflict in Command at Fort Devens, Massachusetts," Feb. 22, 1982.

26. John Friberg, "Flintlock, Unconventional Warfare, and Special Forces Teams," SOFREP, July 12, 2016. https://sofrep.com/news/58701flintlock/

27. Col. Richard J. Kattar, "Memorandum for Record," Jan. 12, 1981, Paris D. Davis Papers.

28. Lieutenant General Robert C. Kingston, letter, Jan. 7, 1982, Paris Davis Papers.

29. Claire E. Aldrich, Letter to Commanding Officer, Headquarters U.S. Army Military Personnel Center, "Authenticity of data contained in a recommendation for the awarding of the Medal of Honor to Col. (then Captain) Paris D. Davis, Commanding Officer, Detachment A-321, A Co., 1st Special Forces Group (Abn)," TDY to Hqs. 5th Special Forces Group (Abn.), Nov. 11, 2011, Lost Medal of Honor Nomination Packet of Colonel (then Captain) Paris Darius Davis, U.S. Army Special Forces, Bong Son, RVN, 17–18 June 1965.

30. William D. Waugh affidavit, "The Missing Medal of Honor Nomination of Colonel Paris D. Davis: Resubmission of the lost 1965 Medal of Honor Nomination," July 2019 Update, 44.

14. "This Just Came Up"

1. James R. Doy, MD, letter, Feb. 15, 1985, Paris Davis Papers.

2. Lt. Col. Allan E. Hesters to Paris Davis, July 12, 1985, Paris Davis Papers.

3. "'Welfare Queen' Becomes Issue in Reagan Campaign," *The New York Times*, Feb. 15, 1976.

4. "Newspaper Set to Begin Publication Monday," *The Baltimore Sun*, March 13, 1999.

5. Sergeant Major (Ret.) William D. Waugh to Commanding Officer, Headquarters U.S. Army Military Personnel Center, "Eyewitness Recommendation for the Medal of Honor for Captain Paris D. Davis," July 22, 1981, Paris D. Davis Papers.

ABOUT THE AUTHOR

Davis Family

Former Green Beret Paris Darius Davis has a storied military career as a highly decorated member of U.S. Special Forces. Born in 1939 in Cleveland, Ohio, he attended Southern University and A&M College in Baton Rouge, Louisiana, where he studied political science on an ROTC scholarship. Commissioned as an Army reserve armor officer in 1959, he graduated from Airborne and Ranger Schools in 1960 and was selected for the Seventh Special Forces Group (Airborne), First Special Forces, serving first in Korea and then Vietnam. In 1965, he was promoted to captain as a detachment commander with the Fifth Special Forces Group (Airborne), First Special Forces. He was one of the first Black Special Forces officers as the civil rights movement gained momentum at home. Tasked with training South Vietnamese villagers, he deployed to Binh Dinh Province in spring 1965. On June 18, Davis commanded a team of South Vietnamese trainees, along with Special Forces soldiers, against a superior enemy force. He led a charge to neutralize enemy emplacements, engaged in hand-to-hand combat, and saved the lives of three American soldiers. He disobeyed a direct order to leave the battlefield until his men were safe. His nomination for the Congressional Medal of Honor was ignored or misplaced at least twice. While the reasons remain unknown, supporters believe that his nomination was disregarded or discarded because he was Black. President Joe Biden awarded him the medal on March 3, 2023, fifty-eight years after the battle in Binh Dinh Province.